Praise for *Aliens & Savages*

"*Aliens & Savages* is a look into these two-way mirrors of the Australian encounters with otherness, and it is not a pleasant sight."
Greg Dening, *The Australian's Review of Books.*

"The writers are particularly good at unravelling the cultural attitudes and the mind set which created the white racism...This is a well-written and easily digested text which enlightens and entertains."
Ray Duplain, *Geelong Advertiser.*

"The granddaughter of Asian migrants, I have been on the receiving end of childish racial taunts and have cringed at the prejudice my family endured when they adopted my country as home. Perhaps I was lucky... *Aliens & Savages* examines the ignorance and fear which drives racial comment in Australian literature. It is a startling insight into how public perception can be shaped by popular writing... Verdict: It should be compulsory reading".
Tine Norman, *Sunday Life Magazine.*

"How quickly we forget. The nation's collective memory had all but banished the shackles of its racist past until the Member for Oxley emerged as a powerful reminder.

In the three decades since Aborigines were given the vote and the last vestiges of the White Australia policy were dropped officially, few bigots have been able to canvass their thoughts publicly. Apart from the rumblings of a handful of outspoken MPs, gun owners and war veterans, racist outpourings have been largely ignored by the general public....

But two Melbourne academics have discovered a few decades of tolerance and political correctness have not buried entirely the early racist writings of Australian literature."
Catherine Fitzpatrick, 'The Big Weekend' - *The West Australian.*

"The book traces the history of 'damagingly racist and xenophobic arguments' that still prevail, acknowledging the prejudice that was the dominant cultural (and political) position of Australia's past."

The Mercury (Hobart)

"Many of the passages of writing have never been seen...because they have been lost or censored from history books...Australia [needs] to face up to its past."

Lin Fong, *Melbourne Leader*.

"*Aliens & Savages*...muses on the question of just who would have been alien to what. Certainly Aborigines were alien to civilisation and savage in looks and behaviour by European standards; but the European settlers were equally alien to the Australian environment and to the Aborigines' highly sophisticated survival techniques, and savage in their treatment of convicts, Aborigines and Chinese."

Wayne Crawford, *The Sunday Tasmanian*.

"The ambition is bold."

Peter Pierce, *Sydney Morning Herald*.

About the Authors

JANEEN WEBB and ANDREW ENSTICE are both literary historians with expertise in popular culture. They have co-authored numerous books and articles, including Kenneth Mackay's 'The Yellow Wave'; The Fantastic Self; and, most recently, an alternate Australian historical novel, The Five Star Republic (2021).

DR WEBB is a multiple award-winning author, editor, critic and academic who has written or edited a dozen books and over a hundred short stories and essays. She is a recipient of the World Fantasy Award, the Peter MacNamara SF Achievement Award, the Australian Aurealis Award and four Ditmar Awards.

She has taught at various universities, is internationally recognised for her critical work in speculative fiction, and has contributed to most of the standard reference texts in the field. She holds a PhD in literature from the University of Newcastle, NSW.

She has lived in various countries, and currently divides her time between Melbourne and a small farm overlooking the sea near Wilson's Promontory.

DR ENSTICE won the Bridport Prize for poetry at the age of nineteen. He was awarded a scholarship to Emmanuel College, Cambridge, graduating MA, and holds a PhD from Exeter University. His first book, Landscapes of the Mind (Macmillan, UK) remains the definitive study of Thomas Hardy's literary landscape in his Wessex books.

He swapped the academic world for life as a scriptwriter and producer with Granada Television in Manchester, UK. He lived for a while in the mountains of Northern Italy, hiked in Sumatra and northern Thailand, and travelled round Australia before settling in Melbourne, where he taught at various universities. He now lives in rural Victoria. He has written and directed for the theatre—his play about the nineteenth-century gold rush, Crossing the River, premiered in Melbourne.

ALIENS & SAVAGES

THE VOICE IN AUSTRALIA

JANEEN WEBB & ANDREW ENSTICE

NORSTRILIA PRESS

NORSTRILIA PRESS
www.norstriliapress.com
11 Robe Street, St Kilda, Victoria 3182, Australia

This revised edition published by Norstrilia Press 2023.
First published in Australia in 1998 by HarperCollinsPublishers Pty Limited ACN 009 913 517. A member of HarperCollinsPublishers (Australia) Pty Limited Group
www.harpercollins.com.au

Copyright © Janeen Webb and Andrew Enstice 1998.
Revised text copyright © Janeen Webb and Andrew Enstice 2023.

This work is copyright. Apart from any use as permitted under the Copyright Act 1968, no part may be reproduced, copied, scanned, stored in a retrieval system, recorded, or transmitted, in any form or by any means, without the prior written permission of the publisher. Every effort has been made to trace copyright holders of material quoted herein. In cases where this has been unsuccessful, please address any inquiries to the authors via the publishers.

Book and cover design by David Grigg.
Cover photograph by Janeen Webb.

Typeset in Sorts Mill Goudy and Avenir Next.

ISBN (paperback): 978-0-645-36966-3
ISBN (ebook): 978-064-536-967-0

Contents

Introduction . . . 1

Part One: Noble or Savage? . . . 19
  1 The Miserablest People in the World . . . 21
  2 The Culminating Ape . . . 58
  3 All That Is Unfit . . . 89

Part Two: White or Yellow? . . . 121
  4 Asian Invasion . . . 123
  5 Federation and Exclusion . . . 157
  6 Austral-Asia? . . . 177

Part Three: Towards Reconciliation? . . . 199
  7 Federation and Empire . . . 201
  8 Stories of a White Australia . . . 218
  9 Cultural Reconciliation . . . 239

Conclusion . . . 252

Endnotes . . . 261
Bibliography . . . 275
Acknowledgements . . . 288

Introduction

> *A country that does not acknowledge the full truth of its history is burdened by its unspoken weight.*
> —Anthony Albanese.[1]

Aliens & Savages is a hands-on historical record of the racism that underpins Australia's growth as a nation. It was first published twenty-five years ago, in response to the rise of Pauline Hanson's One Nation Party, and John Howard's denial of the importance of collective memory. Now, as we approach the referendum on an Aboriginal and Torres Strait Islander Voice to Parliament, we ask: in 25 years, what has changed?

On 10th June, 2023, *The Sydney Morning Herald* offered an historic apology for its brutally racist coverage of the infamous 1838 Myall Creek Massacre of First Nations people.[2] 'Truth is an essential force for reconciliation', said the *Herald* editorial. This statement – like Kevin Rudd's 2008 apology in Parliament to the Stolen Generations – seems to mark a groundswell of change in public sentiment. But the *Herald* wasn't the only one promoting genocide in the nineteenth century, or in the century that followed. And, to judge by some of the language surrounding the forthcoming referendum, the rhetoric of racism is still with us.

When we were first approached about reissuing *Aliens & Savages*, we considered updating the text. To our surprise – and dismay – we found that the arguments haven't changed in twenty-five years. The voices have just got louder, amplified by the echo-chambers of social media. In 1998, overt racism seemed on its way to becoming a thing of the past in Australia. But it has now resurfaced, stronger than before: we would need a separate book just to sample the recent voices of extreme intolerance currently appearing in social media, in right-wing publications, in public speeches and parliamentary debates. The negative voices are everywhere.

Any deviation from the received conservative narrative is savagely attacked. In 2014, publication of Bruce Pascoe's book, *Dark Emu*, triggered extensive denigration of Pascoe's claim to Aboriginal heritage in an attempt to silence his voice. The argument is a familiar one from colonising powers: indigenous culture is systematically sidelined and broken up and, as far as possible, 'bred out'; those claiming to speak for it can then be marginalised as not representing a 'pure' race or culture.

The attacks on Pascoe were deeply personal and deeply destructive. More recently, this pattern was repeated in the vitriolic response by Murdoch media to journalist Stan Grant when his comments just before the recent coronation reminded Australians of the unpleasant, undeniable truths of British colonisation when seen from an indigenous perspective. Similarly, First Nations people supporting the Voice are under attack: as Pat Anderson, one of the architects of the 2017 *Uluru Statement from the Heart* put it in May 2023: 'The hate is raining down on us'.[3]

When *Aliens & Savages* was first published, it was criticised in some conservative quarters for raking up forgotten and marginal writings. This response was a vestige of what used to be called 'cultural cringe', the idea that such writings were somehow unworthy, a disgrace best hidden away while we affirmed our inclusion in a European/Western literary world. No-one today would dispute either the existence or the significance of such writing – especially since there's now a whole 'cultural studies' industry embedded in our Universities.

But there remains the issue of relevance: why should these writings matter to a contemporary audience? As Richard Flanagan remarked in his Closing Address to the 2023 Sydney Writers'

Festival, 'what happened in the foundation of our nation was one great crime composed of countless smaller crimes'.[4] The stories in this book record those crimes.

Aliens & Savages is still the only publication of its kind – a survey of racism and xenophobia in Australian popular writings before the advent of social media. It is a collection of fiction and non-fiction, of personal narratives and official reports, of diaries and media misinformation. In it, you can hear the unguarded voices of the colonists, the squatters, the politicians; you can see the close relationship between the popular press and the prejudices of its readers. They speak the language of futurism. This is because the construction of colonial identity depends on the promise of a different, better future. The narratives of the colonisers create a space which allows the fabrication of a new history – one in which the original inhabitants are written out of their own story. It's uncomfortable reading. But it is necessary reading. It charts the drumbeat of discrimination that persists through the story of Australia.

Because of the sheer volume of such material, *Aliens & Savages* cannot be a complete, exhaustive collection. Rather, it offers a representative selection, concentrating on earlier, less accessible works. Some of the writings discussed here exist only in rare book collections. Many, including pieces by once well-known figures such as William Lane and Marcus Clarke, have never been reprinted since their original publication. And some of these pieces are truly shocking in what they reveal about writers and readers alike.

We did briefly consider, in revising *Aliens & Savages* for release as part of the Voice referendum debate, whether we should focus on materials relating to relations with indigenous communities, and delete the sections devoted solely to Asian immigration. But to do this would narrow the focus to a point where the larger picture of how racism and discrimination have been built into the very foundation story of Australia would be lost.

It was philosopher George Santayana who said in 1905 that those who cannot remember the past are condemned to repeat it.⁵ He referred of course to a collective loss of memory, which occurs when a society or culture loses sight of its past mistakes, and so repeats them – the kind of memory loss that leads to the re-emergence of socially divisive political movements like Pauline Hanson's One Nation Party, American-inspired right-wing evangelical groups and, more recently, the neo-Nazi fringe.

Aliens & Savages tells the story of a dominant Australian culture as reflected in its own writings and, with only a few exceptions, we have not attempted to balance the voices of prejudice with the responses of those targeted by racial discrimination. To do so, we feel, would trespass on territory that more appropriately belongs to present-day descendants of those on the receiving end. There have, of course, always been white voices that dissented from mainstream prejudice, but for much of Australia's modern history, they were in a minority. This book reflects the monocultural world view from which a multicultural Australia emerged.

Cultural discrimination has manifested itself in Australian writing in various forms. Early racism against indigenous communities was part guilt, part defence, part aggression. White land-takers seeking to legitimise their position transferred blame for their actions onto Aboriginal 'savages'. Colonial settlers wrote at a time when it was the intellectually 'correct' position – according to the pseudo-science of Social Darwinism – to assume that the colour of a person's skin was a mark of their place on Nature's human league table. From the very first contact between European explorers and indigenous Australians, 'natives' were observed, captured, examined, scrubbed, clothed, kept as pets, kept as slaves. And – very rarely – treated as fellow human beings. Racial equality was, for a long period of our shared history, almost literally unthinkable.

In the case of Asian, particularly Chinese, immigrants, the racist propaganda was based squarely upon fear of economic competition. Vilified by the British during the Opium Wars, treated roughly in America during the California goldrushes, Chinese immigrants to Australia were regarded as a necessary evil. When growing fear and distrust of all things Asian led to race riots in a number of cities, the popular press had a field day. There was general apprehension that an undefended Australia would be fair game for any foreign invaders (such as the Russians) but most of the literature concentrated on the threat of 'Asian invasion' – in which white Australia is prey to the barbarism of 'Mongol hordes'. And these popular, xenophobic fears were instrumental in determining the nature and timing of Australian Federation in 1901.

Aliens & Savages concentrates on the intimate relationship between popular writing and politics. We no longer need to be convinced (as was the case twenty-five years ago) that popular 'knowledge' is problematic. It is derived from a range of variably reliable sources – nowadays with social media at the forefront. And it directly influences political decision-making. Much of the literature in this book comes from politicians and political apologists, writers who are keenly aware of this interaction. Many of the 'yellow peril' fictions represented in the Asiatic invasion section were written by those in positions of political power, or those aspiring to it. There is fiction by William Lane, who came to Australia with a strong socialist philosophy and anti-Chinese sentiments learned in the United States, and whose prejudices helped to colour the racist foundation policies of the Australian Labor Party. Kenneth Mackay, author of *The Yellow Wave*, was a member of the New South Wales legislature. C.H. Kirmess's fictional guerrilla force, the White Guard, was the model for the right-wing New Guard formed by returned servicemen after World War One. And so on.

Political rhetoric closely resembles the rhetoric of fiction: they use the same language patterns, the same structures. Both are intended to make their readers and listeners believe in the 'truth' of the text. And although today's politicians rarely venture into commercial story-telling, their relationship with popular media is stronger than ever. The power of the novel to reach and persuade a mass audience has largely passed, via television, to the streaming services and social media.

The intimate connection between Australian public life and popular media dates back to the earliest days of settlement. Australia is, in Eurocentric terms, a very long way from anywhere else. And because of our geographical distance from the rest of the world, Australians have tended to think of the first white settlement on our shores as having occurred quietly, in isolation, while the eyes of the world were elsewhere. Nothing could be further from the truth. The British colonisation of Australia was, in effect, an eighteenth-century media event. The communication technology was different from ours, but the imperative to provide sensation for a news-hungry reading public was just the same.

The first settlement voyage to the last unknown continent, the great southern land, excited an extraordinary amount of popular interest. Most of the officers of the First Fleet, from Governor Phillip down, had pre-sold their personal eye-witness accounts to English publishing houses. They had publishing contracts in their pockets well before they sailed from Portsmouth on 13th May, 1787. Governor Phillip and his deputy, Lieutenant-Governor John Hunter, had signed up with John Stockdale of Piccadilly to produce a rather lavish illustrated book; Captain John Davies had contracted with Cadell & Davies in The Strand; Surgeon-General John White had signed with John Debrett at Piccadilly, as had junior officer Captain-Lieutenant of marines, Watkin Tench. This practice continued, with later explorers following suit and signing contracts to pre-sell their stories as a way of financing their explorations of the continent.

This meant that the Australian colonial experience became the best documented colonial settlement in the history of the world. It also meant that the journals, letters and reports were never written as private documents – they were written as dramatic literature, intended for publication, and designed to be read by a popular audience 'back home'.

These writings were never innocent of ideological content. There were always colonial politics to be considered, decisions to be justified, positions to be maintained. Governor Phillip was an interesting choice of leader for the new colony: he had been a spy in France for the British Admiralty, had spent time in the Portuguese navy, and could be expected to appreciate the emerging strategic and political implications of a settlement which was, from the very beginning, rich in primary resources – particularly whale and seal oil – coveted by a European world in the throes of industrial expansion. When questions of racial interaction arose, his duty was clearly to the welfare of the white colonists in his charge, and to his superiors in England, and this is reflected in his records.

So, what exactly counts as 'literature' in the context of the Australian national experience? When the First Fleet sailed in 1787, 'literature' referred to serious writing: it included theology, philosophy, history, biography, editorials, the journals of explorers, but it excluded fiction as too light-minded. Only as the nineteenth century progressed did fiction gradually move into the category of literature. So when writers such as Governor Phillip or Watkin Tench recorded their colonial experiences, their recollections provided us with our first literary pieces.

When it came to the serious expression of sentiment, the acceptable literary form was poetry, the mode of inspiration. Poetry had several advantages in a developing colony, where its relatively short form suited a population that had little leisure for long works, and where materials for publishing were in short supply. So the earliest examples of colonial writing included in this volume are in the form of poetry, and popular journals.

Popular literary taste in Britain and the Americas had an extraordinary influence on the way in which our colonists chose to write. Just as America still retains vestiges of Elizabethan popular lyrics and linguistic constructions of the English spoken at the time of its colonisation, Australia, too, retains evidence of the language and popular forms that dominated literary taste during our early white settlement years. In the case of our poetry, Romantic literature quickly succeeded the staid, urbane rationality of eighteenth-century Augustanism (named for its self-conscious imitation of Roman literature of the period of the

Emperor Augustus). Romanticism, with its emphasis on originality and freedom of self-expression, became the dominant mode in Australia. It was ideally suited to authors asserting their own 'imaginative truths' by recording their personal, emotional responses to a challenging new environment. Moreover, Romantic writers cultivated the appeal of the exotic, the bizarre, even the macabre – and what could be more exotic to the European eye than the wonders of newly discovered Australia?

Along with Romanticism, our early poets and writers adopted a taste for the Gothic, quickly transplanting its trademark sinister motifs of terror and suspense into the Australian environment. And Australian gothic was not confined to literature – it turned up in all manner of domestic and decorative arts. Sydney's Powerhouse museum, for example, houses some of Governor Macquarie's custom-built gothic furniture, including matching hall stands featuring Mr and Mrs Satan holding trays for calling cards, and a set of elaborately carved high-backed chairs, upholstered in kangaroo fur, and sporting the motif of a raised fist holding a knife behind the head of the incumbent. Visitors to the Macquarie establishment do not seem to have recorded their responses.

In the case of eye-witness journal accounts, the literary model was established much earlier. Publishing houses had enjoyed a great deal of success with the journals of adventurers, particularly the memoirs of 'buccaneer and hydrographer' William Dampier, whose book, *A New Voyage Around the World* (1697) had been a runaway bestseller, appearing in four editions in two years. Dampier's account of his voyage was to become the model for subsequent reports of travellers' adventures: it differed markedly from earlier chronicles because it was written in the first person, and because it mixed factual reporting with vivid descriptions of exotic places, peoples, animals, and plants, interlacing the narrative with swashbuckling adventure stories of buccaneering on the high seas and survival in foreign lands.

Fictional versions of such voyages followed Dampier's first-person model, with works such as Daniel Defoe's *Robinson Crusoe*

(1719) and Jonathon Swift's *Gulliver's Travels* (1726) enjoying popular success. Even the Romantic poet, Samuel Taylor Coleridge, used Dampier as the model for 'The Rime of the Ancient Mariner' (1798). Publishers were looking for more of the same, both popular non-fiction and, later, fiction. They were not disappointed.

Then, as now, not all eye-witness accounts were written by the witnesses themselves. There are, indeed, indications that Dampier himself had rather a lot of professional help in preparing his manuscript for publication. Some absolutely verifiable and carefully truthful diaries, like those of Watkin Tench, did become immediate best-sellers. But other popular accounts were more suspect, especially those recounting sensational events. A case in point is the story of the May 1836 shipwreck of the *Stirling Castle* on Swain Reef near Rockhampton. The survivors of the wreck, including James and Eliza Fraser, were captured by local inhabitants on Great Sandy Island (subsequently renamed Fraser Island, until its recent reversion to the indigenous name of K'gari). Many, including Captain Fraser, were killed, and the survivors were rescued after six weeks by members of the Fourteenth Regiment, sent from Moreton Bay. In 1837, a work titled *Narrative of the Capture, Sufferings, and Miraculous Escape of Mrs Eliza Fraser*, purporting to be Mrs Fraser's own account, was published anonymously in New York. On her return to London, Mrs Fraser herself exploited her celebrity status with highly-coloured stories of her 'sufferings'. The events were taken up quickly by other writers: John Curtis, in 1838, published *Shipwreck of the Stirling Castle*. Mrs Fraser's 'experiences' have since become part of Australia's literary folklore, re-told in works such as Robert Gibbing's *John Graham, Convict* (1937), Charles Barrett's *White Blackfellows* (1948), Michael Alexander's *Mrs Fraser on the Fatal Shore* (1971), and, most famously, in Patrick White's *A Fringe of Leaves* (1976). The story was also made into a film, *Eliza Fraser* (1976), with a script by David Williamson. Thus the original facts, whatever they were, have merged with the fictions into a new construct that lives in our popular culture.

The politics of fiction were not confined to questions of exploration and expansion. Side by side with the serious, beautifully produced scientific works written for the educated upper classes, there were tabloid tales of the horrors of Botany Bay, designed to impress the fear of transportation upon the lower classes. Chapbook images of Botany Bay, with its flogging triangles and its gallows, swiftly replaced the fires of hell as pictures to frighten recalcitrant children. As Charles Dickens put it in *Hard Times for These Times* (1854), 'the good grown-up baby invariably got to the Savings-bank, and the bad grown-up baby invariably got transported'.[6] British authorities stressed the severity of punishment in the Australian settlements, and the 'true' accounts of the convicts themselves told of brutality and deprivation, thus reinforcing the official position. Exile was, in itself, seen as a terrible thing, and many homesick letters from the colony, genuine and otherwise, were published in a popular press that had a marked penchant for sentimentality.

Then, as now, the purpose of the cheapest and most widespread forms of publication was commercial, aiming for titillation rather than elucidation. Lurid accounts of depravity and vice in the colony were printed cheaply and in large numbers to reach a popular audience. Their overt moral purpose in warning that such behaviour would lead to transportation was mostly swamped by the detailed depictions of the evil events themselves, and an obligatory scene of penitence by the wrongdoer was usually tacked on at the end. Once again, there seem to have been more eye-witness accounts than there were eye-witnesses, with reports of incidents involving 'savages' thrown in, to add even more spice to the tales. A great many of the first-person accounts, especially those by penitent female ex-convicts, followed a pattern set by Daniel Defoe's entirely fictional *Moll Flanders* in 1722.

The Australian tall tale emerged almost immediately as a hallmark of stories about the new continent. One of the first settlers, Watkin Tench, complained in 1788, the first year of the settlement, that:

...the utmost circumspection is necessary to prevent imposition in those who give accounts of what they see in unknown countries. We found the convicts particularly happy in fertility of invention and exaggerated descriptions. Hence large freshwater rivers, valuable ores, and quarries of limestone, chalk and marble were daily proclaimed soon after we had landed.[7]

The occasion of this remark was the death by hanging of a convict named Daly, whose crime was that he had 'broken up an old pair of buckles and mixed the pieces with sand and stone', and used the resulting composition as evidence that he had found a gold mine.

In retrospect it appears that indigenous spokespersons were also not averse to relating tall tales that evoked surprise and wonder from the white settlers, who appear not to have realised that their informants might have been gently misleading them. But then, how could they realise, when they insisted on regarding the indigenous peoples as too inferior to be capable of such a thing? The stories that the settlers heard from Aborigines, once rudimentary lines of communication had been established, were recorded, verbatim, as undifferentiated 'truth'.

The written word was highly influential in directing popular debate, much more so than it is today. In the early years of the colony, poetry was our 'serious' literary mode, and long novels were mostly imported from Britain and the United States. But literary journals flourished from the 1820s, publishing not only serious poetry, but also adventure stories and romances – the group to which the 'Asian invasion' stories belong. Such stories were used to catch the popular readers considered unlikely to plough through serious political commentary in factual modes. One curious result of this was that Australian fiction was, at times, much more sensationalist than its English counterparts, and some works, such as Fergus Hume's *The Mystery of a Hansom Cab* (1886), were considerably 'toned down' before publication for British audiences.

Australians then, as now, were a very literate community. The publishing industry grew very rapidly, and it is important to remember the large scale of both local publishing and imports of overseas material to Australia in the nineteenth century. Cole's Book Arcade in Melbourne was reputedly one of the largest bookshops in the Empire, and educated Australian audiences could choose from an extraordinarily wide range of material, including much that lay outside the narrow canonical definitions of literature.

Developments in the technology of communications were matched in the 1880s and 90s by the growth of a new mass market, especially in the United Kingdom where the provision of public education created an ideal marketplace for entrepreneurs. A new generation of newspaper proprietors moved rapidly to supply the demand, and publishing houses followed. Even the hack writers were hard pressed to meet this level of demand, and fresh authors were eagerly sought. With the explosion of interest in Australia, following the International Exhibition in Melbourne (1880-81) and the Colonial and Indian Exhibition in London (1886), there was sudden demand by English editors for Australian writing, with the result that expatriate Australians found themselves pressed into service to supply the enormous demand for tales of outback Australian life.

Despite the fact that many Australian writers found a market in writing tales of the bush for a prurient overseas audience, the very nature of life in this new environment made for some interesting variations on the dominant modes. In many ways, the development of our fiction reflects radical changes in scientific thinking – the changes in theory occasioned by the work of Adam Smith, Charles Darwin, Sigmund Freud, and Karl Marx – all of which impacted heavily on white Australian colonisation. The last continent to be 'discovered', Australia was in many ways experimental.

Perhaps the most revolutionary of nineteenth-century changes in the English colonial world lay in its acceptance of a new science: the 'dismal science' of economics. This fundamentally altered the prevailing view of humankind by ascribing to people a monetary value, enabling humans and their labour to be bought and sold in a way no different from any other commodity. This principle had of course always applied to slavery, but now it applied also to the wider community. Concomitantly, since the soul had no identifiable economic value, its existence began to be questioned. Adam Smith's influential book, *The Wealth of Nations*, was published in 1776 – in between the mapping of the east coast of Australia in 1770, and its white settlement in 1788. Smith described the 'labour market' that was emerging hand-in-hand with the advances of the industrial revolution – a situation in which, to put it bluntly, everything was for sale. Profit was identified as the outward and visible sign of efficiency, and success was measured in monetary terms.

Smith made it possible to think in abstract terms of new economic constructs. Australia was the first attempt to model a full modern economy from scratch. The First Fleet was a limited subsistence experiment but, from the time of the Second Fleet (which transported convicts in converted whaling ships designed for immediate reconversion to commercial use), Australia was designed to be a part of the global industrial economy.

This being the case, the attractiveness of Cook's report that the continent was *terra nullius* was incontrovertible. According to this position, the land had no pre-existing medium of exchange, so a new, economically viable structure could be imposed without any real resistance. The Aboriginal inhabitants were simply discounted. The idea of openly destroying an indigenous population was, unfortunately, not a new one. In the islands of the Caribbean, English colonial activity had, at a much earlier date, wiped out the indigenous people, replacing them with imported slaves from Africa, whose task was to grow sugar. England found this a very profitable enterprise, especially as the islands were relatively easy to govern, the slaves having no real means of objecting to their position. The economic analogy with the Australian position, where Aborigines were to be displaced and their lands worked by convict labour, is all too clear.

Smith's economic thinking alone might not have produced radical change but, in combination with the work of Charles Darwin, it was a potent source of justification for exploitation. The scientific thinking espoused in *On the Origin of Species by Natural Selection* (1859) had been around for some time, but it was Darwin who crystallised it. Australia, which could be seen as relatively untouched by civilisation, was seen as a proving ground for many theories, including the earlier work of Lyell's *Principles of Geology* (1830). In terms of Darwinian evolution, Australia's flora and fauna were valuable pieces in the scientific jigsaw puzzle, and hopeful scientists thought this continent a likely home for the 'missing link'. And Australian Aborigines were immediately relegated to the bottom of the human evolutionary ladder. This being so, not only was white exploitation profitable, and 'right', in economic terms, it could also be seen as beneficial for the future of the human species – a convenient combination of ideas in which personal aggrandisement represents a betterment of humanity. Most recently, in comments picked up by news services around the world, former Prime Minister John Howard reasserted the old colonial furphy, that British settlement was the luckiest thing ever to happen to Australia.

In the second half of the nineteenth century, this point of view hardened into the widespread white-race idea of 'The Coming Man': a deeply racist version of social Darwinism popularised in the adventure stories of international writers such as Rudyard Kipling, Robert Louis Stevenson, H. Rider Haggard and Arthur Conan Doyle, and picked up in the *Bulletin*'s Australian 'bush stories'. The Coming Man was the ideology behind the various training groups for boys, from the Boy Scout Movement (which originated in South Africa and spread quickly throughout America and the Commonwealth countries) to the German hostels movement that was eventually to become the Hitler Youth. It was also the philosophy underpinning the Boys' Own Annuals, such as *Young Australia*, which began publication in London in 1893. These books of gripping outdoor yarns, with their emphasis on masculinity, competence in the use of weapons, and the virtues of 'common decency', were sold throughout the Empire, cynically retitled and repackaged for each country. The image of The Coming Man represented an all-white, all-male world view. It excluded women, and was deeply anti-intellectual. Its heroes were men like Scott of the Antarctic and Cecil Rhodes, represented as characters who 'got things done' first, and worried about the ethics later, if at all.

In Australian literature (as in other colonial literatures), The Coming Man merged, quietly, into the figure of The Common Man. He became The Man in the Street, whose virtues of decency and much vaunted common sense were represented as being innately superior to the tainted, if not downright corrupt values of those in positions of power, whether political or military. This is the version of the Australian male that later became the folk-type of the brave Aussie digger at Gallipoli: an ordinary bloke who outraged the British officer class by taking off his shirt when told to dig ditches; the man who prized initiative above obedience, common sense above theory, practicality above manners; a 'man's man' whose respect had to be earned. And this 'common man' in our popular fiction was a firm believer in white supremacy.[8] Today he is the chosen target of demagogues and conspiracy theorists who rail against 'the elite'.

This characterisation points in turn to another of the major changes in nineteenth-century thought that shaped our responses to the world. Australia was, in many ways, a social experiment as well as an economic one, having no aristocracy and no ruling wealthy elite. It was a working colony, where the residents had little time for leisure; a society that drew idealists of all sorts, among them those hoping for a more egalitarian society. The image of Australia as convict hell had quickly given way to the idea of the 'Working Man's Paradise', and the representation of Australia as a land of opportunity – albeit as a place where those who were failures at home could try again – existed side by side with the image of the colony as a 'sink of moral depravity'. In editorials that still sound familiar today, native-born Australians accused Britain of unloading onto the colonial system paupers and emigrants incapable of working. But for skilled white male workers, a number of early advances were made in Australia, with workers achieving the eight-hour day and enjoying living conditions demonstrably better than those of their English counterparts. And despite the various setbacks, a largely egalitarian middle-class society did develop. It might well be argued that the Australian society that evolved is testimony to Karl Marx's wry observation that workers did not want a revolution, just a slightly better life.

Sigmund Freud (1856-1939) was another nineteenth-century thinker who had a profound influence on the development of the Australian identity. Freud's description of the unconscious was more controversial than Darwin's imputation of a simian ancestry. His insistence that sexual desire and fears lay just below the surface was a shocking concept for Victorians. But if they found it hard to credit repressed desires in themselves, they had little difficulty in combining Freudian theory with social Darwinism to consolidate a belief that the 'inferior races' were psychologically as well as physically less developed than themselves. Without properly developed super egos, the 'inferior races' were given over to the gratification of the fleshly desires of the ego, so that their primitive libidos were given free expression, together with other basic instincts. In Australia's first children's book, *A Mother's Offering to her Children*,[9] readers are warned that: 'These poor uncivilized people, most frequently meet with some deplorable end, through giving away to unrestrained passions'.

There were common threads running throughout this peculiar combination of the new economics, social Darwinism, Freudian psychology and Marxist doctrine. The concept of the human body as a machine allowed governments and other institutions to regard human beings as monetary units, as genetic actors in the evolution of the coming race, and as cogs in the machine of capitalism and industry. The determinist position (the theory of natural causality – or, everything that happens must happen) reinforced the notion that the colonisation and direction of Australia, with its displacement of Aboriginal groups, could have happened in no other way for the better advancement of the world. Such 'scientific' thinking formed the basis of the Australian identity and produced a profoundly secular society, dominated by a communal self-interest that defined 'community' in narrowly racial terms.

So it is hardly surprising to find, towards the end of the nineteenth century, that the desire for a White Australia was one of the most powerful driving forces in the move to Federation. So certain were the policy-makers of the rightness of their racist world view that the official policy of Asian exclusion and Aboriginal integration was not relaxed until the 1960s. Decades of multiculturalism have barely begun to ease the grip of a culture of sanctioned racism.

When Governor Phillip set foot on Australian soil and saw his first Aborigine, there would have been no question in his mind as to who was the alien, and who the savage. Indigenous people were 'alien' to civilisation and European culture, 'savage' in looks and behaviour. But when we look back at much of what has been written by the white inhabitants of Australia about contacts with indigenous culture, and then about relations with Chinese immigrants, it is much harder to determine who was what. Clearly European settlers were 'alien' to Australia, 'alien' to the highly sophisticated survival techniques practised by indigenous groups. And these same Europeans were 'savage' in their treatment of convicts, 'savage' in their dealings with Aborigines and Chinese.

Much of the material in this book has slipped from public view. It was largely excluded from formal study because it did not fit twentieth-century ideas of what constituted literature. When the study of Australian Literature at university level finally became respectable, in the 1960s, 'literature' was an exclusive category of excellence, measured by style and by purpose. Politicians who dabbled in mediocre fiction were not serious candidates for literary canonisation – particularly when their racist and xenophobic views were so at odds with the emerging intellectual sensitivities of the 1960s.

By accident and by design, uncomfortable popular fictions which might have reminded us of our embarrassing past were displaced by serious-minded literary fictions. Until recently, overt prejudice and racism seemed in full retreat. But now they are reasserting themselves in social media and in political rhetoric. It is more important than ever that we understand and question the voices which have shaped our status quo. As Janine Burke remarked:

> *Stories that get buried because they do not suit a time and irritate its needs, or because they make the powerful look foolish, or like liars, such uncomfortable stories most often tell the truth. We have to dig them up and restore them to their proper place.*[10]

We did a lot of digging to find the uncomfortable stories presented in this book. The voices in *Aliens & Savages* tells it as it was...and as it still is.

PART ONE
Noble or Savage?

PART ONE
Noble or Savage?

1

The Miserablest People in the World

Terra Australis, the Great South Land, had existed in the European imagination since the end of the Middle Ages. Speculation concerning its whereabouts increased after Columbus' discovery of the fabulous Americas, with trading nations, particularly Portugal and Spain, sending expeditions to locate what they expected to be its southern equivalent, another El Dorado. The motive was straightforward greed – a search for new sources of precious metals, gemstones and spices, and for new maritime trading routes that might prove strategically advantageous. There is much debate about whether or not Portuguese explorers actually reached the Australian coast – they had certainly reached Ceylon (Sri Lanka) and the East Indies (Indonesia) by the 1520s, and had set out in 1521 for the mythical 'islands of gold'. The Spanish attempts are better documented, with Ferdinand Magellan in 1519 leading a Spanish expedition that reached the Philippines via South America. A later Spanish expedition in 1560 found the Solomon Islands, named for the gold they had expected to find; while a 1605 attempt by Fernandez de Quiros landed in the New Hebrides group, where, thinking that he had found a new continent, he claimed 'all this region of the south as far as the Pole'[1], which he named 'Australia del Espiritu Santo'.

The Dutch were more successful. In the course of expanding their trading empire in the East Indies, trading vessels began to plot a course through the southern Indian Ocean, and it was a miscalculation of this route that resulted in the accidental landfall just off the coast of Western Australia in 1616 by Captain Dirk

Hartog, whose pewter plate claiming Dutch sovereignty has entered our national history. But there was still no reason for Dutch traders to consider the area profitable enough to visit, though they continued to chart the coastlines, filling in maps as information became available. In 1623, Dutch captain Jan Carstenz reported to his Batavian superiors, after a voyage charting the Gulf of Carpentaria:

> *In our judgement this is the most arid and barren region that can be found anywhere on the earth: the inhabitants, too, are the most wretched and poorest creatures that I have ever seen in my age or time...*[2]

Likewise, Netherlands explorer and mariner Abel Janzoon Tasman made two expeditions to Australia in 1642 and 1644 on behalf of the Dutch East India Company. After the second voyage, he reported to his sponsor, Anthony Van Diemen (after whom Van Diemen's Land, later Tasmania, was named), that there was nothing of commercial interest in this land, only 'poor and bad-tempered people'.[3]

The Dutch laid claim to Australia, but made no attempt at settlement of this apparently inhospitable land. The popular belief persisted that the real *Terra Australis Incognita*, the Great South Land, must lie somewhere in the South Pacific, east of the barren land that was currently being mapped. The reality of the mariners' observations simply didn't fit the legend – so they kept searching.

Then, in 1688, exactly one hundred years before the First Fleet landed at Botany Bay, the English pirate William Dampier spent six to ten weeks on the north-west coast of Australia. His presence there was part chance, part design: Dampier, who was then a full-time buccaneer, had joined forces in Mexico with Captain Charles Swan on his ship, *The Cygnet*, for a voyage to the East Indies. Swan had succumbed to the sybaritic charms of tropical feasts and dancing girls on the island of Mindanão in the Philippines, where he was fêted by the Sultan of Cotabato, who hoped to retain the buccaneers as a defence against the Dutch. In response to Swan's decline into a life of pleasure, Dampier and some of the crew stole *The Cygnet*, elected John Read captain, and sailed for Manila through the Philippines and the Indonesian islands. This course led them into the path of extreme storms and waterspouts in the South China Sea, which so terrified the seamen that they abandoned their piratical intention to seek out Manila treasure ships, and plotted instead a course for India by way of the Moluccas and Timor then west through the Indian Ocean. On passing Timor, Captain Read decided, out of sheer curiosity, to detour to New Holland – it is probable that they landed in the King Sound area of Western Australia.

Dampier's account of his experiences was published in England in 1697, under the title *A New Voyage Round the World*[4]. He reported that 'New Holland is a very large tract of land. It is not yet determined whether it is an island or a main continent; but I am certain that it joins neither to Asia, Africa, nor America.' His writings reinforced the Dutch view that the land was barren and of no commercial value, and his description of the Aborigines he encountered there became famous:

> The inhabitants of this country are the miserablest people in the world. The Hodmadods of Monomotapa, though a nasty people, yet for wealth are gentlemen to these; who have no houses, and skin garments, sheep, poultry, and fruits of the earth, ostrich eggs, etc. as the Hodmadods have. And setting aside their human shape, they differ but little from brutes. They are tall, straight-bodied, and thin, with small long limbs. They have great heads, round foreheads, and great brows...
>
> They have great bottle-noses, pretty full lips, and wide mouths. The two fore-teeth of their upper jaw are wanting in all of them, men and women, old and young; whether they draw them out, I know not. Neither have they any beards. They are long-visaged, and of a very unpleasing aspect, having no one graceful feature in their faces. Their hair is black, short and curled, like that of the Negroes; and not long and lank like the common Indians. The colour of

> *their skins, both of their faces and the rest of their body, is coal-black, like that of the Negroes of Guinea.*

Dampier's views reflect the cultural prejudices of his time and background. When he calls the Hodmadods 'gentlemen' by comparison, he assumes a concept of civilisation in which the labour of many supports the visible wealth of the aristocratic few. In late seventeenth-century England this wealth was based on agriculture and trade, and reflected in magnificent houses and public buildings. The Great Fire of London, in 1666, had destroyed much of the mediaeval city. Rebuilding had studded the city with major monuments to prosperity, like Sir Christopher Wren's new St. Paul's Cathedral.

What Dampier looks for in New Holland, and does not find, is a civic environment. There is no recognisable formal hierarchy of wealth, no sultans of the sort that had so lavishly entertained Swan at Mindanão. Instead he finds a people who not only have no permanent buildings, but none of the other marks of 'civilisation' either. He is concerned that they are so poor that they lack even clothing, remarking that: 'They have no sort of clothes, but a piece of the rind of a tree tied like a girdle about their waists, and a handful of long grass, or three or four small green boughs full of leaves, thrust under their girdle, to cover their nakedness.'

Dampier, a man who has visited many different cultures in the course of his extensive travels, goes on, in a spirit of scientific observation, to detail the living arrangements of the Aboriginal people. It is clear from the way in which he structures his observations that he is searching his memory, in vain, for a comparable society. He cannot identify either social or religious models, saying that he 'did not perceive that they did worship anything', since Aboriginal culture offered him no equivalent to English prayers. In his view, the 'miserable natives' failed all of his 'civilisation tests':

> *They have no houses, but lie in the open air without any covering; the earth being their bed, and the heaven their canopy. Whether they cohabit one man to one woman, or*

promiscuously, I know not; but they do live in companies, twenty or thirty men, women and children together. Their only food is a small sort of fish, which they get by making weirs of stone across little coves or branches of the sea; every tide bringing in the small fish, and there leaving them for a prey to these people, who constantly attend there to search for them at low water.

Dampier came from an essentially agricultural economy. Hunting in England was then (as now) highly regulated, and reserved largely to the upper classes. Other trading nations of his experience had had fiscal systems of one sort or another. He simply did not recognise the relationship of this society to its environment, even though he recorded it:

When they have eaten they lie down till the next low water, and then all that are able to march out, be it night or day, rain or shine, 'tis all one; they must attend the weirs, or else they must fast: for the earth affords them no food at all. There is neither herb, root, pulse nor any sort of grain for them to eat, that we saw; nor any sort of bird or beast that they can catch, having no instruments wherewithal to do so.

He did in fact see Aboriginal hunting implements, but failed to recognise them as such. Again, his own experience dictated what he could and could not 'see' in this alien environment. Europe was accustomed to violence and warfare, and Dampier himself, as a pirate, had done his share of fighting. So he interprets hunting weapons in familiar terms, describing the unknown boomerang in the only terms he knew, as a curved sword, or cutlass.

These poor creatures have a sort of weapon to defend their weir, or fight with their enemies, if they have any that will interfere with their poor fishery. They did at first endeavour with their weapons to frighten us, who lying ashore deterred them from one of their fishing-places. Some of them had wooden swords, others had a sort of lance. The sword is

> shaped somewhat like a cutlass. The lance is a long straight
> pole sharp at one end, and hardened afterwards by heat.

For their part, the whole basis of European economy, the exchange of labour for goods, is incomprehensible to the tribesmen. In one incident, Dampier attempts to employ the native men to carry water barrels by giving them some cast off clothing, 'thinking that this finery would have brought them to work heartily for us'. The ploy is singularly unsuccessful: 'they stood like statues, without motion, but grinned like so many monkeys... So we were forced to carry our water ourselves, and they very fairly put the clothes off again. Dampier remarks, as Captain James Cook was later to find, that the Aborigines simply did not 'seem to admire anything that we had'.

Yet Dampier, ever curious, persevered with his observations, and did record the communal nature of Aboriginal life:

> There the old people that are not able to stir abroad by
> reason of their age, and the tender infants, wait their return;
> and what providence has bestowed on them, they presently
> broil on the coals, and eat it in common. Sometimes they get
> as many fish as makes them a plentiful banquet; and at
> other times they scarce get everyone a taste: but be it little or
> much that they get, everyone has his part, as well the young
> and tender, the old and feeble, who are not able to go
> abroad, as the strong and lusty.

This aspect of Aboriginal society would later be romanticised by some writers as a paradisal innocence. It was also the basis of contemptuous dismissal of a culture so inferior that it had not developed a proper hierarchy of property. Dampier's account is neutral – though it is worth noting that he does not see this kind of communal existence as proof of any redeeming feature.

Back in England, certainly, his readers preferred to see the 'miserablest people', and not a land of innocence. It was this account which shaped the English vision of Australia as a waste land, a place of inhospitable landscapes and miserable savages. When Jonathan Swift wrote *Gulliver's Travels*, he took part of his description of the Yahoos, the beastlike humans in the land of the Houynhms, from Dampier's account of the Aborigines, and set his fictional country on the latitude of Dampier's New Holland: present-day Australia.

By the time Captain James Cook sailed on the *Endeavour* in 1768, charged with the task of observing the transit of Venus in Tahiti and then searching for *Terra Australis*, ideas about the assumed superiority of European civilisation had changed. The philosophers of the eighteenth-century Enlightenment had moved away from the Old Testament-based view of Europeans as the natural inheritors of the Earth. French philosopher Jean-Jacques Rousseau formulated and popularised the idea of the 'noble savage' – children of Nature whose innocence of the corrupting ways of civilisation made them naturally superior to a corrupted aristocracy. This view of alternative nobility was based in part on European contacts with North American tribes, whose social and economic organisation was easily recognisable to the European colonists.

When Cook made his first voyage, eventually making landfall in Botany Bay in 1770, he took with him the preconceptions of Dampier's account, but tempered these with his own Enlightenment views. He addressed Dampier's description directly when he summarised his views of the Aboriginal groups he had encountered in 1770:

> *They may appear to be some of the most wretched people upon the earth: but in reality they are far more happier than we Europeans; being wholly unacquainted not only with the superfluous but the necessary Conveniences so much sought after in Europe, they are happy in not knowing the use of them. They live in a Tranquility which is not disturbed by the Inequality of Condition: the Earth and sea of their own accord furnishes them with all things necessary for life; they covet not Magnificent Houses, Household stuff &ca they live in a warm and fine Climate and enjoy a very wholesome Air...*[5]

This tension, between a desire by Europeans to see the indigenous inhabitants of Australia as children of Nature and noble savages, and the sense both sides seem to have felt, of alienation from a culture so different as to make each incomprehensible to the other, was to colour European-Aboriginal relations from the very beginning. 'All they seem'd to want,' wrote Cook, 'was for us to be gone'.

Cook's instructions from the British Admiralty were to claim *Terra Australia Incognita*, provided he could reach agreement with the natives. This instruction, however, assumed a civilisation recognisable to European eyes. But Cook found not 'one inch of Cultivated land in the whole Country', no recognisable structure of authority, and no permanent buildings. To his eyes, these children of Nature did not reach a level of culture that would allow them to bargain with him for land. Before leaving, however, Cook had an inscription carved on a tree, facing out to sea, to warn off other potential European claimants.

The reasons behind the British decision in 1787 to establish a penal settlement at Botany Bay were complex. Settlement was the only real way in which Britain could assert a legal right to the continent ahead of Portuguese, Spanish and Dutch claims, and there were further fears of French territorial expansion in the Pacific region. The pressure on Britain to make a claim to the Australian continent increased with the start of the American Revolution in 1776. Once this War of Independence had begun, British convicts could no longer be sent to work the American plantations, and the large numbers of felons sentenced to transportation were clogging British gaols. It was Joseph Banks, the botanist on Cook's voyage, who in 1779 first suggested Botany Bay to the House of Commons as an alternative destination for convicts.

But Botany Bay was more than a convenient 'dumping ground' for convicts, chosen for being so far away as to make it relatively certain that they could never come back. It had been touted as a re-settlement option for displaced American loyalists dispossessed after the American Revolution, and then living in crowded poverty in England. It was also ideally placed to create a secure trade route to China, providing an alternative to the Dutch-controlled East Indies route. And, perhaps most importantly, the natural resources of the new continent were a potential replacement for those lost in the Americas: not only was there abundant timber for the navy, there was also a new supply of the whale and seal oil increasingly demanded by the growing enterprises of the Industrial Revolution – from the Second Fleet onwards, many of the 'convict ships' were merely converted whaling ships, which quickly re-converted and set out in search of whales as soon as the human cargo had been offloaded. So although British Prime Minister William Pitt justified the penal settlement to parliament as the cheapest available option for disposing of convicts, there were underlying political, military and economic concerns influencing his decision.

Strange though it might seem today, the transportation of convicts to Australia was also seen as rational and humane. The eighteenth-century British legal system decreed the death penalty for a wide range of offences, most of which would be considered minor today. Prisons were so overcrowded that old ships were permanently moored in the Thames Estuary to take the overflow. The alternative of transportation allowed convicts to 'redeem' themselves by hard work, and in so doing, to help construct a new colony.

And so the new country of Australia was founded. In the spirit of scientific enquiry, Governor Phillip and the other senior members of the settlement attempted to establish contact with local Aborigines, and to find out more about them. Captain-lieutenant of marines Watkin Tench, a veteran of Britain's war against the rebellious American colonies, was under contract to London publisher John Debrett to produce an account of his experiences with the First Fleet. In *A Narrative of the Expedition to Botany Bay*[6] (published in 1789) Tench recorded his observations of the local Aborigines. In proper scientific manner, he is careful to note:

> ...that all I can here, or in any future part of this work, relate with fidelity of the natives of New South Wales must be made up of detached observations, taken at different times, and not from a regular series of knowledge of the customs and manners of a people with whom opportunities of communication are so scarce as to have been seldom obtained.

Tench's early accounts of the Aborigines are models of dispassionate record. He picks up on descriptions by both Dampier and Cook, comparing and contrasting them with his own observations:

> In their persons, they are far from being a stout race of men, though nimble, sprightly, and vigorous. The deficiency of both of the fore teeth of the upper jaw, mentioned by Dampier, we have seen in almost the whole of the men. But their organs of sight, so far from being defective, as that author mentions those of the inhabitants of the western side of the continent to be, are remarkably quick and piercing. Their colour Mr Cook is inclined to think rather a deep chocolate than an absolute black, though he confesses they have the appearance of the latter, which he attributes to the greasy filth their skins are loaded with. Of their want of cleanliness we have had sufficient proof but, I am of opinion, all the washing in the world would not render them two degrees less black than an African Negro. At some of our first interviews we had several droll instances of their mistaking the Africans we brought with us for their own countrymen.

Only the occasional word or phrase indicates Tench's cultural prejudices at work (note the implied censure for lack of cleanliness, and the casual reference to black Africans having been brought along for the trip). Like both Dampier and Cook, Tench notes the marked Aboriginal disinterest in adopting European clothing, recording 'the disregard they have invariably shown for all the finery we could deck them with', and remarking that:

> *Of the use or benefit of clothing these people appear to have no comprehension, though their sufferings from the climate they live in strongly point out the necessity of a covering from the rigour of the seasons. Both sexes, and those of all ages, are invariably found naked. But it must not be inferred from this that custom so inures them to the changes of the elements as to make them bear with indifference the extremes of heat and cold, for we have had visible and repeated proofs that the latter affects them severely, when they are seen shivering and huddling themselves up in heaps in their huts or the caverns of the rocks, until a fire can be kindled.*

In other words, their lack of practical clothing is seen as proof that they are 'uncivilised', and Tench reports it in conjunction with his observation that 'they are fond of adorning themselves with scars, which increase their natural hideousness. It is hardly possible to see anything in human shape more ugly than one of these savages thus scarified, and farther ornamented with a fish bone stuck through the gristle of the nose'.

Like Dampier and Cook, Tench judges Aboriginal society by European standards, equating lack of material possessions and lack of evidence of perpetual occupation of settled land with lack of culture. He, too, looks for permanent buildings as evidence of civilisation, but finds only temporary shelters, describing Aboriginal huts by opining that 'nothing more rude in construction or deficient in conveniency can be imagined', though he does concede that the people 'depend less on them for shelter than on the caverns with which the rocks abound'.

Nor does he find any evidence of permanent agriculture, observing that 'To cultivation of the ground they are utter strangers, and wholly depend for food on the few fruits they gather, the roots they dig up in the swamps, and the fish they pick up along shore or contrive to strike from their canoes with spears', although he does admire the skill and dexterity with which the fragile canoes are managed. Even at this early stage in European settlement, Tench records that when fish are scarce Aboriginal groups attempt to steal from the settlers, who are prepared to respond with force: 'The only resource at these times is to show a musket, and if the bare sight of it is not sufficient, to fire it over their heads, which has seldom failed of dispersing them hitherto, but how long the terror which it excites may continue is doubtful'.

Importantly for later debates, including the 1997 claims of Aboriginal cannibalism, Tench's description of Aboriginal eating customs goes on to record that:

> *From their manner of disposing of those who die... as well as from every other observation, there is no reason to suppose these people cannibals. Nor do they ever eat animal substances in a raw state, unless pressed by extreme hunger, but indiscriminately broil them and their vegetables on a fire, which renders these last an innocent food, though in their raw state many of them are of a poisonous quality, as a poor convict who unguardedly eat of them experienced, by falling a sacrifice in twenty-four hours afterwards.*

It is worth noting, though, that Tench's careful descriptions of the Aborigines differ very little from his observations on the local wildlife. This is his description of the kangaroo:

> *Of the natural history of the kangaroo we are still very ignorant. We may, however, venture to pronounce this animal a new species of opossum, the female being furnished with a bag in which the young is contained, and in which the teats are found. These last are only two in number, a strong presumptive proof, had we no other evidence, that the kangaroo brings forth rarely more than one at a birth. But this is settled beyond a doubt from more than a dozen females having been killed, which had invariably but one formed in the pouch.*

After giving detailed statistics on the height, growth and weight of the species, Tench goes on to recount the more marvellous aspects of the animal, remarking that 'I shall hardly be credited when I affirm that the kangaroo, on being brought forth, is not larger than an English mouse', and noting that 'At what time of the year they copulate, and in what manner, we know not. The testicles of the male are placed contrary to the usual order of nature...Their bleat is mournful and very different from that of any other animal. It is, however, seldom heard but in the young ones'. Ever practical, he also notes that the young kangaroo 'eats tender and well flavoured, tasting like veal, but the old ones are more tough and stringy than bull-beef.'

The practice of shooting specimens, like the kangaroo, for closer examination was not extended to Aborigines, but the English were certainly not averse to capturing them for the same purpose. In Tench's second book, *A Complete Account of the Settlement at Port Jackson*[7] (published in 1793), he records an incident in which:

> ...the governor on the 31st of December [1789] sent two boats, under the command of Lieutenant Ball of the Supply and Lieutenant George Johnston of the marines, down the harbour with directions to those officers to seize and carry off some of the natives. The boats proceeded to Manly Cove, where several Indians were seen standing on the beach, who were enticed by courteous behaviour and a few presents to enter into conversation. A proper opportunity being presented, our people rushed in among them, and seized two men. The rest fled, but the cries of the captives soon brought them back, with many others, to their rescue, and so desperate were their struggles that in spite of every effort on our side, only one of them was secured; the other effected his escape. The boats put off without delay and an attack from the shore instantly commenced. They threw spears, stones, firebrands, and whatever else presented itself at the boats; nor did they retreat, agreeable to their former custom, until many muskets were fired over them.

> *The prisoner was now fastened by ropes to the thwarts of the boat and, when he saw himself irretrievably disparted from his countrymen, set up the most piercing and lamentable cries of distress. His grief, however, was soon diminished. He accepted and ate of some broiled fish which was given to him and sullenly submitted to his destiny.*

The subsequent treatment of the prisoner, later named Manly, was both kind and cruel, with the settlers attempting to 'civilise' him as a house pet: he was 'soothed', offered food, shown pictures of people, birds and animals to ascertain which he could recognize as having observed – though this was not altogether successful, since he identified the elephant and rhinoceros and several others that most certainly did not exist in his country. He was later given a formal meal at 'a side table of the governor's', so that his captors could observe which foods he would eat, but then the attentions to his person became more invasive:

> *In the afternoon his hair was closely cut, his head combed, and his beard shaved... His hair... was filled with vermin, whose destruction seemed to afford him great triumph; nay, either revenge, or pleasure, prompted him to eat them! but on our expressing disgust and abhorrence he left it off.*

> *To this succeeded his immersion in a tub of water and soap, where he was completely scrubbed from head to foot; after which a shirt, a jacket, and a pair of trowsers, were put upon him. Some part of this ablution I had the honour to perform, in order that I might ascertain the real colour of the skin of these people. My observation was then... that they are as black as the lighter cast of the African negroes.*

His captivity was enforced: 'To prevent his escape, a handcuff with a rope attached to it, was fastened around his left wrist, which at first highly delighted him; he called it 'Ben-gad-ee' (or ornament), but his delight changed to rage and hatred when he discovered its use.' As well it might. Manly slowly became part of the governor's settlement, unable to return to his tribe.

And so began an enforced and unhappy relationship. Aborigines displaced by the fledgling colony responded at first with hostility, but reprisals by the armed colonists (as well as the unprovoked savagery of some) helped push these groups out to the fringes. Little more than a decade after first settlement, European views of the Aborigines had begun to polarise around two familiar stereotypes: the dispossessed and urbanised Aborigine, already affected by alcohol; and the hostile savage.

Early Australian 'literary' writing followed the European model, where poetry was the serious medium for the expression of finer feelings and ideals. It suited perfectly the constraints of the new colony, where no-one had the leisure or material resources to produce longer works. Writers concerned themselves with the lofty issues of building a new civilisation in an alien land – issues which could be suitably presented in the resounding rhetoric of neo-classical verse.

So pervasive was this imported literary vision of the new land that even the first crop of native-born colonial writers subscribed to it. William Charles Wentworth, born in 1790 between Sydney and Norfolk Island, was educated in England, returning to Australia between 1810 and 1817, and again in 1824. At Cambridge in 1823 he wrote 'Australasia'[8], probably the first piece of literature in which an Australian looks back nostalgically to the country of their birth. Wentworth's account of the Aborigines bears all the hallmarks of Rousseau's noble savage, so different from Dampier's view:

> Ye primal tribes, lords of this old domain,
> Swift-footed hunters of the pathless plain,
> Unshackled wanderers, enthusiasts free,
> Pure native sons of savage liberty,
> Who hold all things in common, earth, sea, air,
> Or only occupy the nightly lair,
> Whereon each sleeps; who won no chieftain's pow'r,
> Save his, that's mightiest of the passing hour...

This is the language of a generation that had grown up after the American Declaration of Independence, and the French Revolution, and were far enough removed from the excesses of the guillotine and the Terror to feel comfortable with ideas of individual liberty.

It is also the language of a poet influenced by the ideas of the English Romantics. Wordsworth and Coleridge were, by the 1820s, the established and influential 'older generation' of Romantic poets; Byron and Shelley had been undergraduates at Cambridge only a few years before Wentworth studied there. Wentworth's poem reflects Wordsworth's ideas of Nature as the source of truth:

> Untutor'd children, fresh from Nature's mould,
> No songs have ye to trace the time of old:-
> No hidden themes, like these, employ your care,
> For you enough the knowledge that ye are:-

Clearly, this is a European romanticisation. Only someone centred entirely in a written culture could claim that Aborigines have 'no songs'. Wentworth also imposes on Aboriginal culture an eighteenth-century view of classical virtues when he talks of the battle and the hunt:

> Let Learning's sons, who would this secret scan,
> Unlock its mystic casket if they can,-
> To your unletter'd tastes are sweeter far
> The dance of battle, and the song of war,
> 'Mid hostile ranks the deadly spear to throw,
> Or see the foeman stagg'ring 'neath your blow:-
> To you, ye sable hunters, sweeter too
> To spy the track of bounding kangaroo,
> Or long-neck'd Emu...

The corroboree is also classicised, as an ancient Greek dance of victory:

> And now, the labours of the chase being o'er,
> And Nature's keen suggestions heard no more,

> *In uncouth numbers seated in a ring*
> *Your ancient fathers' warlike feats ye sing,*
> *Or striking each his shield, with clatt'ring lance,*
> *The early night exhaust in Pyrrhic dance.*

Although Wentworth's vision of Aboriginal innocence was heavily romanticised, it did at least acknowledge the presence and significance of the older culture. Other poets, like Charles Tompson, were so concerned with Australia's bright future that Aboriginal culture was simply written out of existence. The land itself was rewritten as a sleeping presence that awaited the touch of the white man to awaken and grow.

Charles Tompson was born in Sydney in 1807, and published the collection for which he is best known, *Wild Notes, from the Lyre of a Native Minstrel*, in 1826 – the first Australian-published collection of verse by someone born in this country. In 'A Song, Written for the XXVIth January Last, being the XXXVIth Anniversary of the Establishment of this Colony'[9] Tompson celebrates the fulfilment of what a later generation of Americans would call 'manifest destiny' – the 'God-given' right to European occupation of vast areas of already inhabited but 'under-used' land. Tompson chooses the kind of high-flown classical rhetoric favoured in the poetry of the previous century to assert his imperial claims. In the tiny colony on the edge of a giant continent, Tompson saw Australia's destiny writ large.

The poem begins with the moment of Australia's creation:

> *When first above the briny surge*
> *AUSTRALIA rear'd her tow'ring crest,*
> *The roaring gales, confounded, fled,*
> *The troubled billows sunk to rest;*
> *And proud, above the azure flood,*
> *Fix'd and immoveable SHE stood.*

Having appeared, Australia is greeted with a fanfare of seashell trumpets, and blessed by the Roman sea god, Neptune:

> *The Tritons, with their writhen shells,*

> Made all the hollow grots rebound;
> Earth, to her inmost caverns shook;
> Old Ocean trembled at the sound;
> And, august, from his crystal caves,
> Rose Neptune, sov'reign of the waves.
>
> ...He rag'd not now, but, with a smile
> Prophetic, thus address'd our isle:-
>
> 'Commerce, on halcyon wings, shall hail
> 'Thy ports, as yet to man unknown,
> 'And loyalty shall stamp Thy name –
> 'The choicest gem in Albion's crown:-
> 'While Thy prolific bosom pours
> 'Her bounteous gifts in lavish show'rs!'

His prophecy delivered, Neptune departs, leaving Australia to await its destiny:

> Ages have roll'd their circling orbs,
> Since dumb creation heard the tale;
> Still each returning year beheld
> Rude darkness o'er our Isle prevail;-
> But now the dawn of Science gleams,
> And Hope streams wide her ruddy beams,
>
> Peace lifts her olive sceptre high;
> Brown Industry assumes the plough;
> Commerce expands her canvas wings,
> Wealth points where honor guards the prow.
> These, HAPPY AUSTRALASIA, these
> Proclaim Thee QUEEN OF SOUTHERN SEAS!

The most striking feature of this poem is the way it presents the occupation of Australia by the British as a God-given, pre-destined right. The Aboriginal presence – 'Brown Industry' – is incidental to ordained commercial development. In this, Tompson's lofty verse foreshadows the political views of the famous radical Presbyterian minister, John Dunmore Lang (an early advocate of an Australian republic). In a speech to the Moreton Bay Friends of the Aborigines Lang justified British expropriation of the original inhabitants by saying that:

> God in making the earth never intended it should be occupied by men so incapable of appreciating its resources as the Aborigines of Australia. The white man had indeed, only carried out the intentions of the Creator in coming and settling down in the territory of the natives.[10]

From the very start, then, literature served a political end. Tompson appears to have shared with many colonists the early hope that Aborigines could be 'civilised', to take their place in the coming nation. By the time he was born, though, the early experiments at integration were already failing. He laments this failure in another poem, 'Black Town'[11], based on Oliver Goldsmith's celebrated eighteenth-century English poem, 'The Deserted Village'. Goldsmith had lamented the decline of traditional rural life in England. Tompson lamented the collapse of early attempts to integrate Aborigines into the colony's agricultural economy. He prefaced his poem with the explanatory comment, that: 'This deserted Hamlet is situate upon the New Richmond Road, distant about twenty eight miles from the Metropolis [Sydney]. These lines were written in the Veranda of the Chapel.' The sense of desolation, of the failure of human effort in the face of 'th'all-conquering scythe of time' was considered a highly appropriate subject for poetic contemplation:

> Ill-fated hamlet! from each tott'ring shed,
> Thy sable inmates, p'rhaps, for ever fled.
> (Poor, restless wand'rers of the woody plain!
> The skies their covert – nature their domain.)
> Seek with the birds, the casual dole of heav'n,
> Pleas'd with their lot – content with what is giv'n
> Time was, and recent memory speaks it true,
> When round each little cot, a garden grew;
> A field whose culture serv'd a two-fold part, –

> *Food, and instruction in the rural art;*
> *The lordling tenant, and his sable wife*
> *Were taught to prize the sweets of social life...*

To Tompson, teaching the 'sable inmates' the arts of polite society, and introducing them to the advantages of Christianity, was the noblest of achievements. He laments the indifference of many colonists to this higher purpose:

> *Lost child! shall we the savage part pursue?*
> *Shall all despise thee for thy sable hue?*
> *Will Charity no warm viceregent send*
> *To own thee brother, or to call thee friend?*
> *True, there are some, whose panting bosoms thirst*
> *With holy zeal, to raise thee from the dust,*
> *T'infuse those truths to burden'd sinners giv'n,*
> *And fix thy wand'ring, reckless thoughts on heav'n.*
> *But these bright thoughts th'unwilling fates deride,*
> *The will is theirs – th'ability deny'd.*

Finally, despite his desire to acknowledge Aborigines – at least, in their 'improved' form – as brothers, Tompson opts for the poetic way out of the dilemmas posed by clashing cultures. He blames it all on the inevitable passage of time:

> *Thus shall man's proudest, noblest project fade,*
> *And with its founder in the dust be laid.*
> *Th'imperial palace, and the lowly cot*
> *Alike must share this universal lot,*
> *And bow before th'all-conquering scythe of time,-*
> *Such was proud Ilion's [Troy's] fate, and such, alas! is thine!*

Which was always less of a comfort to the inhabitant of the 'lowly cot', or the failed social experiment, than it was to the rulers in their palaces and mansions.

It would be a mistake to think that all the colonists shared a common view of the inferiority of Aboriginal culture. One anonymous contributor to the *Colonial Times* in 1826 extolled the happy existence of the Aboriginal children of Nature in their unspoilt paradise before the white people came:

> *Oh! where are the wilds I once sported among,*
> *When free as my clime through its forests I sprung;*
> *When no track but the few which our fires had made,*
> *Had tarnished the carpet that nature had laid;*
> *When the lone waters dashed down the darksome ravine;*
> *O'erhung by the shade of the Huon's dark green;*
> *When the broad morning sun o'er our mountains could roam,*
> *And not see a slave in our bright Island home.*
>
> *When our trees were unscath'd, nor our echoes awoke,*
> *To the hum of the stranger, or woodman's wild stroke;*
> *When our rocks proudly rose 'gainst the dash of the main,*
> *And saw not a bark on the wide, azure plain;*
> *When the moon through the heavens roll'd onward and*
>   *smil'd,*
> *As she lighted the home of the free and the wild.*[12]

This idyllic existence is contrasted with the savage and alien ways of the invaders:

> *Oh! my country, the stranger has found thy free clime,*
> *And he comes with the sons of misfortune and crime;*
> *He brings the rude refuse of countries laid waste,*
> *To tread thy fair wilds and thy waters to taste;*
> *He usurps the best lands of thy native domains,*
> *And thy children must fly, or submit to his chains.*

The poet also criticises the free settlers for their imposition of an alien culture on the land, and for their petty pride. The vision of white Australia here is far different from Tompson's lofty rhetoric:

> *He builds his dark home, and he tricks it about,*
> *With trinkets and trifles within and without;*
> *When the bright sun of nature sinks into the main,*
> *He lights little suns to make day-light again;*

> And he calls a crowd round him, to see him preside,
> And our tyrant himself is the slave of his pride!
>
> ...Oh! I would not exchange the wild nature I bear,
> For life with the tame sons of culture and care,
> Not give one free moment as proudly I stand,
> For all that their arts and their toils can command.
> Away to the mountains, and leave them the pains,
> To pursue their dull toils, and to forge their dark chains.

This rejection of the invading culture is one of the most heartfelt in the early literature. It is tempting to speculate that, for the poet, Aboriginal life represented the freedom the 'sons of misfortune' had been denied by transportation.

The contrast of free and noble Aborigines with the 'rude refuse' of the convicts – the best and worst of two cultures meeting – is a theme that recurs in a number of early literary works. Unfortunately for the Aborigines, there is usually an underlying assumption of their inevitable decline in the face of superior force.

Nevertheless, sympathy for the vanishing and perhaps superior life of the noble savage was to prove very persistent. As late as 1886 Ettie A. Ayliffe (Mrs. J.A. Bode) published a collection entitled *Original Poems*, which included the poem 'Lubra'[13], in which she attacks hypocritical attempts at 'justification' of Aboriginal dispossession on religious grounds. The poem is interesting for another reason too: it attempts to create an identifiable 'Aboriginal' voice in English. It actually has more in common with biblical language, but it does manage to avoid the neo-classical or romantic distortions of the earlier poetry:

> Ours was the land, all ours, mine and my peoples': the tribes'
> To roam at will, to dwell, to hunt and to fish in.
> We were the lords of the soil, the inheritance ancient
> Owned by our fathers, and theirs, who handed it down to
>   their children.
> Ours, plenteous game: the life of the free in the forest;

> *Happy were we in the wild, and our wigwams builded at*
> *pleasure.*
> *Joy, we could call it at will, guest of the careless and simple;*
> *Joy of feasts at our fire when the tribes in corroboree mingled,*
> *Joy of rest in the woods, where the wild birds screeched*
> *through our dreaming;*
> *Simple our pleasures, but sweet; and care had no word in our*
> *language.*

Into this blissful life comes the invader, the alien, the culture that cannot be understood:

> *The white man, he makes many things: too many; has care,*
> *and is weary.*
> *...Why should man labour and sweat, and groan out his life*
> *to no profit?*
> *Why make innum'rable things, when his wants are so few*
> *and so simple?*
> *...Happy were we, more than he who builds; makes great*
> *things, and has burden.*
> *...Would he had sunk in the sea, and the waters gone foaming*
> *above him,*
> *Before he had stepp'd on the land...*

Ayliffe reverses the usual picture, of the dangerous native lurking on the edges of civilisation, an ever-present menace:

> *Houses and farms, and the fields of his tillage our hunting*
> *grounds fill;*
> *The game has slipped from the way, is scant and diminished;*
> *We have no country to roam, to dwell therein in abundance:*
> *He drives us for evermore onward, ever circling us nearer;*
> *Chicken are we as the game that the hunter has trapped in its*
> *hiding.*
> *We dare not kindle our fires; to camp on the bounds of his*
> *pastures;*
> *See, we are fading away; we wither and pass into shadow!*

Tompson's assertion of a God-given British right to occupy Australia is also reversed by Ayliffe:

> Even the scrublands uncleared we scarcely are suffered to rest in,
> We, the possessors from first of this country made all for us black men.

The poem achieves, in part at least, a turning of the tables on the usual white arguments. Australian poetry had frequently offered sympathetic identification with the plight of the Aborigines, but Ayliffe forces the reader to take on something of the other cultural perspective too. It portrays the white invader as hunter, the Aborigine as prey:

> He is the eagle whose eye ranges afar, and thro' heaven,
> Wings his strong flight: the prey sees, and is swift to devour it;
> He is the dingo that prowls and lurks all night through the forest:
> Howls to the moon in his caves, for he scents and he ravins for carcase.

At this point the poem turns again, and directly accuses the invader on his own self-justifying terms:

> They talk of their God and His law; we, we know naught of things Christian:
> Yet we know this was all ours, and would be so still but for white men.
> If we had owned that great force sufficient to conquer them fighting,
> Then we, too, might understand this prate of the justice of Heaven.

The voice of the poem changes, becoming more overtly biblical, even Old Testament. Its condemnation is a response to those squatters who justified their actions on the grounds that they were like Moses and his tribe, moving to take possession of the Promised Land:

> No sense of justice restrains, no balance made equal arrests him:
> That which his eye hath desired, lo, he makes haste to possess it;
> Thus he erases us out for his pleasure, his gain, his convenience:
> And preaching in many big words, he says that his God bids him do it.

Ayliffe identifies the huge discrepancy between the real motives and their justification. In this she foreshadows some of the more self-interested debate surrounding the 1997 Wik High Court decision on native title and pastoral leases. 'God' and 'white destiny' are today no longer advanced as the primary justifications. But the god of economic rationalism is. The concept of 'certainty of title' (a certainty which appears to apply largely to the pastoralists, and which is argued on purely economic grounds) has replaced the idea of 'natural inheritance' in the rhetoric of dispossession. But the sense that the white occupiers are best fitted to make use of the land remains unchanged. Ayliffe points unerringly to the real causes of dispossession when she says, of the white man, 'he erases us out for his pleasure, his gain, his convenience'.

Vague sympathy for the dispossessed was first brought sharply into focus by the massacre at Myall Creek, New South Wales, in June 1838. Twenty-eight Aborigines – old men, women and children – were murdered, and their bodies burnt, by a dozen white men. Governor George Gipps insisted (for the first and only time) on applying the policy of equal treatment for murderers, black or white, and the seven men found guilty were hanged. There was enormous opposition in the colony, with newspaper editorials condemning Gipps outright. It is therefore all the more surprising to find a white woman, Eliza Hamilton Dunlop, taking a courageous stand with the publication, only five days before the executions, of 'The Aboriginal Mother (from Myall's Creek)'[14]. The rhetoric is entirely English, but the mother's bitter recrimination in the face of the awful savagery of race war is universal:

> Oh! hush thee – hush my baby,
> I may not tend thee yet.
> Our forest home is distant far,
> And midnight's star is set.
> Now, hush thee – or the pale-faced men
> Will hear thy piercing wail,
> And what would then thy mother's tears
> Or feeble strength avail!
>
> Oh, could'st thy little bosom,
> That mother's torture feel,
> Or could'st thou know thy father lies
> Struck down by English steel;
> Thy tender form would wither,
> Like the kniven in the sand,
> And the spirit of my perished tribe
> Would vanish from the land.

The mother is presented like a heroine from a Walter Scott novel, unable to play the warrior, but bravely defying the attackers in the vain attempt to save her children:

> For thy young life, my precious,
> I fly the field of blood,
> Else had I, for my chieftain's sake,
> Defied them where they stood;
> But basely bound my woman's arm,
> No weapon might it wield:
> I could but cling round him I loved,
> To make my heart a shield.

But there is nothing romantic in the portrayal of what she has just escaped:

> I saw my firstborn treasure
> Lie headless at my feet,

> *The goro on this hapless breast,*
> *In his life-stream is wet!*
> *And thou! I snatched thee from their sword,*
> *It harmless pass'd by thee!*
> *But clave the binding cords – and gave,*
> *Haply, the power to flee.*

This is the gruesome reality of massacre. The stroke of the sword which beheads the elder son gives the mother a moment of grace, just sufficient to escape with her baby, drenched in the blood of the slaughtered child. What follows is more haunting still. It foreshadows the aftermath of genocide, when the survivors attempt to rebuild their lives:

> *Now who will teach thee, dearest,*
> *To poise the shield, and spear,*
> *To wield the koopin, or to throw*
> *The boommerring, void of fear;*
> *To breast the river in its might;*
> *The mountain tracks to tread?*
> *The echoes of my homeless heart*
> *Reply – the dead, the dead!*

Dunlop's position is interesting. She arrived in Australia in 1823, a mother of four children married to the man who became protector of Aborigines at Wollombi and Macdonald River. She published poetry in most of the leading newspapers of the day, and was the first Australian poet to attempt to reproduce Aboriginal songs in written form. Like a number of other interested and sympathetic people of her time, she also carried out research into Aboriginal languages. This early form of ethnography sought to record – that is, in European terms, to write down – the oral traditions of a vanishing culture. But given the attitude of most colonists – that the Aborigines were a worthless menace – good intentions were, from the very start, inextricably bound up with the certainty of destruction. What most people like Dunlop felt they were recording was a doomed people.

Ironically, one of the most complete accounts of Aboriginal culture comes not from the official attempts at scientific documentation, or from the sympathetic individual responses of well-placed colonists, but from – apparently – the pen of a convict.

James Tucker was transported for life after writing a threatening letter to his cousin. He was sent to Sydney in 1827, and worked in the Blue Mountains, then later in the colonial architect's office where Francis Greenway was building his reputation as Australia's first significant architect. Tucker was twice granted his ticket-of-leave – the conditional pardon that meant he could live freely in the colony, but not return to England – but lost it again both times. His life after the mid-1850s is unclear, but he probably died in Sydney in 1888.

The book Tucker is now associated with, *Ralph Rashleigh*[15], was probably written about 1844-5. It was not published until 1929, in London, when it was taken to be a book of actual reminiscences of the convict experience. A publishers' note records how the story came into their hands, as a typescript from 'Mr. Charles H. Bertie, the well-known librarian of Sydney', who later sent the manuscript, 'an aged foolscap book of undoubted antiquity'. Assuming the account to be real, the publishers decided to rewrite it in a style more 'acceptable to modern readers'. Not until 1952 was it finally published in its original form, as a novel.

The book uses the device of fictionalised 'reminiscences', like Jonathan Swift's satirical *Gulliver's Travels*. The story is reported by a squatter (an authoritative voice), who acts as a kind of narrative frame, within which the actual book of Rashleigh's adventures is set. Like many such books, it combines detailed observations of local customs with its fictional events, creating an effect that is somewhere between novel and documentary account – what we might now call 'faction'.

The Aborigines and their ceremonies are described without sentimentality, and with a curious blend of fascinated acceptance and revulsion. In this, the book brings together the usually polarised views of early colonists towards Aboriginal culture. It represents one of the few attempts at genuine understanding of an alien society, rather than dispassionate recording, idealisation, or flat rejection.

The book traces the story of Rashleigh's life, from his first arrest for passing counterfeit coins, through his transportation and adventures among bushrangers and Aborigines, to his return to white Australian society, and finally his death during an Aboriginal attack.

In the following passage, which begins with the epigraph: 'Untamed, as nature first formed free-born man, When wild in woods the noble savage ran', the runaway Rashleigh has been caught in a flash flood. He is washed ashore on a beach somewhere to the north of what would later become Port Macquarie. He recovers consciousness to find himself surrounded by Aborigines. He fears for his life, until the intervention of the elder of the tribe. The elder is described in terms that recall observations by Dampier, Cook and Tench:

> *The black who now approached was one of the most revolting specimens of humanity that can possibly be conceived. A very few white hairs remained upon his polished skull, forming a thin circle around it. His beard, however, was more luxuriant than usually falls to the lot of any Australian aboriginal. One of his organs of vision had been utterly extinguished, leaving in its room only a raw and bloody cavity. His other eye appeared to be more than half obscured by rheum. His body was emaciated by sickness until it scarcely possessed more substance than a shadow.*
>
> *Add to the above that he was gashed and scarred all over, but particularly about the face, also that, though last not least among a race supereminent for uncleanliness, he appeared even more conspicuous for personal filth than any of his fellows, and you may conceive some idea of the unattractive appearance of this old black.*

The old man, or 'carandjie', wields great authority and, following his intervention, Rashleigh is adopted into the tribe, undergoing ceremonies of tooth-removal and ritual scarring at a tribal ritual conducted at sunrise:

> At a motion from the old black, Rashleigh's arms were secured by two of the bystanders, and the carandjie put on such an indescribably demoniac look that our exile now quite gave himself up for lost. His race was not yet run, however, for the ancient black magician, taking the implements of stone in his hand, approached, speaking very earnestly and... making signs as if he wished the prisoner to open his mouth. Rashleigh at last complied with the direction, and the old man placed the chisel against one of his single teeth... a smart tap on the chisel from the stone forced out the tooth, the patient's head having been supported behind by one of his guards.

This part of the ceremony was followed by 'a dance, called by the colonists a *corroboree*', at the conclusion of which Rashleigh is again seized, and feels gashes inflicted upon his back and chest, though as an escaped convict he is able to bear it bravely, as 'being almost indurated to torture by the cats of the Coal river, he did not betray any susceptibility to pain.' On being raised up again, Rashleigh 'found that he had received no less than thirty six deep cuts, regularly placed, before and behind him, in four rows of nine each, from his shoulders to the bottom of his ribs, but none lower than this.' The tribe then celebrates, with food and an intoxicating drink that had 'a taste something similar to fermented Spanish liquorice, but with a certain pungent acridity which it imparted to the palate after it had been swallowed.' The effect is to render the tribe 'completely dead drunk'.

Once formally accepted in this manner, Rashleigh is given pigment with which to anoint his skin, which darkens to the point where he looks not unlike his fellow tribesmen. He is resigned to living the native life, remaining 'in this state of willing barbarism for four years' as a 'white blackfellow'. He is given a wife, dogs, hunting implements, and rapidly becomes 'tolerably proficient in most of the simple arts of the aborigines', having learned enough of their language to get by. His narrative includes detailed descriptions of tribal justice, marriage and burial customs; descriptions which bear a remarkable similarity to the reports of other later observers (such as Pemberton, whose account appears in chapter 3). Here is Tucker's description of 'courtship' and 'marriage':

> *These aborigines have no marriage ceremony whatsoever. When a youth has undergone his initiation and is declared to be a man, the first use he makes of the weapons he has prepared is to go upon a sort of foray to hunt for a wife. With this view he steals cautiously towards some swamp, near which he has lain in wait all night in readiness for this enterprise at day dawn, and from among the young gins belonging to another tribe, whom he thus surprises while searching for food, he selects one to his mind whom he perceives by her head-dress to be unmarried. Her he instantly pounces upon and bears off by force, maugre her struggles or the outcries of her companions. If he can succeed in conveying her safely to his camp before any of her male relatives can rescue her, she becomes his bride, never afterwards being owned by her own tribe, who will not even allow her to approach them.*
>
> *The young gins, who seem to consider it a point of honour to offer as much resistance to this customary kind of abduction as they can, do not fail to bite, kick and scratch their captors as furiously as possible in their transit, which the latter retaliates by blows upon the female's head, of force nearly enough to stagger a horse, for should any of them alight upon a leg or an arm it invariably breaks the limb; and thus, by the time they reach the camp the bride is at least insensible and the bridegroom streaming with blood from the effects of this truly savage courtship...*

Remarkably, Rashleigh's narrative also includes an account of his own life with his Aboriginal wife, Lorra. This appears to be the only nineteenth-century account of a genuine love match between a white man and a black woman. The marriage ends with her death, Rashleigh mourning her as 'the only female to whom himself was ever dear, except his sister and his mother.'

The uneasy acceptance of difference which Tucker's work reveals could not last. The technique of combining observation and narrative to form a compelling tale, however, was much more persistent. It proved irresistible to the popular writers of the 1890s, who serviced the enormous English market for Australian adventure stories.

This market had come into existence following the Colonial and Indian Exhibition in London's South Kensington, in 1886, which was attended by some five million people. The public impact must have been something similar to the 1980s release of Paul Hogan's *Crocodile Dundee* in New York. Things Australian were suddenly in fashion. The exotic world of the Australian outback, revealed in black and white photographs and displays, was brought to life for ordinary Londoners by the cheap publication of highly-coloured and romantic stories of bush life. Established Australian writers who had been unable to sell a single collection of short stories to English publishers suddenly found that tales of mateship and the bush were in hot demand. Collections were compiled in London by minor Australian writers solely to cater to this new market. Anthologies with titles like *Under the Gum Tree* (1890), *Coo-ee* (1891) and *In Australian Wilds* (1889) were an instant success. In this imperial and popular market, where mass public education had created a newly literate working class, much of the 'decorum' of middle-class taste did not apply. The idea that romances should be both entertaining and morally improving was insignificant to people hungry for fictional escape from intolerable working conditions. Sensationalism became an acceptable aspect of the popular novel, and sensational tales of encounters with savage tribes were one of the staples of such fiction.

One writer who tapped into this new market was Simpson Newland. Like many other writers of popular Australian fiction, he was first and foremost a public figure. Born in England in 1836, Newland came to Australia as a child, and became a member of the South Australian parliament, and chair of a commission on the development of the River Murray. In 1893 in London he published *Paving the Way*[16], a novel based loosely on his experiences of outback life. Like Tucker's book, it took liberties with the facts, tailoring its narrative to the new public taste. His object, Newland said, was 'to blend truth and fiction in a connected narrative'. His form 'partakes largely of a romance', but the details are apparently 'mainly authentic'.

The book commences with the story of an early shipwreck on the South Australian coast and the massacre of survivors by Aborigines, led by a 'tall and brawny savage, with a broad scar down the right side of his fierce face, which increased its natural hideousness'.

The massacre – based on an isolated incident in the history of white settlement – is generalised by Newland as representative of Aboriginal savagery:

> The dead and dying white men were alike hacked and speared in the blood-frenzy and love of slaughter common to all the aboriginals of Australia.
>
> ...They rushed upon the bodies of the white men with brutal, abusive cries; their clothes were torn away and every indignity and horror that ingenuity could devise was perpetrated on the slain. Then, when their furious spite was appeased or spent, the mutilated remains were dragged down and cast into the sea...

Newland's account shares with Dampier and Cook a Eurocentric code of 'civilised' human behaviour. Those writers had looked in vain for signs that Aboriginal groups wore clothes, built houses, had a social hierarchy. Newland's fiction goes further, and imposes on Aborigines a European sense of anti-civilised behaviour in the mutilation of dead enemies. It also portrays the victors as incapable of 'civilised' enjoyment of the spoils of war:

> The whole of the band presently came in, staggering under the booty they had taken. Everything eatable was thrown

about in the reckless manner of the Australian black in the time of abundance; some of the food was tossed away with contempt, while more met with the decided appreciation of the aboriginal appetite. Flour was voted unpalatable, and no wonder, since in their ignorance they essayed to devour it dry; but for the purposes of personal adornment it was much valued, particularly when preparing for the festive 'Corroboree.'

Unlike Tucker's fairly factual account of the corroboree, Newland's version cannot resist the opportunity to emphasise the essential savagery of the participants:

On special occasions, when feminine visitors or captives are present, they are of a distinctly festive and immoral tendency; then proceedings are indulged in that polite society would shudder at, but which the laws of the Australian aborigine sanction. Again, when the theme is war, the warrior is painted and bedizened with tenfold elaboration from the soles of his feet to the crown of his head. Weapons in hand, he parades proudly before his people, boasting of past exploits and vaunting of his prowess in the future. Hideous, grotesque, yet striking, he forms one of the whirling, bounding throng of warlike figures, passing before the bewildered eyes of the spectator with brandished arms and waving plumes in swift and strange evolution. Again, they form in line, square, or other intelligible order and foot it featly, all the time uttering suppressed, fierce cries to the accompaniment of their trampling feet, the clash of weapons and the beat of their rude music. Hour succeeds hour; often the whole night long, or indeed successive nights, are thus spent and the excitement lasts until nature can no more. It is the same with all the black-fellow's pleasures – eating, drinking, sleeping or the tender passion; in all alike he knows or acknowledges no law to limit his full indulgence.

And when the time comes for division of the final spoils – two captured white women – the warriors inevitably come to blows. 'An aged, tottering old man, who exercised great influence over his people' settles matters by killing both women, 'an act quite in accordance with the usages of the tribe'.

Newland's account, though set in much the same period as Tucker's, was written almost half a century later, when settlement was an accomplished fact, and the displacement of the Aborigines largely complete. It makes no attempt to examine Aboriginal custom as an alternative social system. Instead it takes the high imperial position of the later nineteenth century, of innate European superiority. The fictional narrative places all indigenous culture in a position of inferiority – at best unpleasant, at worst inhuman.

In the chapter ironically entitled 'Civilizing the Blacks', Newland records the reality of the official policy of co-existence on pastoral leases (the policy confirmed by the 1997 Wik decision, but rarely practised). This is the voice of Mr. Buckstone, Protector of Aborigines – a far cry from Eliza Dunlop's sympathetic voice some sixty years earlier:

> *'Pray, gentlemen,' said he, 'recollect that your mission is twofold, to recover the stock and to pacify the natives, in which laudable and benevolent objects I wish you every success. If you feel a disposition to be hard upon them, remember that you have implanted a taste for mutton deep down in their unsophisticated stomachs and no savage is good at controlling his appetite. Think what grilled chops, done to a turn, must mean to him after lean opossum and tough kangaroo.'*

Competition between hunters and graziers could have, from the graziers' point of view, only one result. The men to whom Buckstone speaks are in no doubt what he means by 'pacification':

> *'A 'cute man is the Protector of Aborigines,' observed Mr. Danker; 'he wants us to exterminate the fighting men of the*

> *Rufus tribe, but he won't say so. He knows that when I was in Adelaide little more than a week ago, the Government had nearly determined to send him up with a strong body of police to subdue them, which simply means a stand-up battle in which they would be shot down without quarter...'*

Official policy was still – at least in theory – governed by the established principle of equality before the law in cases of murder. Newland's story makes no bones about the South Australian government's pragmatic hypocrisy:

> *The authorities have been vacillating as usual on the aboriginal question. Very possibly if we make a slaughter and thus finally settle the ever-recurring trouble on this track, they may yield to popular clamour and prosecute us.*

But although he points the finger at such double standards, Newland's primary concern is not with the Aboriginal victims of dispossession. In his story, the failure by white settlers ruthlessly to stamp out all resistance merely causes further Aboriginal attacks:

> *Disdaining to seek cover, the savage warriors came fearlessly to the attack, leaping, dancing and clashing their shields and clubs together in bravado and scorn of men they had learnt to despise. Their yells and derisive shouts showed that they were confident in their numbers and bravery and looked for another easy victory.*

There is a certain grudging admiration for the warriors who, in their 'glory of paint and feathers', echo popular images of the 'American Indian' (as did Ettie Ayliffe's more sympathetic portrait, with its Aboriginal 'wigwams'). But admiration is not sympathy. Although he ironises some of the myths of British heroism popular at the time, Newland will not go so far as to join in the romanticisation of the Aboriginal past. His warriors are not noble. They are savage competitors in the struggle to fulfil the destiny of the white race. And in this struggle, there can only be one outcome:

When the troopers returned to the battle-ground, the old chief was still alive. As they approached, he raised himself on his elbow and after looking in vain for a weapon, spat with all the savage contempt of his race at the victors, then sank back with an abusive epithet on his lips and died. Had his colour been white and had he fallen at Bannockburn or Hastings, or any other famous fight for fatherland in the old world, his name would ring in the ears of posterity; but being a mere Australian savage, who died fighting against our religion and civilization, we can see nothing heroic in that. Perhaps he saw dimly, as many of his people have clearly seen since and as the American Indian has had occasion to know, that the success of the white man entailed the ruin of the aboriginal race. So he preferred to die defiant and free, rather than to linger on for a few miserable years in degradation and servitude.

White settlement in Australia had begun with cautious good intention, combined with a sense of the God-given destiny of the white race to 'inherit' the land from the (possibly) noble savage. But by the end of the nineteenth century, relations between invaders and invaded had hardened into violence, mistrust and mutual incomprehension. Attempts to include the original inhabitants in the noble task of civilising a continent were abandoned.

Newland represents the defiant death of his Aboriginal chieftain as some kind of choice by the mortally wounded man. In reality, there was no choice, except for the colonists, who could choose between the rapid extermination of Aboriginal culture, or its lingering decline. In either case, they would be now be guided by one of the most significant shifts in European thinking since the Renaissance: the theory of natural selection.

2

The Culminating Ape

Nineteenth-century relations between the settlers and indigenous peoples were inevitably affected by developments in European thinking. Enlightenment ideas of the 'noble savage' were supplanted by evolutionary theories which allowed scientists to begin developing rank orders of humanity. In the often difficult, sometimes hostile, conditions of colonisation, Australian settlers abandoned with some relief the official effort to embrace Aborigines as idealised children of Nature. It was far simpler and more convenient to regard them as superseded branches of humanity fated to be displaced by a superior culture.

It was probably inevitable that Governor Phillip's idealism would be tempered by the harsh realities of a colony struggling to establish itself under difficult conditions. He carried the responsibility for the lives and fortunes of the whole group, convict and free. When it came to any clash of interests with the indigenous inhabitants, his ultimate choice must always be with the wellbeing of the colonists.

Successive governors adopted varying positions on relations with the Aborigines, and Governor Lachlan Macquarie went so far as to establish a special school and a model village settlement for them, at Black Town on the Parramatta Road, where they could learn European farming practices. Neither experiment succeeded, however, and shortly before his departure in 1821, Macquarie instead recommended the creation of an Aboriginal reserve (a suggestion not acted on).

The problems had been exacerbated by a rapid increase in the numbers of colonists (up from 15,000 in 1815 to 30,000 in 1821). The inevitable expansion into the interior led to further clashes, which Macquarie attempted to deter with 'punitive' expeditions designed to terrorise the Aborigines. In clashes with the Wiradjuri, for example, an unknown number of Aborigines (probably in the hundreds) and some twenty British were killed. Macquarie also banned the carrying of weapons by Aborigines near the British settlements, on pain of armed retaliation. Under these hostile conditions, any perception of the Aborigines as 'noble savages' who could be incorporated in the new Australian order was quickly abandoned.

The lack of sustained large-scale armed resistance to settlement – a result of the very different social structures of the two societies – encouraged the colonists to view the tribes more as an irritation, dangerous at times but susceptible to firm action. Within a relatively short time of the first settlement in Australia, colonists were largely agreed that relations with indigenous people were to be a matter of displacement of tribes from disputed land, absorption of surviving individuals into the fringes of white society, and the rapid decline of an indigenous culture. Individual concerns had more to do with the essential humanity of the process itself, rather than any perception that the process should – or could – be halted.

Once it was accepted that the 'inferior' race would inevitably be superseded by the invaders, even the most sympathetic account of mistreatment of the Aborigines could do little more than lament their passing, and hope for minimal standards of respect for the conquered. This, for example, is the 1847 poem 'The Tasmanian Aborigine's Lament and Remonstrance When in Sight of His Native Land from Flinders Island'[1], by an anonymous author writing under the pen-name of 'Auster' (many such anonymous contributions adopted names which suggested their connection with the new land). The poem assumes an Aboriginal voice which accepts the genocide of Tasmania's Aborigines, asking only to be buried in 'native land'. It marks the shift in

European perception of the Aborigines, from children of Nature to relics of the past:

> Thou, white man, with thy ever growing store
> Of learning, maks't a home in every land;
> For thee all countries forth their treasures pour,
> And Nature waits, the servant of thine hand.
>
> Not so with us; linked with our native earth
> Are all pleasures, and is all our care:
> The state our fathers lived in at our birth,
> Is but the lot that we are born to bear.
>
> ...
>
> Our race is fast decaying; – far and wide
> Extend thy riches, and increase thine heirs:
> Oh! let us die where our forefathers died,
> That we may mix our wretched dust with theirs.

Enlightenment views had created a problem for the settlers, by setting up an impossible tension between the idealised image of the noble savage in a pristine land, and the pragmatic necessity of change and displacement. The revival in religious sentiment early in the nineteenth century did not really help: it just shifted the debate from arguments of inevitability and necessity to arguments of moral rectitude.

It was another scientific development which gave white Australia the means to resolve its dilemma, and addressed both rational and moral arguments to the satisfaction – and ultimate benefit – of the colonists.

In farming, eugenics – the selective breeding of animals to emphasise particular desired characteristics – has been practised since earliest times. It had been developing as a science since the agricultural revolution in Britain in the early eighteenth-century. Despite the scientific rationalism of the late eighteenth-century, however, this obvious evidence of how species could be changed and adapted over time was not initially seen as the operation of a general principle of evolution. Belief in the Old Testament version of creation was simply too deeply embedded in the culture to be displaced. Nevertheless, the signs of imminent change were there.

Frenchman Jean Lamarck was born in the middle of the eighteenth-century – before the decline of the French kingdom – and lived through the violence of the Revolution, into the great changes of the nineteenth century. He rose to prominence under the monarchy, but it was not until 1809 that he published the book which first called into question the generally accepted Biblical view of creation as a hands-on single event. That book, *Philosophie Zoologique*, helped to shape the thinking of the next generation of scientists. Among them was Charles Lyell, who between 1830 and 1833 published *Principles of Geology*. In it he examined the increasing body of scientific evidence that forces of geological change, rather than ending after the creation, were still at work in the world.

Ideas like these rapidly gained popular currency. In 1844 Robert Chambers (joint founder of the publishing house of W & R Chambers) wrote *Vestiges of Creation*[2]. He published the book anonymously, fearing the backlash of criticism from the religious community. Although he had never carried out research of his own, Chambers argued strongly from the available scientific work:

> *We have seen powerful evidence, that the construction of this globe and its associates, and inferentially that of all the other globes of space, was the result, not of any immediate or personal exertion on the part of the Deity, but of natural laws which are expressions of his will. What is to hinder our supposing that the organic creation is also a result of natural laws which are in like manner an expression of his will?*

Shortly after publication of the first part of Lyell's work, a young Cambridge graduate called Charles Darwin was given a chance to make something of his fairly directionless life. He was offered the unpaid post of naturalist on a round-the-world expedition aboard HMS *Beagle*. The trip lasted five years, and Darwin's now famous observations of the enormous range and diversity of species he saw on his travels formed the basis of his best known work, *The Origin of Species by Natural Selection*, published in 1859[3].

Darwin delayed publication of his theories for some time, fearing, like Chambers, the anger of the religious community. He was finally pushed into action when in 1858 he received an essay from the young biologist, Alfred Wallace, entitled 'On the Tendency of Varieties to depart indefinitely from the Original Type'. Wallace had independently reached almost precisely the same conclusions as Darwin, drawing on his own research in the Malay archipelago (present-day Indonesia).

'New and improved varieties will inevitably supplant and exterminate the older, less improved and intermediate varieties,' wrote Darwin. 'And as natural selection works solely by and for the good of each being, all corporeal and mental endowments will tend to progress towards perfection... Thus, from the war of nature, from famine and death, the most exalted object which we are capable of conceiving, namely, the production of higher animals, directly follows.'

What Darwin never argued was that human societies operate according to the same laws of natural selection. His theory was concerned solely with biological principles of evolution. Nevertheless, part of his conclusion to *The Origin of Species* does speculate about possible future directions for the development of his ideas: 'Psychology will be based on a new foundation, that of the necessary acquirement of each mental power by gradation. Light will be thrown on the origin of man and his history'.

This suggestion was seized upon by another advocate of evolutionary development, Herbert Spencer, who in 1852 had written:

> ...*supporters of the development hypothesis...can show that any existing species – animal or vegetable – when placed under conditions different from its previous ones, immediately begins to undergo certain changes of structure fitting it for the new conditions. They can show that in*

> successive generations these changes continue until
> ultimately the new conditions become the natural ones.
> They can show that in cultivated plants, in domesticated
> animals, and in the several races of men, these changes have
> uniformly taken place.⁴

Spencer was a theoretical psychologist. Darwin may well have had him in mind when he added that rider about future directions in psychology. In 1855 Spencer had published his book-length study, *Principles of Psychology*, arguing for an evolutionary theory of development. He became an ardent advocate of Darwin's ideas, and was one of those responsible for the formation of perhaps the most pernicious extension of them – what came to be called 'social Darwinism' – which assumed that human societies behave according to the principles of natural selection, and evolve by competition for resources. In this view, 'survival of the fittest' becomes a basic precept of human behaviour. Dispossession – even extermination – of 'inferior' societies has a scientific basis.

And even more significantly, from a nineteenth-century perspective, this rational law has all the authority of moral justification. As Robert Chambers had argued, evolutionary theory was not anti-religious, merely an adjustment of human thinking to the discovery of higher principles at work. If competition between societies was a natural part of evolution, it followed that it was divinely sanctioned. Nineteenth-century creationists might argue against the new ideas just as vehemently as their twentieth-century counterparts, but their arguments were doomed. A God-given model of natural selection, of survival of the fittest, made far too effective a justification of imperial and colonial expansion to be denied.

The new science of anthropology contributed to the debate by establishing a 'rank order' of humanity. In the *Anthropological Review* for 1870 Max Muller divided human racial groups into seven classes, with Aborigines at the bottom, followed by Papuan, Malayo-Polynesian, Negro, American Indian, Higher

Asiatic, Mediterranean, Semitic, and Indo-German (the Aryan type later idealised by the Nazi party).

This position reinforced another branch of pseudo-science which enjoyed considerable popularity in the nineteenth century. Phrenology – reading an individual's character from the shape of their skull – had also begun to explore the issue of 'species' differentiation. The general principles of a 'scientific' reading of human appearance had been developed in *Physiognomische Fragmente* (1775-8), by the Swiss writer Johann Kaspar Lavater (and it is interesting to note that Charles Darwin was almost turned down for his post on the *Beagle* because of a Lavaterian interpretation of the shape of his nose!). Phrenology extended these principles into a systematic study of both individual and racial difference. It also led to the long-lasting fashion among European museums for collecting specimen human skulls from around the world, for comparative anatomical study.

The columnist 'Aeneas', writing in the *The Colonial Literary Journal* on 29th August and 5th September 1844,[5] gives a lengthy phrenological account of the 'reading' of Aboriginal skulls. 'Aeneas' reports that 'the brain of the New Hollander as in all savage nations, lies in the posterior parts of the head – the seat of the passions, and inferior sentiments; the moral and intellectual portions, with few exceptions, are very deficient'. The article notes the 'deficiency of the organ of Constructiveness', which explains the Aboriginal 'want of constructive ingenuity...and mechanical genius'. The prominence of the 'organ of Locality, with Individuality' explains the Aboriginal ability in tracking and their talent for observation, as they 'chase the nimble-footed kangaroo over the flower-enamelled plains of their country'. The article also notes that their 'Time is much more largely developed in their forehead than Tune – hence their comparative skill in the modulations of time displayed in their grotesque dances and corroborries, and the almost total want of any thing like melody in the discordant noises which form their national music.'

It was the difficulty of fitting Australia's indigenous inhabitants into the comfortable Enlightenment model of the noble savage that contributed to the local popularity of such tools of racial discrimination as phrenology and social Darwinism. The belief that different races of the human species represented rungs on the evolutionary ladder, with white Europeans at the top, was extremely attractive to a society based on dispossession of an indigenous culture. It could be reassuringly argued that the very fact that white people had come to dominate the economic, military and political life of the globe was sufficient demonstration that they had been selected by Nature (or God) for that position.

So the idea that the Aborigines were the lowest on the evolutionary scale of being rapidly entered the Australian public consciousness. Aboriginal people were soon being described as 'living fossils', to be studied and recorded before they became, inevitably, extinct as a result of 'natural law'. And since they were held to be closest of all humanity in the great chain of being to our primate ancestors, there were frequent unflattering comparisons made between Aboriginal people and apes. In this context, historian Henry Reynolds cites, in *Frontier* (1987), the example of the New South Wales poet and politician, William Charles Wentworth, who argued in 1844 against allowing Aboriginal evidence in court on the grounds that it would be 'quite as defensible to receive as evidence in a Court of Justice the chatterings of the ourang-outang as of this savage race'[6]. Those who opposed the heresy of early evolutionary theory, such as outspoken Presbyterian minister J. D. Lang, thundered against the 'damnable doctrine' held by some of the squatters '...that the black man of the forests of Australia is originally no better than the ourang-outang or monkey'.[7]

This 'Darwinian' comparison certainly caught the imagination of the writers of scientific romances. As early as 1872 Marcus Clarke was satirising the idea of the 'missing link'. This brief account appeared in a special 1872 supplement to the *Australasian*, in which the leading literary figures of Melbourne were invited to write speculative reports from Melbourne a hundred years in the future. Entitled *The New Era*, it was dated as though appearing on April 29th 1972:

> The wonders of the Universe will never cease. From the
> North Pole we have just received information of the
> discovery of a tribe of beings claiming brotherhood with us,
> who are web footed and handed, living in holes on the banks
> of the land, and subsisting on raw fish, which they plunge in
> after and eat voraciously when occasion requires them to
> appease their appetite. A hundred years ago Professor
> Darwin agitated the theory of a connecting link between the
> lower order of animals and man. Might this not be the
> connection with the fishes? Pity Darwin is dead.[8]

In 1873, the anonymously written *Account of a Race of Human Beings with Tails*[9] extrapolated its own missing link hypothesis and reported the remarkable discovery in central Australia of 'a community of men walking upon two legs, but bent forward, with a considerable amount of hair on their bodies, long arms, claw-like fingers, and real tangible tails, more or less long'. More imaginatively, the American writer Austyn Granville returned home from his travels in Australia to depict in *The Fallen Race*,[10] published in 1892, the discovery of a hidden island where a white queen rules an extraordinary species of ovoid kangaroo-Aborigines, developed from the unlikely primaeval union of the two groups. Again, this is clearly a view of indigenous peoples which relegated them to such an inferior evolutionary status that their interbreeding with animals was possible.

One writer who did know Australia well was Ernest Favenc. He emigrated from England in 1865, when he was in his late teens. For fourteen years he worked on stations in north Queensland, and then led an expedition to investigate a possible Queensland-Darwin rail link. He moved on to open up grazing country on the Gulf of Carpentaria and in Western Australia. This background was put to use in a number of studies of Australia and its explorers, and in rather more adventure romance novels and stories.

One collection of these stories, *Tales of the Austral Tropics* (1894), contained a story titled 'A Haunt of the Jinkarras'.[11] This tale is presented, like Tucker's *Ralph Rashleigh*, as a personal account framed by a narrative which gives the unlikely events an air of credibility. It is prefaced by an 'editorial' note:

> In May, 1880, the dead body of a man was found on one of the tributaries of the Fluke River, in the extreme North of South Australia. The body, by all appearances, had been lying there some months and was accidentally discovered by some surveyors making a flying survey with camels. Amongst the few effects was a Lett's Diary containing the following narrative, which, although in many places almost illegible and much weather-stained, has been since, with some trouble, deciphered and transcribed by the surveyor in charge of the party.

That circumstantial detail, 'a Lett's Diary', is a nice touch, lending a thoroughly believable ordinariness to what follows. The story unfolds through the diary entries:

> March 10, 1888. – Started out this morning with Jackson, who is the only survivor of a party of three who lost their horses on a dry stage when looking for country; he was found and cared for by the blacks, and finally made his way into the telegraph-line, where I picked him up when out with a repairing-party....

> March 18. – Amongst the ranges, plenty of water, and Jackson has recognised several peaks in the near neighbourhood of the gorge, where he saw the rubies.

> March 19. – Camped in Ruby Gorge, as I have named this pass, for we have come straight to the place and found the rubies without any hindrance at all...

> March 20. – Been inspecting some caves in the ranges. One of them seems to penetrate a great distance – will go tomorrow with Jackson and take candles and examine it.

> March 25. – Had a terrible experience the last four days. Why on earth did I not go back at once with the rubies? Now I may never get back. Jackson and I started to explore the cave early in the morning. We found nothing

> extraordinary about it for some time. As usual, there were numbers of bats, and here and there were marks of fire on the rocks, as though the natives had camped in it at times... Suddenly the passage opened and we found ourselves in a low chamber in which we could scarcely stand upright. I looked hastily around, and saw a dark figure like a large monkey suddenly spring from a rock and disappear with what sounded like a splash. 'What on earth was that?' I said to Jackson. 'A jinkarra,' he replied, in his slow, stolid way. 'I heard about them from the blacks; they live underground.'
>
> ...The splash was no illusion, for an underground stream of some size ran through the chamber, and, on looking closer, in the sand on the floor of the cavern we could see tracks like those of human feet.

They return to their campsite for the night, and tackle the cave again the next day, wading through the underground stream to reach another cavern, where they discover the reality of the jinkarras:

> The air was laden with pungent smoke, the place illuminated with a score of smouldering fires, and tenanted by a crowd of the most hideous beings I ever saw. They espied us in an instant, and flew wildly about, jabbering frantically, until we were nearly deafened. Recovering ourselves, we waded out of the water, and tried to approach some of these creatures, but they hid away in the dark corners, and we could not lay hands on any of them. As well as we could make out in the murky light, they were human beings, but savages of the most degraded type, far below that of the common Australian blackfellow. They had long arms, shaggy heads of hair, small twinkling eyes, and were very low of stature. They kept up a confused jabber, half whistling, half chattering, and were utterly without clothes, paint, or any ornaments. I approached one of their fires, and found it to consist of a kind of peat or turf;

> some small bones of vermin were lying around, and a rude club or two.

More than a hundred years after Cook, Favenc's narrative still searches for those marks of human civilisation: clothes, ornaments, sophisticated tools. The jinkarras are even denied (as so many writers had denied the Aborigines) a fully-formed human language. It is not our explorer who is 'confused', but the jinkarras themselves, despite the fact that they are, presumably, communicating with each other. What sets Favenc's story apart from its rationalist precursors, however, is the passage that follows, where the two white men take a closer look at the jinkarras, handling them as though they are dealing with an unusual species of possum they have just discovered:

> While gazing at these things I suddenly heard a piercing shriek, and, looking up, found that Jackson, by a sudden spring, had succeeded in capturing one of these creatures, who was struggling and uttering terrible yells. I went to his assistance, and together we succeeded in holding him still while we examined him by the light of our candles. The others, meanwhile, ceased their clamour and watched us curiously.
>
> Never had I seen so repulsive a wretch as our prisoner. Apparently he was a young man about two or three and twenty, hardly five feet high at the outside, lean, with thin legs and long arms. He was trembling all over, and the perspiration dripped from him. He had scarcely any forehead, and a shaggy mass of hair crowned his head, and grew a long way down his spine. His eyes were small, red and bloodshot; I have often experienced the strong odour emitted by aborigines when heated or excited, but never did I meet with anything so offensive as the rank smell emanating from this being. Suddenly Jackson exclaimed: 'Look! look! he's got a tail!' I looked and nearly relaxed my grasp of the brute in surprise. There was no doubt about it,

> this strange being had about three inches of a monkey-like tail.
>
> 'Let's catch another,' I said to Jackson after the first emotion of surprise had passed. We looked around after sticking our candles upright in the sand. 'There's one in the corner,' muttered Jackson to me, and as soon as I saw the one he meant we released our prisoner and made a simultaneous rush at the cowering form. We were successful, and when we dragged our captive to the light we found it to be a woman. Our curiosity was soon satisfied – the tail was the badge of the whole tribe, and we let our second captive go.

Long arms, low forehead, hair that extends down the back, and a short tail: Favenc's composite creature is another 'missing link' in the Darwinian model of human evolution. Conveniently, it demonstrates by its inferior relationship with the Aborigines, not that they are fully human, but that they are simply the next step up on the ladder towards that distant summit of perfected humanity, the Englishman (or, in the Australian context, the Britisher, part of that wider English-speaking racial group now spread around the globe).

Certainly the narrator feels no kinship with the jinkarras. His immediate response after releasing the female is 'to go and rinse my hands in the stream, the contact had been so repulsive to me'.

Given the confident popular belief in natural selection, it is hardly surprising that colonists now saw themselves as the natural inheritors of the Australian continent.

Henry Kingsley was the younger brother of the Reverend Charles Kingsley, author of *The Water Babies* and chief proponent of Christian Socialism (nicknamed 'muscular Christianity') – an attempt to balance spiritual and physical health, and so improve the lot of ordinary people. The Kingsley family was adventurous: Henry the elder, uncle to Charles and Henry, had travelled extensively in the South Pacific; and Mary, their niece, was later to make a solo expedition through an area of West Africa unexplored by any European male. Henry (the younger) came to Australia in 1853, attracted, like many others, by the gold rush. Like most others, he failed to make his fortune, and returned to England in 1858.

In England, he took advantage of his brother's publishing connections to sell a novel based on his knowledge of Australian life, *The Recollections of Geoffry Hamlyn*.[12] It appeared in 1859, shortly before the release of *The Origin of Species*, and was enormously successful in both Britain and Australia. For many years it was regarded as one of the most significant of 'Australian' novels.

The moment at which the novel moves from its early English setting to its Australian location is couched in the language of the King James Bible, where in his *Revelation* St. John the Divine says:

> *I saw a new heaven and a new earth: for the first heaven and the first earth were passed away... And I John saw the holy city, new Jerusalem, coming down from God out of heaven, prepared as a bride adorned for her husband. And I heard a great voice out of heaven saying, Behold, the tabernacle of God is with men, and he will dwell with them, and they shall be his people...*[13]

Kingsley's version of this in *The Recollections of Geoffry Hamlyn* makes the abstract visions of John into the concrete realisation of Australia:

> *A new heaven and a new earth! Tier beyond tier, height above height, the great wooded ranges go rolling away westward, till on the lofty skyline they are crowned with a gleam of everlasting snow. To the eastward they sink down, breaking into isolated forest-fringer peaks, and rock-crowned eminences, till with rapidly straightening lines they fade into the broad grey plains, beyond which the Southern Ocean is visible by the white sea-haze upon the sky.*
>
> *All creation is new and strange.*

Kingsley breathes new life into the metaphor of Old and New Worlds, first used about the discovery of the Americas:

> ...*so we sat and watched them debouche from the forest into the broad river meadows in the gathering gloom: saw the scene so venerable and ancient, so seldom seen in the Old World – the patriarchs moving into the desert with all their wealth, to find a new pasture ground. A simple primitive action, the first and simplest action of colonisation, yet producing such great results on the history of the world as did the parting of Lot and Abraham in times gone by.*

This passage has been frequently quoted as one of the reasons for twentieth-century rejection of Kingsley as an English, rather than an Australian, writer, reflecting essentially alien colonial values. But in fact *Geoffry Hamlyn* perfectly reflected the attitudes of the Australian colonists themselves (a fact confirmed by its commercial success in Australia).

The early settlers wrote of a land preserved by God and destiny for their coming. A hundred years later, descendants of those settlers had become agents of Darwinian evolution, Nature's destiny. The fact that these white 'heirs' to Australia had inherited their continent through displacement and massacre was soon forgotten. They were, by self-definition, the fittest race to survive and prosper in 'undeveloped' lands. Genocide could be rationalised as genetic improvement.

The irony of this situation was not lost on popular writers such as H. G. Wells. A pupil of Darwin's advocate, Thomas Huxley, Wells subscribed to the modified form of Darwinism that rank-ordered humanity. But unlike many nineteenth-century writers, who added a Biblical separation of the fully human Europeans as God-decreed inheritors of all the earth, he maintained a clear sense of the close relationship between humans and other species, describing 'Man' as 'the culminating ape'. He argued that Europeans had a clear duty to exercise responsibility as the 'superior' race.

Wells wrote at a time when many believed intelligent life might be found on Mars, and he drew on the example of European genocide of Tasmanian Aboriginal people to form the basis for his cautionary novel *The War of the Worlds*[14], in which Martians colonise the Earth. If Europeans take uncivilised advantage of their natural superiority over other races, he argued, then they will inevitably be subject to the same natural laws of selection when they themselves finally come into contact with a superior species:

> ...*we must remember what ruthless and utter destruction our own species has wrought, not only upon animals, such as the bison and vanished dodo, but upon its own inferior races. The Tasmanians, in spite of their human likeness, were entirely swept out of existence in a war of extermination waged by European immigrants, in the space of fifty years. Are we such apostles of mercy as to complain if the Martians warred in the same spirit?*

In Australia, however, the genocide of the Tasmanian Aborigines did not give rise to a warning sense of general human impermanence. Many writers persisted in the romantic interpretation of Aboriginal decline as an inevitable, if regrettable, process in the ascent of the human species.

The romantic sensibility was peculiarly suited to the shift in scientific thinking from the Enlightenment to evolutionary theory. This poetic vision foregrounded the emotions and point of view of the observer-poet. The individual subjects of the poetry became secondary to the heightened sensibility of their representation. Each was one aspect of a higher, universal Truth.

In the Australian context, this displacement of attention from the plight of the threatened Aborigine to the fine sensibilities of the poet and the reader allowed both to achieve a neat resolution of the paradox that they were mourning the loss of a romantic past that was actually still present. There could be no help for a people already doomed, by 'Darwinian' process, to extinction. There was only the valedictory requiem.

Henry Kendall was born in 1839 near Milton, in southern coastal New South Wales, and grew up among some of the spectacular rainforest scenery which later figured largely in his romantic interpretations of the Australian bush. He worked in whaling ships for two years in his late teens, but then went to Sydney, where he struggled to establish himself as a writer. The rest of his short life (he died at the age of forty-three) was marked by the difficulties of pursuing this career, and by the problems of extended alcoholism. He enjoyed a high reputation in his lifetime and for a while after his death in 1882, but then fell from favour, for very similar reasons to those that had made his reputation: the powerful romantic themes, language and form of his poetry.

Kendall published a range of poems on the theme of the Aboriginal past. He applied to the Australian context a central theme of Victorian romantic writing: nostalgia for a heroic but vanished age. The mediaeval or classical stories of English authors became, in Kendall's poems, tales of bygone Aboriginal heroes. So completely Europeanised are these poems that Kendall's 'Aboriginal Death Song' uncannily echoes his elegiac lament for J. D. Lang. This is from the 'Aboriginal Death Song':

> *Far by the forested glen,*
> *Starkly he lies in the rain;*
> *Kings of the council of men*
> *Shout for their leader in vain.*
>
> *Yea, and the fish-river clear*
> *Never shall blacken below*
> *Spear and the shadow of spear,*
> *Bow and the shadow of bow.*
>
> *Hunter, and climber of trees,*
> *Now doth his tomahawk rust*
> *(Dread of the cunning wild bees),*
> *Hidden in hillocks of dust...*[15]

Compare this with 'John Dunmore Lang':

The noise of thy battle is over,
Thy sword is hung up in its sheath;
Thy grave has been decked by its lover
With beauty of willowy wreath.
The winds sing about thee for ever,
The voices of hill and of sea;
But the cry of the conflict will never
Bring sorrow again unto thee...[16]

The celebration of individuals was matched by a requiem for a race. In 1864 Kendall published 'The Last of His Tribe', in which a lone, bewildered Aborigine close to death recalls 'the hunts of yore'. The poem concludes with a dream of the warrior restored to his tribe and his woman, like some antipodean King Arthur borne across the lake by the mysterious maiden to an Aboriginal Avalon:

Will he go in his sleep from these desolate lands,
Like a chief, to the rest of his race,
With the honey-voiced woman who beckons and stands,
And gleams like a dream in his face –
Like a marvellous dream in his face?[17]

This equivalent valorisation of white and black did not last. Kendall's personal life collapsed in the early 1870s. *Leaves from an Australian Forest*, his second volume of verse, was published in 1869, after his move to Melbourne. It was not a commercial success, and his alcoholism grew markedly worse as he tried to cope, first with increasing poverty, then with the death of his infant daughter in 1870. He returned to Sydney, where he was treated at the Gladesville asylum, and separated from his wife. In the aftermath of depression, he turned to lighter verse, adopting the mocking tone of James Brunton Stephens' 1873 volume, *The Black Gin*. Kendall and Scottish immigrant poet Stephens were soon in competition to produce poetry that ridiculed Aborigines, and Kendall was boasting he could 'out-Blackfellow Stephens'.

Stephens had come to Queensland in 1866, at the age of thirty-one. He was a university-educated schoolmaster, and taught for three years in Brisbane before taking a private tutoring post at a cattle station on the Logan river. He read and wrote extensively as a defence against what he called 'the land of monotony'. The publication of several volumes of verse brought him to official attention and he was appointed to the civil service, becoming acting under-secretary to the Queensland colonial secretary. He and Kendall were regarded as the leading literary figures of their time, and Stephens' reputation rose further after Kendall's death, but fell further still after his own, in 1902.

Unlike Kendall, Stephens never romanticised the Aborigine. His poetic voice was largely satirical, servicing the racist bias of the Queensland periodicals for which he wrote. 'To a Black Gin', often represented as an exercise in literary satire, is uncompromising in its stereotyping of the female Aborigine:

> *Thy rugged skin is hideous with tatooing,*
> *And legible with hieroglyphic wooing –*
> *Sweet things in art of some fierce lover's doing.*
>
> *For thou some lover hast, I bet a guinea,*
> *Some partner in thy fetid ignominy,*
> *The raison d'être of this piccaninny.*
>
> *What must he be whose eye thou hast delighted?*
> *His sense of beauty hopelessly benighted!*
> *The canons of his taste how badly sighted!*[18]

Kendall's own version of this theme, 'Ode to a Black Gin', appeared in the *Town and Country Journal* for 17th March 1877. Like Stephens' satires, it offered the occasional conciliatory gesture towards its subjects (the equivalent of statements such as 'I'm not a racist, but...'):

> *And though I've laughed at your expense*

> *O Dryad of the dusky race,*
> *No man who has a heart and sense*
> *Would bring displeasure to your face.*[19]

In 'Jack the Blackfellow', published two years later, Kendall was less concerned to achieve even this tenuous balance. The poem depicts a male Aborigine without redeeming feature:

> *He go to church! His Paradise,*
> *My simple friend, is yonder bar,*
> *There is no heaven in his eyes*
> *But where the grog and 'bacca' are.*[20]

And in 'Black Jemmy', Kendall offered to expose the 'reality' concealed by the religious sentimentalism of 'Nigger Missionaries': 'I have a big buck darkie here, I'll draw a sketch of him'.[21]

Although Kendall's vision swerved from his original romanticisation, other poets of the time were producing poems that celebrated a romantic European vision of the Aboriginal past. George Gordon McCrae was brought to Australia by his parents in 1841, settling with them at Arthur's Seat on the Victorian Mornington Peninsula (a period described in the journal of his mother, Georgiana McCrae). He worked in the civil service, becoming deputy registrar-general, and was part of a literary circle that included Henry Kendall, Marcus Clarke and Adam Lindsay Gordon. In 1867 McCrae published 'Mamba ('The Bright-Eyed'): An Aboriginal Reminiscence' and 'The Story of Balladeadro', long poems on Aboriginal subjects. Like some of the earlier attempts at sympathetic identification with the Aboriginal perspective, 'Mamba' adopts an Aboriginal voice. It might be argued that this device allowed the poets to relegate their Aboriginal subjects to a safely poetic status: admired from a distance; in need of protection; and to be kept firmly in check in case their natural passions got the better of them. As this section from Canto I, XXVIII shows, however, McCrae's treatment is much more complex:

> *Within the circle of the camp*

> *Blazed the clear fire, while measured tramp*
> *Of dancing warriors shook the ground,*
> *To song and time-sticks' throbbing sound.*
> *There twice two hundred feet advanced,*
> *There twice a hundred malkas glanced*
> *Bright in the moon, that silvered o'er*
> *The arms that all those malkas bore.*[22]

That repeated 'twice two hundred...twice a hundred' echoes the fantastic setting of Samuel Taylor Coleridge's romantic poem, 'Kubla Khan', with its 'twice five miles of fertile ground'. And McCrae immediately goes on to include a reference to his American contemporary, Longfellow, whose poem 'Excelsior', with the 'youth who bore, 'mid snow and ice,/ A banner with the strange device,/ Excelsior!' had captured the popular imagination a couple of decades earlier, and become a favourite drawing-room recitation piece. This is McCrae's version:

> *Wild the device, and strange the sign*
> *That stared in many a snowy line*
> *From beaming face and heaving breast,*
> *And limbs that seldom paused to rest;*
> *Whilst all the rib-like lines laid on,*
> *Made each man seem a skeleton.*

The references to other romantic writers are supplemented by a direct appeal to the image of Aborigines as part of the natural scene:

> *Nodded the feathers from the red*
> *And netted band that bound each head,*
> *And hoarsely rustling leaves of trees*
> *Shook round dark ankles in the breeze.*
> *The singers with their time-sticks rang*
> *The cadence of the song they sang;*
> *And every face and limb below,*
> *And tree above them, caught the glow*
> *That spread from camp-fire's rising blaze,*

> *Lighting the yapeen's wond'rous maze*
> *Of feet and ankles in the dance*
> *With fitful gleam or twinkling glance.*

In this setting, Mamba himself appears as a fascinating mixture of the wild, the natural, the exotic, the inspiring, and the sensual:

> *Conspicuous 'mid the dancing crowd,*
> *Whose ranks alternate swayed and bowed,*
> *Shone Mamba, tricked with wild design,*
> *And symbol traced in waving line.*
> *No limbs more active wore the green*
> *At yon great Ghim-boboke yapeen;*
> *And no two arms more graceful there*
> *In circling motion cleft the air*
> *Than his – and hit the eagle-eye*
> *Inspiring all the minstrelsy.*
> *The young and old in groups around*
> *Drank in the sight, the joy, the sound;*
> *And Mamba's form throughout the dance*
> *Attracted every wondering glance.*

McCrae's work, much admired at the time by Kendall, soon fell from favour as over-romanticised. Nevertheless 'Mamba' shows less direct Europeanisation than Kendall's romantic heroes. It has many similarities to Longfellow's much better-known poem of native American life, 'Hiawatha', published in 1855, which became an icon of American identity. No doubt McCrae hoped for something similar from 'Mamba', with its adopted Aboriginal terms and its descriptions of Aboriginal ceremony, set in a popular poetic style.

But 'Hiawatha' could not prevent the destruction of the native American way of life, as settlers pushed out into the West. The poem was an elegy for a dying culture. And 'Mamba', too, was finally an elegy, a celebration of what had been lost – or rather, what was in the process of being destroyed, even as McCrae was writing.

This elegiac mood, with its sense of helplessness in the face of historical inevitability, was to become ingrained in the Australian poetic consciousness. Mary Gilmore, writing in 1932, and again adopting an Aboriginal voice, mourned what seemed by now a lost culture:

> *Harried we were, and spent,*
> *Broken and falling,*
> *Ere as the cranes we went,*
> *Crying and calling.*
>
> *Summer shall see the bird*
> *Backward returning;*
> *Never shall there be heard*
> *Those, who went yearning.*
>
> *Emptied of us the land,*
> *Ghostly our going,*
> *Fallen, like spears the hand*
> *Dropped in the throwing.*
>
> *We are the lost who went*
> *Like the cranes, crying;*
> *Hunted, lonely, and spent,*
> *Broken and dying.*[23]

The sense of unavoidable loss expressed in this poetry has proved so powerful and enduring a literary metaphor of the clash between cultures that it even coloured the development of Aboriginal literary voices in the later twentieth century. When, finally, Oodgeroo Noonuccal (formerly known as Kath Walker) came to write of her people's experience of displacement and dispossession, her cry of outrage was couched in surprisingly similar terms of inevitability:

> *We are the shadow-ghosts creeping back as the camp fires*
>   *burn low.*
> *...*

> *The eagle is gone, the emu and the kangaroo are gone from*
> *this place.*
> *The bora ring is gone.*
> *The corroboree is gone.*
> *And we are going.'*[24]

Not all nineteen writers subscribed to the dominant and – for white society – convenient view of 'natural decay'. For some, also aware of pre-Darwinian debate about 'superior' and 'inferior' human races, moral and personal responsibility for the decline of Aboriginal society could not be so easily evaded.

Henry Kingsley's novel, *The Recollections of Geoffry Hamlyn*, reflected many of the ideals of Christian Socialism at the heart of the Kingsley family. It also dealt with Australian conditions with a surprising lack of sentimentality. Kingsley's desire to present a realistic picture had been tempered by pressures from his publisher, Macmillan, for a more 'acceptable' text, and the result was a loosely structured adventure romance that drew on its Australian materials for entertaining and exciting accounts of life in the colonies.

Despite this constraint, Kingsley managed to find ways to undermine the comfortable certainties of his audience. The Aborigines of *Geoffry Hamlyn* appear as conventional racist caricature, but in this description, for example, with its direct comparison of European beauty and grotesque Aboriginal degradation, the voice of the narrator still manages to raise some uncomfortable speculations about the role of prejudice and racial stereotyping in blinding us to the truth:

> *God save us! What imp's trick is this? There, in the porch in the bright sun, where she stood not an hour ago in all her beauty and grace, stands a hideous old savage, black as Tophet, grinning; showing the sharp gap-teeth in her apish jaws, her lean legs shaking with old age and rheumatism.*
>
> *The collie shakes out her frill, and raising the hair all down her back, stands grinning and snarling, while her puppy barks pot-valiantly between her legs. The little kangaroo*

> rats ensconce themselves once more in their box, and gaze
> out amazed from their bright little eyes. The cockatoo hooks
> and clambers up to a safe place in the trellis, and Sam, after
> standing thunder-struck for a moment, asks what she wants.
>
> 'Make a light,' says the old girl, in a pathetic squeak.
> Further answers she makes none, but squats down outside,
> and begins a petulant whine: sure sign that she has a tale of
> woe to unfold, and is going to ask for something.
>
> 'Can that creature,' thinks Sam, 'be of the same species as
> the beautiful Alice Brentwood? Surely not! There seems as
> much difference between them as between an angel and an
> ordinary good woman.' Hard to believe, truly, Sam; but
> perhaps, in some of the great European cities, or even nearer
> home, in some of the prison barracks, you may chance to
> find a white woman or two fallen as low as that poor,
> starved, ill-treated, filthy old savage!

The voice of the narrator takes issue with Sam's gothic imaginings and ill-considered evolutionist assumptions. And the appearance of the radiant Alice offers a model of womanly concern for the disadvantaged, in the new Christian Socialist mould:

> Alice comes out once more, and brings sunshine with her.
> She goes up to the old lubra with a look of divine compassion
> on her beautiful face; the old woman's whine grows louder
> as she rocks herself to and fro. 'Yah marah, Yah boorah, Oh
> boora Yah! Yah ma!'
>
> 'What! old Sally!' says the beautiful girl. 'What is the
> matter? Have you been getting waddy again?'
>
> 'Baal!' says she, with a petulant burst of grief.
>
> 'What is it, then?' says Alice. 'Where is the gown I gave
> you?'
>
> Alice had evidently vibrated the right chord. The 'Yarah
> moorah' coronach was begun again; and then suddenly, as
> if her indignation had burst bounds, she started off with a
> shrillness and rapidity astonishing to one not accustomed to

blackfellows, into something like the following: 'Oh Yah (very loud), oh Mah! Barkmaburrawurrah, Barmamurrahwurrah Oh Ya Barkmanurrawah Yee (in a scream. Then a pause). Oh Mooroo (pause). O hinaray (pause). Oh Barknamurrwurrah Yee!'

Alice looked as if she understood every word of it, and waited till the poor old souls had 'blown off the steam,' and then asked again:

'And what has become of the gown, Sally?'

'Oh dear! Young lubra, Betty (big thief that one) tear it up and stick it along a fire. Oh, plenty cold this old woman. Oh, plenty hungry this old woman. Oh, Yarah Moorah,' etc.

'There! go round to the kitchen,' said Alice, and get something to eat. Is it not abominable, Mr. Buckley? I cannot give anything to this old woman but the young lubras take it from her. However, I will 'put the screw on them.' They shall have nothing from me till they treat her better. It goes to my heart to see a woman of that age, with nothing to look forward to but kicks and blows. I have tried hard to make her understand something of the next world: but I can't get it out of her head that when she dies she will go across the water and come back a young white woman with plenty of money. Mr. Sandford, the missionary, says he has never found one who could be made to comprehend the existence of God.

The picture of Alice is highly romanticised, to suit conventional English stereotypes of the ideal woman. But there is nothing romantic in Kingsley's vision of Aboriginal life as a displaced culture on the fringes of white society. Traditional tribal relationships have broken down, and the old woman is reduced to begging for handouts. The well-meaning attempt to Christianise the Aborigines is met with mutual incomprehension. This is the harsh reality of 'natural selection'.

Marcus Clarke had still less sympathy with the advocates of social Darwinism. In 1877 he turned the tables on the racists in a satirical look at The Future Australian Race.²⁵ In this short piece he applied an evolutionary model to Europeans living in the Australian environment. For his 'reasoned' eugenic argument Clarke drew, tongue in cheek, on sources as diverse as the *North American Medico-Chirurgical Review*, reproductions of Hogarth and Rowlandson, and back copies of *Punch*. He wrote:

> The quality of a race of beings is determined by two things: food and climate. The measure of that quality is the measure of the success in the race's incessant struggle to wrest nature to its own advantage. The history of a nation is the history of the influence of nature modified by man, and of man modified by the influence of nature.
>
> ...
>
> Now let us consider what climate and food will do for Australians.
>
> In the first place, we must remember that the Australasian nation will have an empire of many climates, for it will range from Singapore and Malacca in the north, to New Zealand in the south. All varieties of temperature will be traversed by the railroad traveller of 1977. The enormous area of Australia, that circle whose circumference is the sea, and whose centre is a desert, is a strong reason against federation. It is more than likely that what should be the Australian Empire will be cut in half by a line drawn through the centre of the continent. All above this line – Queensland and the Malaccas, New Guinea, and the parts adjacent – will evolve a luxurious and stupendous civilisation only removed from that of Egypt and Mexico by the measure of the remembrance of European democracy. All beneath this line will be a Republic, having the mean climate, and, in consequence, the development of Greece. The intellectual capital of this Republic will be Victoria.

> *The fashionable and luxurious capital on the shore of Sydney Harbour. The governing capital in New Zealand.*

But food and climate will not only affect the political systems, according to Clarke:

> *The inhabitants of this Republic are easily described. The soil is for the most part deficient in lime, hence the bones of the autochthones will be long and soft. The boys will be tall and slender like cornstalks. It will be rare to find girls with white and sound teeth. A small pelvis is the natural result of small bones, and a small pelvis means a sickly mother and stunted children. Bad teeth mean bad digestion, and bad digestion means melancholy. The Australians will be a fretful, clever, perverse, irritable race. The climate breeds a desire for out-of-door exercise.... The boys, brought up outside their homes' four walls, will easily learn to roam, and as they conquer difficulties for themselves will learn to care little for their parents. The Australasians will be selfish, self-reliant, ready in resource, prone to wander, caring little for home ties. Mercenary marriage will be frequent, and the hotel system of America will be much favoured.*

His discussion of the effects of immigration reads at times like a selective breeding manual:

> *The best bone and sinew of Cornwall, the best muscle of Yorkshire, the keenest brains of Cockneydom... the daring spendthrift, the young cavalry officer who had lived too fast for the Jews, the younger son who had outrun his income. Barristers of good family and small practice, surgeons having all the Dublin Dissector in their heads and all the hospital experience of Paris in their hands, met each other over a windlass at Bathurst or a drive at Ballarat. If there was plenty of muscle in the new land, there was no lack of blood.*

Clarke's text seductively offers the popular view of Australia as the coming nation, but immediately questions its own premise:

> ...deny, if you can, that there is here the making of a great nation. You do not deny it; but –. But what?
>
> 'There are many factors in the sum of a nation's greatness – Religion, polity, Commerce.'
>
> Granted; but these are controllable. There is only one influence which we cannot escape, though we may modify it, and that is the influence of Physical Laws. Let us consider what climate the Australian nation will live in, and what food it will be prone to eat, and, having arrived at a distinct conclusion upon those two points, we can predict, with positive certainty, their religion, their polity, their commerce, and their appearance. You stare? Attend for a moment, and you will see that a proposition of Euclid is not clearer.

Clarke's modern proposition describes the influence on the future Australasian character of soil (affecting bones, teeth and digestion to produce '...a fretful, clever, perverse, irritable race'); climate (with its inducement to outdoor life encouraging men who are 'selfish, self-reliant, ready in resource, prone to wander, caring little for home ties'); meat and alcohol consumption (we will be 'content with nothing short of a turbulent democracy'); the high level of oxygen in the air (we will have big chests, but produce no poets, being 'freed from the highest burden of intellectual development'); the sun (producing 'deep-set eyes with overhanging brows', and a short upper lip with the 'whole mouth made fleshy and sensual'); and carnivorous habits (which 'will square the jaw and render the hair coarse but plentiful').

The text maintains its inflating seriousness of tone for much of its length, with only the occasional aside:

> Men who habitually eat non-nitrogenous substances and pay little attention to the state of their bowels are always prone to gloomy piety. This is the reason why Scotch-men and women are usually inclined to religion.

In summary:

The Australasian will be a square-headed, masterful man, with full temples, plenty of beard, a keen eye, a stern yet sensual mouth. His teeth will be bad, and his lungs good. He will suffer from liver disease, and become prematurely bald; average duration of life in the unmarried, fifty-nine; in the married, sixty-five and a decimal.

...in another hundred years the average Australasian will be a tall, coarse, strong-jawed, greedy, pushing, talented man, excelling in swimming and horsemanship. His religion will be a form of Presbyterianism; his national policy a Democracy tempered by the rate of exchange.

His wife will be a thin, narrow woman, very fond of dress and idleness, caring little for her children, but without sufficient brain power to sin with zest.

In five hundred years – unless recruited from foreign nations – the breed will be wholly extinct; but in that five hundred years it will have changed the face of nature, and swallowed up all our contemporary civilisation.

Perhaps unwilling to depress his audience entirely, he added:

It is, however – perhaps fortunately – impossible that we shall live to see this stupendous climax.

Clarke's satire attacks both ill-judged social Darwinism and the often ludicrous predictions of a glowing Australian future, as well as the gloomier class-bound prognostications about creeping democratisation of the populace. In retrospect, however, the form of this attack also reminds us of the role of scapegoating in our society. It suggests the disturbingly large part which outward appearance played – and still plays – in the displacement of social tension onto those of different appearance. It is all too easy to blame onto racially and culturally different groups problems which are actually rooted in those circumstantial categories: religion, politics and commerce.

Nineteenth-century theories of the connection between physiognomy and character fitted all too neatly into a desire to relegate the indigenous population to a marginal status. The theory of natural selection gave the white Australian colonists the justification they needed for the displacement of Aborigines from disputed land, and the active extermination of Aboriginal cultures. In its anthropological form it also gave European culture a self-fulfilling belief in itself as the pinnacle of all creation. To possess the world was proof of one's natural right to possess it.

It was not a long step from this position to a more active attempt to speed up the processes of Nature. Why wait for the natural decline of the current owners when their dispossession was clearly inevitable?

A further conclusion that may be drawn from such a view of the world is that it is also reasonable to speed up the natural 'improvement' of the human species in much the same way as domestic animals are 'improved': by selective breeding, and the prevention of cross-breeding.

And if selection works, how much more efficient to eliminate the undesirable characteristics altogether.

The stage is set for genocide.

3

All That Is Unfit

'To see yourself as a force of History is to be freed from pity and from guilt', said art critic Robert Hughes, writing of the displacement of native Americans by the spread of white settlement into the West.[1] Unfortunately for Australia's indigenous inhabitants, most settlers in inland areas shared this view of themselves as agents of history through natural selection. As forces of divine will and historical inevitability working in a difficult, sometimes hostile, environment, they did not feel they could afford the luxury of undue consideration for the doomed Aboriginal peoples.

The European presence was well established in coastal areas by the second half of the nineteenth century, but exploration of the interior continued. The first crossing from Adelaide to Alice Springs and then to the north-west coast of Western Australia was made by Peter Warburton, travelling with his son, Richard, and five other men, in a train of seventeen camels. The trip from Adelaide to Alice Springs (then just a repeater station on the newly-completed international telegraph cable line) took from September to December 1872. The group remained at Alice Springs until April 1873, and finally reached the west coast on December 29th that year.

Warburton was born in England in 1813, began his career as a midshipman in the Royal Navy, and then spent twenty-four years in the Indian Army before taking up a post as commissioner of police in Adelaide in 1853. He was dismissed in 1867, but appointed colonel of the South Australian Volunteer Military Force in 1869. He made a number of journeys out to the area around the salt lakes, but when the South Australian Government fitted out an expedition to attempt the inland crossing, Warburton, by then fifty-eight years old, was passed over for command. Undaunted, Warburton managed to find private backers. In the event, it was his expedition which completed the crossing. The official party, led by William Gosse, had to be content with finding and naming Ayers Rock (now Uluru).

When Warburton made the trip described in his 1875 book, *Journey Across the Western Interior of Australia*,[2] the spirit of scientific inquiry which had characterised the first settlement had given way to a general impatience with Aborigines as an uncooperative nuisance. As this extract clearly shows, indigenous peoples had also learned from earlier encounters, showing a caution fully understandable in the circumstances:

> *September 1st... On the 30th, just before reaching the lake, we had captured a young native woman; this was considered a great triumph of art, as the blacks avoided us as though we had been plague-stricken. We kept her a close prisoner, intending that she should point out native wells to us; but whilst we were camped to-day the creature escaped from us by gnawing through a thick hair-rope, with which she was fastened to a tree. We were quickly on her tracks, directly we discovered our loss, but she was too much for us, and got clear away...*
>
> *4th. Marched six miles west, and found a native camp and well. Could not catch a native there, they being too quick for us; not far, however, from the camp a howling, hideous old hag was captured, and, warned by the former escape, we secured this old witch by tying her thumbs behind her back, and haltering her by the neck to a tree. She kept up a frightful howling all night, during which time we had to watch her by turns, or she would have got away also. I doubt whether there is any way of securing these creatures if you take your eyes off them for ten minutes...*

> 6th. We let the old witch go. She was the most alarming specimen of a woman I ever saw; she had been of no use to us, and her sex alone saved her from punishment, for under pretence of leading us to some native wells, she took us backwards and forwards over heavy sand-hills, exhausting the camels as well as my small stock of patience.

Warburton's gothic references to the 'hag' and 'witch' are familiar European literary concepts which help distance him from any human sympathy for the woman. The 'consideration' shown to her sex seems ironic in the face of treatment that might barely have been considered appropriate for an unmanageable dog.

Like many of the Europeans making contact with hostile or uncooperative Aborigines, Warburton seems in retrospect blind to any view of the situation but his own. The fact that the old woman has clearly been successful in diverting hostile intruders from precious water supplies does not evoke respect, only impatience.

Similarly, Norwegian naturalist and ethnographer Carl Lumholtz (after whom the extraordinary Lumholtz's tree kangaroo is named) spent four years living with Aboriginal groups in northern Queensland, but remained often painfully unaware of what might lie behind some of the incidents he experienced and recounted in his study, *Among Cannibals*.[3] Woken by Aborigines with whom he was camped, and told, in great distress, that an attack by another group was imminent, Lumholtz at first dismissed the idea as nonsense. He was eventually persuaded to fire his rifle, which he did with great reluctance, and only so he could get back to sleep. Only later did he decide that his companions had probably been right, and firing his gun had scared off the potential attackers. His conclusion, however, was not that the superior skills and foresight of his Aboriginal friends had saved his life as well as theirs, but that the rapid flight of the other group on hearing a gun demonstrated the innate superiority of Europeans over Aborigines.

This sense of superiority was given 'scientific' credibility by another developmental model, derived in part from Darwin's observational methods, in part from phrenology. Human skulls were collected and scrupulously measured, to produce comparative tables of human development. Lumholtz himself recounts in *Among Cannibals* collecting a 'specimen', from the measurement of which he determined that 'the small development of the cranium, and the low receding forehead, which is unfavourable to a development of the frontal lobes, indicate the low plane of intellectual development of the Australian natives.'

This belief that Aborigines were scarcely human led to them being regarded by many as just another animal species. Lumholtz records offers by pastoralists 'to shoot blacks for me so that I might get their skulls.'

In one area, however, Europeans were fascinated by indigenous custom. Cannibalism was such a deeply-felt taboo in European society that the very idea of other societies in which it was routinely practised retained a lasting, slightly horrifying, appeal. It had become one of the markers by which the level of humanity and civilisation in any group could be determined. And since Aborigines were classified as the lowest form of humanity, lower than the known cannibal groups of Melanesia, they were widely assumed to be cannibals as well.

The down-to-earth Lumholtz devoted his four years in Queensland to an 'ethnographic' study of Aborigines, observing the customs and practices of a people he assumed to be dying out. He gives no indication that he actually witnessed cannibalism. The closest he comes is to say that one old man was stoned to death by another tribe, and his 'flesh was brought in baskets to Herbert Vale' – an account which does not make it clear whether Lumholtz himself even saw the flesh in question. Despite this, Lumholtz called his resulting book-length study *Among Cannibals*, a title which had obvious sales potential in its European marketplace.

To the modern reader, Lumholtz's technique is more like fiction than scientific reporting. He constructs his story from personal experience, second-hand accounts, and tales told to him over the camp fire by his various Aboriginal companions. Out of these materials he weaves a compelling narrative. The possibility that his hosts might be doing something similar does not seem to have occurred to him, when he comments that cannibalism 'was the leading topic of their conversation, which finally both disgusted and irritated me'. One of the difficulties for a serious-minded 'ethnographer' like Lumholtz would clearly have been how to distinguish fact from fiction in the information he was given, especially when it was transmitted in the form of camp fire yarns. Unfortunately his book does not often give specific sources for information offered as factual and, where it does, that source is usually hearsay. His account of Aboriginal cannibalism, for example, is quite detailed, but gives no evidence of a source. Says Lumholtz:

> *On Herbert river, expeditions are sometimes undertaken for the special purpose of securing talgoro – that is, human flesh.*
>
> ...
>
> *When they have found a small family tribe to be attacked, they try to stay near their camp in the evening. Nothing having happened to cause apprehension during the day, the family sits comparatively secure round the camp fire. Early in the morning, before sunrise, a noise is suddenly heard and the family wakes up in a fright. The black man's highly-wrought fancy always makes him imagine that his enemies are far more numerous than they are in reality. Each one tries to save his life as best he can: resistance being out of the question, there is no gallant defence of women and children. Each one has to look after himself; and it is generally worst for the old individuals, who are killed and eaten. A woman is as a rule splendid booty; if she be young her life is generally spared, but if she be old she is first ravished and then killed and eaten.*

One source of information was clearly the camp-fire tales told for Lumholtz's benefit when he was living with one of the Aboriginal groups:

> The natives of Northern Queensland and of many other parts of Australia are cannibals. My people never made any secret of this, and in the evenings it was the leading topic of their conversation, which finally both disgusted and irritated me.

The Aborigines were apparently quite specific in their accounts:

> The greatest delicacy known to the Australian native is human flesh. The very thought of talgoro makes his eye sparkle. When I asked my men what part of the human body they liked best, they always struck their thighs. They never eat the head or the entrails. The most delicate morsel of all is the fat about the kidneys. By eating this they believe that they acquire a part of the slain person's strength, and so far as I could understand, this was even more true of the kidneys themselves. For according to a widespread Australian belief, the kidneys are the centre of life.

To bring the gruesome 'evidence' closer to home for his readers, Lumholtz links this account to another story that had wide popular circulation for a time:

> It happened years ago in Victoria that a white policeman was attacked by the blacks. They struck him with their clubs until they believed him dead, and then they took out his kidneys and ran away. The man came to his senses again for a moment and was able to relate what had happened, but a few hours afterwards he died.

And this piece of hearsay is linked back again to the tales told to Lumholtz by his Aboriginal acquaintances, who assured him that human body tissue was used as a good-luck charm:

> A man told me that immediately after beginning to wear a
> small piece of human fat, he waded across the river, and
> came at once to a tree where he found a large edible snake.

Despite his claim to factual reporting, Lumholtz is not scrupulous in his adherence to evidence drawn from his own observations. He comes to Australia with a thesis, and looks for any 'evidence' to support it:

> As a rule the Australian natives do not eat persons
> belonging to their own tribe. Still, I know instances to the
> contrary, and I have even heard of examples of mothers
> eating their own children. Besides the circumstance already
> related, it happened in 1883, about a hundred miles from
> Townsville, that a child which had died a natural death was
> eaten, and that the mother herself took part in the feast. A
> day or two later she too died and was eaten.

At this point Lumholtz makes some attempt to distinguish between different Aboriginal groups, saying that 'the killing of children rarely happens on Herbert river, for the mothers are invariably fond of their children'. He does, he says, 'know of examples of their killing their children because they were a burden to them, but such things also happen in civilised countries'. But still the hearsay evidence continues: 'Mr. White has informed me...; Many of the white people at the station were witnesses of this event.'

At times the temptation to read between the lines of Lumholtz's account, and see there a picture of the humourless ethnographer having his leg pulled, becomes almost overwhelming. In a statement that contradicts his earlier 'evidence' about the killing of a white man for his kidneys, he reports that:

> The blacks do not like to eat white people. When Jimmy
> had killed the white man near my headquarters, my
> question as to whether the dead man had been eaten caused
> great surprise. The answer was: Kolle mah! komorbory
> kawan! – that is, By no means! terrible nausea! At the
> same time the person pointed at his throat to indicate his

> disgust for the flesh of a white man. The other persons present agreed with him...I have heard it stated by 'civilised' blacks that the white man's flesh has a salt taste, which the natives do not like.

Lumholtz reports with equal seriousness the rumours of cannibalism during the Palmer River gold rush of the 1870s and 1880s, picking up the popular myth of the superior taste of Chinese flesh:

> This also seems to harmonise with their fondness for the flesh of the Chinese, whose food consists largely of rice and other vegetables. Farther north in Queensland it twice happened during my sojourn in Australia that the blacks killed the Chinese in great numbers. It was said that ten Chinamen were eaten at one dinner.

It is worth noting that Simpson Newland, no particular supporter of Aborigines, flatly contradicts Lumholtz's assertions of cannibalism among the tribes. In *Paving the Way*[4] – published just five years after *Among Cannibals* – Newland says that: 'The Australian aboriginal was erroneously supposed by the early settlers to have a craving for the kidney-fat of the white man... [To] do them justice,' says one of Newland's characters, 'I never knew them in their direst straits resort to that or contemplate anything like cannibalism.'

Other interpretations are also possible of some of the 'evidence' gathered by Carl Lumholtz. The 'splendid booty' of a young woman, whose life is spared during a raid for human flesh, for example, carries the implication of raiding for a very different purpose: to secure wives. In his certainty about Aboriginal cannibalism, Lumholtz does not even consider this alternative. A very similar account of Northern Territory Aborigines, written some sixty years later, does, however, record exactly this motivation for intertribal raids that capture young women.

R. J. Pemberton was a soldier stationed in the Northern Territory as part of Australia's Second World War preparations. In his unpublished reminiscences of that period,[5] he describes the way 'war' is waged between two Aboriginal groups, for the express purpose of capturing women (the details match quite closely the description of 'marriage' in *Ralph Rashleigh*):

> It was the fourth week of our sojourn at the outpost and Bungeye came up at about lunchtime very concerned and very perplexed and very sweaty – finally we worked out the fact that the Brinkines and the Wogites were about to have a war. Evidently they knew what day the war would start and the day was tomorrow. 'Brinkines very bad men,' he said – of course Bungeye was a Wogite – he said, 'Yes, we have big war – throw spears.'

The day for the 'war' arrives. The diggers stay well out of the way, letting events take their course:

> We saw the Brinkines sneaking through the sparse trees, and we saw the Wogites lining up on the other side – about 15 in all each – they seemed to be well matched – all the young bucks of the tribes. And they had different spears – these were not their hunting spears – these were throwing spears – very fine, very light and heavy on one end.

The fighting itself is ritualised, the two sides taking it in turns to hurl their spears:

> ...and they whooshed through the air at great pace and the Wogites retaliated with another fusillade of spears and they were equally as good at it. This went on all day. There were a few people pierced by the spears – legs, arms, shoulders, nothing to kill them, nothing deadly – it was just a pre-arranged play.

Unlike Lumholtz, whose narrative never questions its underlying assumption of European superiority, Pemberton – faced with the reality of modern warfare – is far less convinced of the advantages of 'civilised' behaviour:

> When it was all over, the next day, Bungeye came up all smiles and I said, 'Who won?' He said, 'Nobody, nobody

> won. They go home. We go home.' I said, 'That's a good idea. That's the best way to have a war.'

It takes Pemberton some time to discover the reasons for this 'war'. Some of the boys had recently been accepted into the status of men, and:

> ...when a young boy comes in from his learning – his teacher brings him in and he won't bring him in until he considers he's a man and when he's a man he needs a wife, and wives have to be worked out by the old men of the tribe.

This 'working out' follows a traditional pattern:

> ...during the war some of the old men went into the Brinkines territory and abducted two of the young women – two marriageable young women – and they scouted around down the outskirts of the war and brought them back into the camp and there they were married to the young boy who had been brought in from his learning. This is the way it's done – it's the way it's always done for many thousands of years.

Despite the slippery nature of the 'evidence', rumours of cannibalism amongst indigenous groups have proved very persistent. They have also regularly been advanced as 'evidence' for the inferior status of Aborigines, particularly as part of the rhetoric of justification for their mistreatment or exclusion. The popular revulsion from this taboo makes it a useful device for denigrating and demonising a cultural or racial group. In one of the more infamous sections of *Pauline Hanson: The Truth*,[6] 'evidence' of cannibalism is used as part of a systematic discrediting of Aboriginal culture. Lumholtz's book is mentioned in a footnote, but the main source of quotation is a 1967 text, Hector Holthouse's *River of Gold: The Story of the Palmer River Gold Rush*.[7]

Hector Holthouse is the author of a number of local histories of Queensland. Like Lumholtz, he draws together his varied materials to form a compelling narrative. He is more precise than Lumholtz about acknowledging sources, though he is also not averse to a strategic disposal of his material, to achieve the greatest impact. In a passage from his opening chapter (quoted verbatim in *The Truth*) Holthouse offers a brief account of:

> Chinese coolies hung from trees by their pigtails for days, in batches of half a dozen or more, waiting their turn to be knocked on the head, roasted, and eaten.

Holthouse uses this unsubstantiated assertion as a useful narrative hook to justify the sensational title of his first chapter, 'Cannibal Country'.

The Truth presents this quotation as undisputed truth. And in her 'Surrendering Australia' chapter, Hanson also quotes selectively from the 'Asiatic Invasion' chapter in *River of Gold*, where the issue of cannibalism is taken up in much more detail. This time, the passage quoted from Holthouse's book states that: 'To the cannibal blacks, the new-chum Chinese were manna from heaven. Hundreds of them were ambushed, captured and eaten at leisure in gloomy canyons like Hell's Gate'.

The fictional device of imprisoning humans in a 'larder' prior to eating them is a stock-in-trade of European oral folk and fairy tales, occurring for example in such favourites as 'Jack and the Beanstalk' and 'Hansel and Gretel'. Holthouse's book clearly acknowledges the connection of the Palmer River rumours to bush mythology:

> Somewhere near the Gate there was supposed to be a large mountain cave which was given the name of the Devil's Kitchen. Rumour was that captured Chinese were taken there by the dozen and hung on trees outside by their pigtails until they were needed for killing and eating. In later years many miners looked for it, believing that some of the gold the captured Chinese would have been carrying would be found there. If the cave ever existed, it was never located.

Neither was the beanstalk.

For parts of his narrative, Holthouse draws on newspaper accounts and miners' reminiscences which report the Palmer River gossip. Unlike *Pauline Hanson: The Truth*, however, *River of Gold* does not fail to mention a further important qualification, that much of the wilder rumour was motivated by conflicts arising from claim-jumping on the goldfields: stories of Aboriginal cannibalism made a convenient cover to divert suspicion from European killings of rival Chinese fossickers:

> *The blacks were in fact blamed for some killings, particularly of Chinese, that they never committed. 'A spear sticking through a Chinaman's body was no evidence that he had been speared to death by a blackfellow,' one old hand from the Palmer wrote. 'Many a man was shot dead and then a barbed spear poked through the hole the bullet had made.'*

Despite such contrary evidence, rumours of cannibalism remained fixed in the popular imagination for many years. They served a useful purpose for settlers and miners alike, justifying maltreatment of Aborigines, and displacing blame for ordinary murders motivated by greed onto convenient Aboriginal groups.

This displacement followed a tradition of scapegoating which Marcus Clarke, and later Holthouse, highlighted. It began of course with the earliest settlement when fear of the alien environment was personified in representations of the indigenous inhabitants. Any lingering Rousseauesque conceptions of the noble savage were displaced in the later nineteenth century by a focus on the relationship between 'regressive' appearance and 'regressive' culture. The pseudo-scientific attempts to rank-order humanity had led to the development of a range of physical indicators that were supposed to demonstrate the degree to which any given racial group had advanced in the scramble up a Darwinian ladder. A progressive culture (like the British) gave evidence in its achievements of advanced development, and the general physical characteristics of the members of that culture could therefore be used as a yardstick by which to measure others. Equally, the reverse was true. The lack of 'progress' in Aboriginal culture was indicative of inferior development, and the appearance of Aborigines was therefore seen to offer a model of an older, superseded form of humanity, so close in appearance and behaviour to the apes from which we had sprung as to be scarcely human at all (remember Peter Warburton's dehumanising description of the old woman he captured). If this tendency to equate appearance and cultural development was implicit in factual accounts, it was quite explicit in some of the fiction that appeared later in the century.

One of Ernest Favenc's novels of romantic adventure was a speculative account of very early European contact with Australia, entitled *Marooned on Australia: Being the narration by Diedrich Buys of his Discovery and Exploits in Terra Australis Incognita about the year 1630*.[8] The story draws on the wreck of the *Batavia* in Western Australia in 1629, and the incidents which followed, using these as a jumping-off point for a fanciful story of a lost civilisation in the outback. In it Favenc describes the moment of encounter with this civilisation, when Diedrich Buys and his companion discover a carved rock head:

> ...we both were struck by observing that this head was not a copy of the natives of the country we had passed through. For these Indians are all most ugly, having blubber lips, flat noses, and low foreheads; but this head was that of a handsome man although without any beard.

This description takes us right back to William Dampier's 1697 account, with its reference to 'great Bottle Noses, pretty full lips, and wide mouths...Hair...like that of the negroes; and not...like the common Indians'.[9] Favenc adapts Dampier to social Darwinism, with a clear grading of humanity that includes the standard reference points of 'civilisation' – clothing, agricultural economy, a built environment, and a social hierarchy. Favenc's pre-existent antipodean civilisation has strong echoes of Arab oasis settlements:

> We saw green patches like cultivated fields, thickets of tall trees, low houses with white walls, and, above all, human beings, clothed and apparently wearing a kind of headdress.

Note that four years of living among 'savages' does not constitute contact with human beings – a not uncommon discrimination in this period. The anonymous author of *The Bat-*

tle of Mordialloc[10] – one of the earliest invasion scare fictions written in Australia – for instance, treats his introductory description in similarly pseudo-Darwinian fashion, with a metaphorical gesture towards the spiritual sanction of material and expansionist ambitions:

> *Where, a hundred years before, the land was practically a vast solitude, scantily peopled by the lowest savages, noble cities had sprung up with thriving industries, halls of learning, and spires rising heavenwards.*

Just as the early settlers offered literary justifications of invasion that claimed divine predestination, by the late nineteenth century writers of popular fiction were expressing the common view that European civilisation – and the British in particular – was ordained by both Nature and God to bring a better way of life to all parts of the globe. Marginal cultures, like the Aboriginal, would simply die out naturally.

Of course, if Nature was a little slow about the process, then white civilisation could always lend a helping hand. Carl Lumholtz might not have found much direct information to support claims of Aboriginal cannibalism, but his records of white atrocities against blacks are many and detailed: '...it is necessary for the white man to defend himself,' he agrees, 'but there is no doubt that in this respect he has gone further than necessity demanded'. He records the Sunday afternoon 'sport' of 'hunting the blacks', and at least one instance of mass poisoning by strychnine, at Long Lagoon in Queensland. The threat of legal process was generally scorned, with one farmer boasting that, like the Myall Creek killers earlier in the century, he had cremated the blacks he had shot. 'He looked upon this as a most excellent precautionary measure, for it made proof against him impossible', Lumholtz writes.

The sheer pragmatic callousness of the squatters is at times breathtaking. One man:

> *...shot all the men he discovered on his run, because they were cattle killers; the women, because they gave birth to*

cattle killers; and the children, because they would in time become cattle killers. 'They are unwilling to work,' I have heard colonists say, 'and hence they are not fit to live.'

Lumholtz reports one atrocity in some detail, concealing the names as a reluctant courtesy to the white murderers:

> A cedar-cutter in Northern Queensland had one day left one of his white workmen in charge of the camp, while he and his other labourers went to the woods to work...In the course of the day two blacks came to the guard, and as the latter had no ill-will to the natives, he treated them in a friendly manner and gave them tobacco. When the master returned in the evening he became very angry on account of what had happened, and the next day he set a Kanaka to watch the camp. The natives of course thought the white man was friendly, as he had given them tobacco, and so they did not hesitate to visit the camp again the next day; but they soon found out their mistake. One of the blacks who tried to make his escape was wounded in the leg, while the other one was captured and tied to a tree. This done, the wounded man was seized and killed with a butcher's knife. When the Kanaka came back to the camp the master had returned, and the latter at once ordered, in cold blood, that the prisoner who was tied to the tree should also be killed. They did not even waste a bullet on the poor fellow, who was pierced with a knife.

Not all colonists were so brutal. Some people, Lumholtz says:

> ...look upon the blacks as human beings with a right to live in the land which is in fact their own. 'Were I a black man, I would kill all the whites,' an Australian gentleman once said to me.

Lumholtz makes no secret of his own belief that Aborigines are destined to die out, but he is no believer in artificially hastening the process. He records a similarly pessimistic Darwinian view among some at least of the white colonists:

> One of these protectors of the blacks writes to me –
>
> 'If I thought that anything I might say on the treatment of the aborigines would in any way tend to ameliorate their present wretched condition, I would not for a moment grudge my lost health, and would plead their cause to my last breath. But alas! it were vain to hope for any improvement in their condition; for it is an immutable law of nature that the strong will prey upon the weak. I always look upon the condition of the lower order of 'whites' as a fearful satire on Christianity. The English nation is continually casting stones at other nations for the treatment of conquered races, but nothing could be more barbarous than their own treatment of the aborigines of Australia.'

Lumholtz notes that some 'reservations' have been set aside for Aborigines to 'raise crops and cattle, and receive instruction'. But the outcome, he believes, is not in doubt:

> 'When civilised nations come into contact with barbarians, the struggle is but short, excepting where a dangerous climate helps the native race,' says Darwin, and history corroborates his statement.

The problem, according to Lumholtz, is that Aborigines are too low down the scale of humanity to be saved:

> They have proved themselves almost incapable of receiving either culture or Christianity, and they have not the power to resist the onward march of civilisation. They are therefore without a future, without a home, without a hope, – a doomed race...The philanthropist is filled with sadness when he sees the original inhabitants of this strange land succumbing according to the inexorable law of degeneration. Invading civilisation has not brought development and progress to the Australian native; after a few generations his race will have disappeared from the face of the earth.

While Lumholtz might not have approved the process of extinction, others did, and were not afraid to say so. This is the solution to the 'Aboriginal problem' advocated in 1883 by the *Bulletin*:

> Gather them all together on an immense reserve in North-Western Australia...Let them have no rum and no religion, but fight and frolic in their own way. And by the time the Whites would be closing upon them, they would have reduced their own numbers so much by internal quarrels that the boundary line of their reservation could be shifted inwards far enough to allow four or five 'runs' in the space vacated. So the process of closing in could go on until the last survivors, two or three in number, were frozen out altogether. Some showman by that time could make a good thing of taking them around the other colonies and exhibiting them as curiosities. This is the way to let the Black race die out easily and naturally. The present efforts to ameliorate their conditions only result in killing them out sooner, and making their lives miserable while they do last... the relentless logic of the history of all our past dealings with the natives is summed up concisely in the dictum of the Northern Miner – 'the nigger must go'.[11]

Even the 'relentless logic' of this ferocious 'solution' pales by comparison with another, fictional response to the 'nigger' problem. G. Read Murphy's *Beyond the Ice: Being a Story of the Newly Discovered Region Round the North Pole*[12] was written in 1894 as a 'utopian' fiction: a picture of a supposedly perfected society. In this tale, the narrator, Dr Frank Farleigh, the sole survivor of an expedition to the Pole, finds himself marooned in the Arctic. Here he discovers a complex and highly technologically advanced society of polar people, the Fregidans, whose country is divided into three city states with differing social views. 'Scientific thinking' is in the political ascendancy, with the result that a previously liberal-minded state has decided upon ruthless extermination of the already marginalised 'savages', the Rodas, who (foreshadowing some of the representations of the supposed 'Aboriginal welfare industry' in the 1990s) are characterised as useless and ungrateful recipients of public charity.

Since it is known that the Rodas, armed with primitive weapons, are about to raid an outpost, the Fregidan preparations to meet them are murderous. In an incident that looks forward to Nazi gas chambers, the defenders of 'civilisation' have prepared to 'fill the [entry] tunnel with gas that will kill every man or animal in it'. In the course of the raid, the Fregidans expect to 'slay at least four out of every five of them in a few hours'. When challenged on the ethics of this, the commander responds: 'What matter?... They are murderous savages, who are too lazy and selfish to accept civilization'.

The intended genocide of the Rodas is justified in terms of scientific eugenics:

> *In our society no thing or animal that is detrimental to the general welfare is allowed to increase its species. And yet the community maintains in its midst human beings who are ill-fed, ill-housed, and often diseased... We misinterpreted liberty to mean that a man who does no active wrong must be allowed to do all the passive wrong that suits him.*

This blaming of the victim is another disturbing and familiar response to social problems. When a marginalised group becomes restive, one temptingly simplistic 'solution' is to eliminate the problem by eliminating the human results, rather than the social and economic causes.

In the imaginative spaces of literature, the desired absence of Aborigines could become a reality. In fiction, it was possible to rewrite the past so thoroughly that the 'problem' had never existed at all. The great open spaces of the continent of Australia, ordained for white exploitation, could become blank pages, virgin brides, spirits of place wakened for the first time to themselves. This is Ernest Favenc again, in poetic mood this time:

> *A cloudless sky o'erhead, and all around*

The level country stretching like a sea –
A dull grey sea, that had no seeming bound,
The very semblance of eternity.

All common things that this poor life contained
Had passed from them, leaving no sign nor token;
My footfall first broke the stillness that had reigned
For centuries unbroken.
...
Then came strange sounds, as if a spirit walked,
Wringing its hand in pain,

Crying, 'No rest! no rest! Who dares intrude,
And waken silence that for countless years
Has been unbroken? Must our solitude
At last know human tears?...'[13]

And this is Joseph Furphy ('Tom Collins') in his famous Australian novel, *Such is Life*,[14] like Henry Kingsley echoing the words of St John the Divine in the *Revelation*, seeing the new land 'as a bride adorned for her husband':

> To me this wayward diversity of spontaneous plant life bespeaks an unconfined, ungauged potentiality of resource; it unveils an ideographic prophecy, painted by Nature in her Impressionistic mood, to be deciphered aright only by those willing to discern through the crudeness of dawn a promise of majestic day. Eucalypt, conifer, mimosa; tree, shrub, heath, in endless diversity and exuberance, yet sheltering little of animal life beyond half-specialised and belated types, anachronistic even to the Aboriginal savage. Faithfully and lovingly interpreted, what is the latent meaning of it all?
>
> Our virgin continent! how long has she tarried her bridal day! Pause and think how she has waited in serene loneliness while the deltas of the Nile, Euphrates, and Ganges expanded, inch by inch, to spacious provinces, and

> the Yellow Sea shallowed up with the silt of winters
> innumerable – and waited while the primordial civilisations
> of Copt, Accadian, Aryan and Mongol crept out, step by
> step, from palæolithic silence into the uncertain record of
> Tradition's earliest fable – waited still through the long eras
> of successive empires, while the hard-won light, broadening
> little by little, moved westward, westward, round the
> circumference of the planet, at last to overtake and
> dominate the fixed twilight of its primitive home – waited,
> ageless, tireless, acquiescent, her history a blank, while the
> petulant moods of youth gave place to imperial purpose,
> stern yet beneficent – waited whilst the interminable
> procession of annual, lunar and diurnal alternations lapsed
> unrecorded into a dead Past, bequeathing no register of good
> or evil endeavour to the ever-living Present. The mind retires
> from such speculation unsatisfied but impressed.
>
> Gravely impressed. For this recordless land – this land of
> our lawful solicitude and imperative responsibility – is
> exempt from many a bane of territorial rather than racial
> impress. She is committed to no usages of petrified injustice;
> she is clogged by no fealty to shadowy idols, enshrined by
> Ignorance, and upheld by misplaced homage alone; she is
> cursed by no memories of fanaticism and persecution; she is
> innocent of hereditary national jealousy, and free from the
> envy of sister states.
>
> Then think how immeasurably higher are the possibilities of
> a Future than the memories of any Past since history began.

This is the messianic foundation of the sense of 'national culture' born in the 1890s and fostered by overtly racist periodicals like the *Bulletin*, which sponsored Furphy's writing. Furphy's vision of a land of innocence, freed of memory, looking only to the future and not to the past, is an Australia where the past of dispossession and extermination has been written out of existence. The 'Aboriginal savage' is a mere bystander to the consummation of the union between a virgin continent and her far-sighted white bridegrooms.

⁓

But while the Aboriginal presence was being written out of Australian fiction, or rewritten to a more comfortable nostalgia for a vanished past, commercial interests in Queensland were importing another racial group to use as cheap labour. The Kanakas – Pacific Islanders (the term comes from the Hawaiian word for 'man') – first came to Australia as crew on whaling ships in the early part of the nineteenth century. When the sugar and cotton industries really began to expand in Queensland, much larger numbers were imported as 'indentured labour' – fixed contract labourers, tied to their employer for the term of the contract. A fee was usually paid to the contractor who supplied the labour, while the workers themselves received little. The system was, in effect, a form of limited slavery.

The rural industries preferred to import cheap labour, since Aborigines had generally proved unwilling workers. The system was eventually ended, not by concern for the welfare of the Kanakas, but by pressure from the white labour organisations which wanted to protect their own members from cheap competition.

While it lasted, however, 'blackbirding' brought huge profits to the shipowners and captains engaged in the trade. It also provoked its share of sea shanties, the popular songs of the sea. This is 'Recruiting':

> *Far, far, upon the sea, looking out for blacks are we,*
> *We've got a decent cargo in the hold,*
> *If a hurricane don't blow, we'll soon back in Queensland*
>   *show,*
> *With a good lot of kanakas to be sold.*
> *We have to watch each isle, for the niggers, though they smile,*
> *Will knock you over if they get a chance,*
> *For though rifles we don't sell they can get them just as well*
> *From ships that hail from Germany or France.*

> Far, far, upon the sea, and the agent's on the spree,
> The captain don't know what is to be done,
> For unless he has his glass he won't let the niggers pass,
> And back without a cargo we must run.
> The planters they will cuss and lay the blame on us,
> Although in our losses they don't share,
> But we're bound to have our day if we only peg away,
> Oh gaily goes the ship when the trade is fair.[15]

One of the most famous of the blackbirders was 'Bully' Hayes, an American-born captain. His lasting reputation comes from the books and stories about him by Australian writer Louis Becke (George Lewis Becke). Becke made his way to America in 1869, at the age of fourteen, and spent the next quarter-century working with the Pacific island traders. He claimed to have sailed with Hayes, to have been charged with piracy (but acquitted), and shipwrecked a number of times.

Becke returned to Sydney in 1893. There he met Ernest Favenc, who introduced him to J. F. Archibald of the *Bulletin*. It was Archibald who helped Becke begin writing about his experiences, in short stories which were first published in the *Bulletin*, and then collected in *By Reef and Palm* (1894), *His Native Wife* (1895) and *The Ebbing of the Tide* (1896).

Although Becke's reputation has proved more lasting overseas than in Australia (perhaps because his South Pacific tales are perceived as less 'Australian' than the outback tales of writers like Henry Lawson), he is one of the more sensitive writers about inter-racial relations. His tales of marriages between Pacific Islander women and white men do not shy away from the difficulties of such relationships, and the cruelty of many of the men. Even where the relationship is positive, the cross-cultural marriages portrayed by Becke often do not survive the hostility of both cultures.

In 'A Dead Loss',[16] Becke explores another side to blackbirding – the buying and selling of Islander women as sexual partners. The tale begins with a conventional narrative frame that locates it within the real world, and tells its story of exploitation in a very down-to-earth way:

> Denison, the supercargo of the Indiana, was sent by his 'owners' to an island in the S. W. Pacific where they had a trading business, the man in charge of which had, it was believed, got into trouble by shooting a native. His instructions were to investigate the rumour, and, if the business was suffering in any way, to take away the trader and put another man in his place.

Note that the 'investigation' is concerned only with the commercial side of the matter. 'Shooting a native' was clearly of no great moment, provided it did not interfere with business.

The 'savage and morose' young captain of the trading vessel, working under the pseudonym of 'Captain Chaplin', is something of a mystery man, who turns out to know the island and its drunken trader well (drunkenness, like violence and the buying and selling of sexual favours, was clearly an occupational hazard of life as a white trader living on an isolated South Pacific island). He is recognised by the trader as 'that —— nigger-catching skipper that was here from Honolulu four years ago'.

Martin, the trader, tells a story of a visit by a whaling ship that had rescued the survivors from 'a big canoe with a chief's retinue on board', including the dead chief's wife and daughter, to whom the trader takes a fancy:

> Martin gave the captain trade and cash to the tune of five hundred dollars for the two women, and came ashore. Pensioning off his other wife, he took the young girl himself and sold the mother to the local chief for a ton of copra.

The dismissed wife's brother comes looking for Martin and, in the ensuing fight, the brother is shot and Martin stabbed. He is tabooed by the villagers, who withdraw to the other side of the lagoon leaving the trader and Lunumala, his new girl, to their own devices. 'And Martin gave himself up to love and drink, and, since the fracas, had not done a cent's worth of trading.'

Martin is given the company's ultimatum: give up the girl, or leave the island. When he refuses, the captain makes his move:

> 'Now, I don't want to make any man feel mean, but she don't particularly care about you, and –'
>
> The graceful creature nodded her approval of Chaplin's remarks, and Martin glared at her. Then he took a drink of gin and meditated.
>
> Two minutes passed. Then Martin turned.
>
> 'How much?' he said.
>
> 'Fifty pounds, sonny. Two hundred and fifty dollars.'
>
> 'Easy to see you've been in the business,' mumbled Martin; 'why, her mother's worth that. 'Tain't no deal.'
>
> 'Well, then, how much do you want?'
>
> 'A hundred.'
>
> 'Haven't got it on board, sonny. Take eighty sovereigns and the rest in trade or liquor?'
>
> 'It's a deal,' said Martin; 'are you game to part ten sovereigns for the girl's mother, and I'll get her back from the natives?'
>
> 'No,' said Chaplin, rising; 'the girl's enough for me.'

Any thought that such illegal dealing in human beings might be frowned on by the owners is quickly dismissed. Again, only one thing counts – the bottom line:

> I know our godly owners would raise a deuce of a row about my buying the girl if I couldn't pay for her keep while she's on board, but I've got a couple of hundred pounds in Auckland, as they know, besides some cash on board.

And the reason for the captain's interest? Not a sexual one (such human weaknesses being merely something to exploit). In the world of the blackbirder there is only the ultimate motive of profit:

> ...there's a friend of mine in Honolulu always willing to give a few thousand dollars for a really handsome girl. And I believe that girl will bring me nearly about three thousand dollars.

The girl's co-operation is easy to obtain, with the promise of an early return to her home island. Not until the ship heads for Fiji does she realise she has been tricked. And then, without a word:

> ...she turned and looked aft at us, and her long, black hair streamed out like a pall of death. Suddenly she sprang over.
>
> With a curse Chaplin rushed to the wheel, and in double-quick time the whaleboat was lowered and search was made. In half an hour Chaplin returned, and gaining the deck said, in his usual cool way, to the mate: 'Hoist in the boat and fill away again as quick as possible.' Then he went below.
>
> A few minutes afterwards he was at his accustomed amusement, making tortoise-shell ornaments with a fretsaw.
>
> 'A sad end to the poor girl's life,' said the supercargo.
>
> 'Yes,' said the methodical ex-Honolulu blackbirder, 'and a sad end to my lovely five hundred dollars.'

Part of the impact of Becke's story comes, of course, from its contrast of the impersonal, profit-motivated Chaplin and the drink-sodden, self-centred Martin with the noble figure of Lunumala. There is, however, nothing romanticised about the situation. Becke's stories do not indulge in the elegiac nostalgia of so much 'Aboriginal' poetry of the period. They coldly spell out the misery and human cost of exploitation, and sheet home the blame to where it really lies.

Another writer who addressed some of the realities of the completely unequal contest between black and white was Mrs Aeneas (Jeannie) Gunn. Jeannie Taylor grew up in Melbourne, where she established a private school with her sister. She married Aeneas Gunn in 1901 and moved with him to the very different world of a station on Roper River in the Northern Territory. She spent a little over a year there, until the sudden death of her husband in 1903, after which she returned to Melbourne, where she published her two books *Little Black Princess* and the much better known *We of the Never Never*, which draws on her brief experience of station life.

We of the Never Never,[17] published in 1908, paints extensive and sympathetic portraits of station characters, and has become something of an icon in the literature of outback white Australia. In its treatment of contacts with local Aborigines, however, the book reflects something of the complexity of attitudes current at the turn of the century. In this passage, Mrs Gunn tackles the issue of cattle-killing, proposing a level of peaceful co-existence between pastoralists and native owners which acknowledges prior claims. Her solution goes much further than the 1997 High Court Wik decision which provoked such controversy, and is scathing of white hypocrisy:

> *The white man has taken the country from the black fellow, and with it his right to travel where he will for pleasure or food, and until he is willing to make recompense by granting fair liberty of travel, and a fair percentage of cattle or their equivalent in fair payment – openly and fairly giving them, and seeing that no man is unjustly treated or hungry within his borders – cattle killing, and at times even man killing, by blacks will not be an offence against the white folk.*

> *A black fellow kills cattle because he is hungry and must be fed with food, having been trained in a school that for generations has acknowledged 'catch who catch can' among its commandments; and until the long arm of the law interfered, white men killed the black fellow, because they were hungry with a hunger that must be fed with gold, having been trained in a school that for generations has acknowledged 'Thou shalt not kill' among its commandments; and yet men speak of the 'superiority' of the white race, and, speaking, forget to ask who of us would*

> go hungry if the situation were reversed, but condemn the black-fellow as a vile thief, piously quoting – now it suits them – from those same commandments, that men 'must not steal', in the same breath referring to the 'white man's crime' (when it finds them out) as 'getting into trouble over some shooting affair with blacks'. Truly we British-born have reason to brag of our 'inborn sense of justice'.

Sympathetic though this position is, another aspect of *We of the Never Never* looks, to modern eyes, distinctly racist. This is what immediately precedes the first passage:

> 'River tonight, Sambo,' he said airily; but after that one swift glance Sambo rode after us as stolid as ever – Sambo was always difficult to fathom – while Dan spent the afternoon congratulating himself on the success of his dust-throwing, proving with many illustrations that 'it's the hardest thing to spring a surprise on niggers. Something seems to tell 'em you're coming,' he explained. 'Some chaps put it down to second-sight or thought-reading.'

The 'surprise' is a dispersal party:

> The Maluka was on the river, and when the Maluka was about, it was considered wisdom to be off forbidden ground; not that the blacks feared the Maluka, but no one cares about vexing the goose that lays the golden eggs.

Or, to put it another way, co-existence is dependent on the Aborigines acknowledging who is master in this land:

> On stations in the Never-Never the blacks are supposed to camp either in the homestead, where no man need go hungry, or right outside the boundaries on waters beyond the cattle, travelling in or out as desired, on condition that they keep to the main traveller's tracks...
>
> Of course no man ever hopes to keep his blacks absolutely obedient to this rule; but the judicious giving of an odd bullock at not too rare intervals, and always at corroborree times, the more judicious winking at cattle killing on the

> boundaries, where cattle scaring is not all disadvantage,
> and the even more judicious giving of a hint, when a hint is
> necessary, will do much to keep them fairly well in hand...

'The Maluka' – Aeneas Gunn – sets out to teach a lesson to blacks who fail to adhere to his rules. *We of the Never Never* assumes that the Maluka's 'nigger hunt' will 'only involve the captured with general discomfiture', rather than the all-too-common random killings. But any concern for Aboriginal welfare is clearly dependent on their acceptance of white dominance on this shared land.

The references to 'Sambo' and 'niggers' are a sharp reminder of the generalised racism prevalent in most white societies prior to and just after the First World War. In its most contemptuous form, this racism lumped together all non-Europeans as 'coloureds', and added a general category within this, for the lowest form of humanity, 'blacks' or, in American slang, 'niggers'.

In Australia, the term 'nigger' had been applied, off and on, to indigenous peoples since the 1840s. It was always used as a term of denigration, as a reduction of their essential humanity, a distancing device that allowed the application of the kind of double-standards to which Mrs Gunn refers. Ernest Favenc, for example, in his 1894 story, 'Spirit Led',[18] glosses the term 'dispersing-match' with the footnote 'nigger raid', meaning an attack by a party of armed whites on an Aboriginal encampment. And D. H. Lawrence, writing the novel *Kangaroo*,[19] based on his short visit to Australia in 1922, fell easily into the idiom:

> ...the landscape is so unimpressive, like a face with little or
> no features, a dark face. It is so aboriginal, out of our ken,
> and it hangs back so aloof. Somers always felt he looked at
> it through a cleft in the atmosphere; as one looks at one of
> the ugly-faced, distorted aborigines with his wonderful dark
> eyes that have such an incomprehensible ancient shine in
> them, across gulfs of unbridged centuries. And yet, when
> you don't have the feeling of ugliness or monotony, in
> landscape or in nigger, you get a sense of subtle, remote,

> formless *beauty more poignant than anything ever experienced before.*

The 'Kangaroo' of the book's title is eminent Sydney lawyer Benjamin Cooley, leader of a secret right-wing association of returned First World War servicemen. Lawrence's novel traces his own encounters with the New Guard, a real-life right-wing organisation. One of the New Guard's leading figures, Captain F. E. de Groot, later became famous when he galloped forward, sword in hand, and dramatically severed the ribbon at the opening of the Sydney Harbour Bridge. De Groot's action was a deliberate affront to the Labor premier of New South Wales, John Lang (in Lawrence's novel, published in 1923, the digger movement disrupts a labour meeting, causing heavy casualties).

The New Guard itself was modelled on the fictional 'White Guard' formed in a 1909 novel, *The Australian Crisis*, by C. H. Kirmess.[20] In that novel, the Guard is a guerrilla movement fighting to free northern Australia from a British-approved Japanese colony. Certainly the New Guard saw itself is as a bastion against any such threat to the new white Australian identity confirmed at Federation.

Aborigines had by this stage been largely relegated to a forgotten or inferior status; they were no real threat like the 'hordes' of Asia. But the violent right-wing tendencies of the White and New Guards are a sharp reminder of Australia's involvement in radical developments of political racism. In 1925, two years after the publication of *Kangaroo*, Adolf Hitler published *Mein Kampf*. And in the same year, Australian writer Erle Cox released a scientific romance he had been working on for several years, called *Out of the Silence*.[21]

Erle Cox was born in Melbourne in 1873, educated at Melbourne Grammar, and became a major figure in Melbourne journalism, writing variously for the *Australasian*, the *Argus* and the *Age*. His fiction-writing career began in 1910, when he won a short story competition in Frank Fox's *Lone Hand*. In *Out of the Silence* Cox revisited the social Darwinist variant on the theory of natural selection, looking forward rather than back, to the possible future of the human species. The story is chilling in its implications.

Out of the Silence opens with a brief account of a highly advanced humanoid society on Earth somewhere in the very distant past. Faced with imminent planet-wide catastrophe which will wipe out all life, these people take out insurance against their common future. Three carefully selected individuals are sealed into capsules which preserve them and the full range of their technology and knowledge in stasis, so that 'the wisdom of our race' can be handed down to a future human society.

The story then switches to twentieth-century Australia where Cox's narrator, excavating a waterhole on his homestead, discovers one of the capsules. When he finally breaks through to the inner sanctum, he faces a woman from this distant past, with awe-inspiring but entirely rational powers at her disposal. She is possessed of extraordinary beauty and physical grace – a scientifically updated version of Victorian spiritual grace. She stands for a genetically refined 'humanity', for which the laws of natural selection obviate any requirement for moral justification.

Representations of such superior beings in scientific romances always seemed somehow to refine or distill the essences of European upper-class 'beauty'. Here for example is Cox's breathless description of his alien sleeping beauty, awakened in the outback when two regular blokes dig up her high-tech time capsule:

> *Slowly as the dawn a faint flush of colour spread over the pale cheeks, and a deeper hue to the perfectly curved lips. But with the flush of pink came something more, that seemed as if a veil that had rested on the pale features had been drawn aside. It appeared as if a soul had entered, and found a resting place...the white hand stirred restlessly, and fell across the golden cascade of her hair...the long lashes trembled on her cheeks, and the white lids fluttered ever so slightly, and then... Slowly the eyes opened, glorious deep, grey orbs...*

Naturally she enslaves them, and implements an alien plot to take over and 'improve' the world. After all, to this advanced being, Cox's hero and his friends appear as primitive as their perception of the Aborigines. To her, all but the white races are subhuman. This is spelled out in her interview with the Prime Minister, Sir Miles, when she demands that he surrender Australia to her implementation of the Final Solution:

> '...you have the means, and intend to use them, of destroying the coloured races in the world?' asked Sir Miles.
>
> Earani answered without hesitation. 'That is right, inasmuch as I intend to eliminate all that is unfit in the world.'
>
> '...you have the means, and will use them, of imposing your will and your own ideas of civilisation on the world?'
>
> 'That is my mission', she answered quietly, 'and I regard it as a sacred mission.'

The Prime Minister argues against such a solution to the problems of the world, even while he acknowledges the human perfection of Earani herself. But the argument she advances is tempting:

> This world of yours is full of pain and misery. Is any price too great to pay to cure it? Is any price too great that buys a perfect and wholesome humanity?

To Sir Miles, in return for his collaboration, she offers a Faustian contract:

> ...fifty years of absolute power, backed and guided by ten thousand years of experience, and this people of yours to work for. To lay the foundation of a work that will knit them into a perfect humanity; a race that will eventually become without blemish, morally or physically. My friend, would such a work be the work of the fiends you would have us appear?

The muddled and imperfect world of humanity is finally saved by chance. The jealous girlfriend of the man Earani has chosen as her consort stabs and kills her rival. The men themselves were helpless, adapting themselves to the apparently inevitable.

So the question is unresolved: given the opportunity, and official release from the constraints of conscience, would Australians in the 1920s have followed the route taken by Nazi Germany? Would they have willingly assisted in genocide to preserve the racial purity of a White Australia?

On the evidence of the literature, with its insistence on the racial inferiority of 'the coloured races', and the God-given right of white settlers to possess the land they had colonised, by any means at their disposal, the possibility was all too real.

Part Two
White or Yellow?

4

Asian Invasion

Antipathy to the indigenous peoples of Australia had its roots in a sense of European racial and cultural superiority. There were economic issues involved on occasion, especially when pastoralists moved deeper into the remote areas of the north and west of the continent, coming into contact with actively hostile Aboriginal groups. In general, however, the Aboriginal presence was regarded as a temporary nuisance, rather than a lasting threat to the new economic order.

In the case of the Chinese immigrant community, however, the situation was very different. Immigration from China began in 1848, just before the first gold rush, and only a decade before the publication of Darwin's *The Origin of Species by Natural Selection*. The Chinese quickly became subject to the same kind of rank-ordering as the Aborigines (though much further up the ladder), and were therefore regarded as naturally inferior. To the annoyance of white miners and traders, however, Chinese immigrants proved efficient, hard-working and perfectly capable of dealing with the peculiarities of European culture. With many of them coming from the same areas of southern China, they also maintained a degree of social cohesion that was denied to the polyglot white miners, who came from a wide range of cultural and linguistic backgrounds.

As a distinct group, the Chinese immigrants represented a real economic threat to the struggling diggers and to the many small business people who flourished by supplying their wants. Where Aborigines had been dismissed quite early as incapable of being absorbed into a European economic model, the Chinese were vilified for the very efficiency with which they fitted in. Cultural and racial differences were merely convenient ways of identifying and attacking what – from the point of view of the individual European immigrant trying to establish a sound economic base – was soon perceived as the economic enemy.

Many diggers and small business owners came to Australia to escape the economic limitations of class-bound European social systems. Their resentment of the Chinese was not lessened by the enthusiasm of British capitalists investing in the developing colonies for what appeared to be a limitless source of cheap, industrious and compliant labour.

The economic value of importing cheap 'coolie' labour into Australia had been suggested as early as 1829, in Edward Gibbon Wakefield's *A Letter from Sydney*.[1] Wakefield (1796-1862) was a colourful English character whose abduction of and marriage to an under-age heiress led to his serving a three-year term in London's Newgate prison. This experience so changed him that he devoted his life to the critical study of transportation and colonisation and the publication of various works on criminal justice. One of his early books, *A Letter from Sydney*, written in prison and edited by Robert Gouger (founder of the National Colonisation Society), canvassed ideas for increasing 'systematic colonisation' – a blueprint for assisted migration. The book was controversial in Sydney, where it was taken to be the work of an Australian colonist. Wakefield went on to become a major figure in colonisation debates: he was involved in the establishment of the 1831 assisted migration scheme in New South Wales, and later the formation of the South Australian colony in 1836. He was also part of Sir Charles Molesworth's 1837-38 British parliamentary investigation into transportation, convened in response to controversial argument between its supporters and emancipists, and conducted amid growing concerns about the brutality of 'The System'. The investigation led to the eventual abandonment of transportation. The last east coast convicts arrived in

Tasmania in 1843, although Western Australia, desperately short of labour, continued to receive convicts until 1858.

The idea of importing coolie labour grew in popularity in the eastern states when the transportation of convicts ceased, coincidentally at a time when Britain and the United States had new treaties in place with China, following the Opium Wars (waged by the United Kingdom against China to enforce the opening of Chinese ports to trade in opium). British consumption of Chinese commodities, particularly tea, silk and porcelain, had increased, and when China refused to accept payment in opium from India, Chinese ports were blockaded. The First Opium War (1839-42) resulted in the cession of Hong Kong to Britain, and the opening of five treaty ports; the Second Opium War (1856-60), the consequence of further Chinese resistance to trade in opium, resulted in greater trading privileges for European states, together with treaties which guaranteed, among other things, free movement of Chinese nationals within the Empire and the United States of America.

Isolationist China was forced to open her doors, and many Chinese nationals now chose to seek a new life elsewhere. The first (all male) group of Chinese workers arrived in Australia in 1848, and the number of Chinese immigrants increased dramatically during the gold rushes in the second half of the nineteenth century. In Victoria, there are reports of 10,000 Chinese on the goldfields in 1855, increasing to 25,000 by 1857. In Queensland, Chinese significantly outnumbered European diggers at the Palmer River Goldfields in 1875.[2] The industry and efficiency of the Chinese caused enormous resentment at what many saw as unfair competition (Chinese were popularly supposed to be capable of working in climatic conditions that would cripple a white man). Their numbers threatened to swamp a nervous white culture which was not prepared to adapt itself to what it saw as an inferior race. The stage was set for racial conflict.

The 1855 report into the Eureka gold-miners' rebellion in Victoria had warned of a future in which vastly outnumbered white colonists would be swamped by a 'countless throng of Chinamen'. In response, the Victorian government imposed a Poll Tax of ten pounds per head on every Chinese immigrant, with the result that shipping owners, always careful businessmen, simply unloaded their profitable cargo of Chinese in New South Wales or South Australia, leaving the hapless immigrants to trek overland to the diggings. Many illustrations from the period depict immigrants trudging along with their possessions suspended in two baskets from a pole carried across the shoulders. J. Chandler, recording the events in his *Forty Years in the Wilderness* (1893) describes them as 'winding across the plain like a long black mark'.[3]

The Eureka report's concerns about the racial future of the colony were, in part, a reflection of the more immediate economic concerns of the white miners, who saw their chance for prosperity threatened by the influx of Chinese. Their fears were reflected in popular songs of the time, like this one, called 'Chinese Immigration',[4] by goldfields entertainer Charles Thatcher:

> You doubtless read the papers,
> And as men of observation,
> Of course you watch the progress
> Of Chinese immigration –
> For thousands of these pigtail chaps
> In Adelaide are landing;
> And why they let such numbers come
> Exceeds my understanding.

Thatcher was born in Bristol in 1831 and began his career playing the flute in London theatre orchestras. Like many others, he followed the lure of gold to Melbourne, and then to the diggings at Bendigo where he arrived in 1852. He was to remain in Victoria until 1861, and returned for a further three years from 1866. He was not successful as a miner, but when he reverted to the entertainment field his fortunes changed. He rapidly gained a large following for his songs on local subjects, set to popular tunes. He finally returned to England in 1869, but did not settle, dying in Shanghai in 1878.

During his years on the goldfields, Thatcher published many of his songs in local newspapers, writing enough to release three volumes: *Thatcher's Victoria Songster* (1855), *Thatcher's Colonial Songster* (1857) and *Thatcher's Colonial Minstrel* (1859). 'Chinese Immigration' was one of his goldfield pieces, sung to the miners of Bendigo to the tune of 'Dicky Birds'. It was also published in his *Colonial Songster*, and effectively caught the popular mood of the time.

Thatcher had an unerring eye for the causes of the miners' fears. When an unassuming weatherboard temple was built in 1855 at Emerald Hill (present-day South Melbourne) and began dispensing meals to weary Chinese diggers on their way to or from the goldfields, neighbours complained of the stench from foreign cooking. Goldfields money paid for the present imposing temple, completed in 1866, and the new building was designed to blend with other grand public structures springing up throughout Melbourne. But inoffensive externals could not deflect resentment. Even the low-key presence of the hospitable little weatherboard temple had represented something disturbingly alien. Thatcher's song pinpointed and exploited deep European suspicion of a culture so different from their own:

> *On Emerald Hill it now appears*
> *A Joss House they've erected;*
> *And they've got an ugly idol there –*
> *It's just what I expected;*
> *And they offer nice young chickens*
> *Unto this wooden log;*
> *And sometimes with a sucking pig*
> *They go the entire hog.*

Like the Eureka report, Thatcher predicted an Asianised future for Australia:

> *Now some of you, perhaps, may laugh,*
> *But 'tis my firm opinion,*
> *This colony some day will be*
> *Under Chinese dominion.*

They'll upset the Australian government,
The place will be their own;
And an Emperor with a long pigtail,
Will sit upon the throne.

He also foreshadowed, in humourous vein, the more specific fears that would come to obsess writers of the 1880s and 90s, when persecution of the Chinese immigrants gave real cause to fear punitive intervention:

Of the stations up the country
They'll quickly take possession.
The squatters will be used as slaves,
By the celestial nation;
And growing tea or rice will be
Their only compensation.

The mandarins will seize for wives
The fair Australian girls...

But in 1857 such fears were in their infancy, and Thatcher concludes on an upbeat note, in the tongue-in-cheek voice of the eternal opportunist:

If it comes to pass, these English songs
Away I'll quick be flinging,
And learn their language; and come out
In Chinese comic singing.

The European colonists were given more immediate and substantial cause for alarm by the 1872 completion of the cable telegraph link to Britain, which destroyed forever the illusory security of distance from involvement in larger world events. Some of the first telegraph news reports from Britain, for example, covered the unfolding events of a national coal miners' strike. Australians, unused to hearing about such crises as they occurred, panicked at the apparently imminent collapse of Britain.

The traffic of news, of course, went both ways. Atrocities committed on Chinese diggers were reported overseas just as readily as world news came to the colonies. So resentment of Chinese industry and success was compounded by ever-increasing terror at the prospect of invasion by an avenging Chinese horde: the basic scenario for a number of lurid Australian fictions which were published from the 1880s onward.

The voice of local Chinese reason, published in *The Chinese Question* (1879),[5] went largely unheard. Three Chinese gentlemen – L. Kong Meng, Cheok Hong Cheong and Louis Ah Mouy – presented a pamphlet outlining 'the primary cause of the immigration of Chinese subjects into these colonies, and...their perfect right to settle in any part of the British Empire'. Describing themselves as 'natives of China and citizens of Victoria', they reminded their fellow Victorians of the events leading up to their immigration:

> Up to the year 1842, we lived in contented isolation from the rest of the world. The nations of Western Europe – England more particularly – said 'This shall not be.' By force of arms a treaty was extorted from the Government at Pekin, in virtue of which a certain number of Chinese ports were thrown open to British commerce. In 1844, the United States demanded and obtained similar privileges. In 1860, the English and French Governments, acting in concert, overcame the resistance which his Imperial Majesty and the chief Mandarins of the country offered to an extension of these extorted rights, and they dictated a second treaty at Pekin, which guaranteed to the people of both nations the utmost freedom of ingress and egress, and which reciprocally bestowed upon the Chinese a similar freedom as regards the territories of France and the British Empire. In 1868, the Government of the United States concluded with the Emperor of China what is known as the 'Burlingame Treaty,' which assured to Americans the same access to our country...and opened the United States to Chinese immigration.

The forceful nature of the actions of Britain, France and America was emphasised:

> Western powers, armed with the formidable artillery with which modern science has supplied them, battered down the portals of the [Chinese] empire... They said "We must come in, and you shall come out. We will not suffer you to shut yourselves up from the rest of the world...

The terms of these treaties are of great relevance to us today. We can see just how far the nature of the agreement has been modified over the years as Britain officially returned Hong Kong to China at the end of June 1997 – without, by any means, allowing free immigration of Hong Kong citizens. But back in 1879, reminding Australian colonists that Britain and America had forced China to open its borders, and had actively encouraged free emigration, merely increased local resentment at Imperial interference. *The Chinese Question* touched directly on the real fears of European colonists when it described the Australian continent in terms of a promised land that would support the 'redundant millions of Europe and Asia':

> When we heard...that there was a great continent nearly half as large again as China, and containing only a few hundreds of thousands of civilized people thinly scattered around the coast; that it was only a few weeks' sail from our own country, numbers of Chinese set out for this land of promise.

This position was historically and politically reasonable, but European settlers did not find it at all reassuring. Nor did they wish to be reminded of the industry of Chinese settlers, which they saw also as a direct threat. *The Chinese Question* asserts that its settlers have been model colonists – 'They came to work, not to beg or steal' – and cites their success as market gardeners, fishermen, traders and hawkers of useful wares as evidence of their benefit to the health of the colony.

Ironically, the reasons advanced in the Chinese pamphlet for their acceptance were the same reasons given for their exclusion by the xenophobes who feared the relative lack of white settlers in a huge continent and distrusted the obvious industry of their Chinese rivals.

The Chinese Question also pleads for the traditional Australian right to 'a fair go':

> *Surely, justice is justice, right is right, and fair play is fair play, all the world over. The laws of morality do not vary with the variation in the degrees of latitude; and if it be lawful for the Englishman...to compete with our countrymen in China, it must be equally lawful for the Chinaman...to compete with Englishmen in Australia.*

The white settlers in Australia didn't think so. Economic self-interest was rapidly justified by appeals to racial purity, and resentment at ways in which distant Imperial policy was impacting on the economic and social lives of the white settlers was growing.

There was some support for the reasonable voice of the Chinese community. *Melbourne Punch* responded to *The Chinese Question* with a plea for a more considered approach:

> *Three Chinese merchants in Melbourne have put forth an appeal to the reason, the justice, the right feeling, and the calm good sense of the British population of Australia, as against the clamour which has been raised by anti-Chinese agitators, here and elsewhere. Such an appeal is entitled to a respectful hearing. Let us listen before we strike.*[6]

Far from moderating their stance, however, the colonies began to assert their right to pursue racial purity as a matter of policy. There were calls for a union of the colonies that would give them power fully to control internal affairs, especially the contentious issue of immigration. The twin concepts of Australian Federation and a White Australia of pure British stock became inextricably linked in the popular imagination.

The nationalistic, anti-Asian mood is reflected in popular doggerel rhymes of the time, like this one, reportedly chanted by

European diggers after the New South Wales Government enacted the Chinese Immigration Bill (1861):

> *Rule Britannia! Britannia rules the waves*
> *No more Chinamen will enter New South Wales*[7]

The anonymous 'Dick the Digger: A Tale of the Buckland' draws on the writer's experience of the Buckland River (Victoria) anti-Chinese riots:

> *For pick, pick it made him sick*
> *To think that he was getting daily, a*
> *Heap of these accursed Chinese*
> *And he cried 'They'll ruin Australia'*[8]

The Chinese were often depicted as degraded habitués of opium dens, regarded as locations for all manner of vice. In the nineteenth century opium was not illegal – Britain and her allies had fought and won two wars to ensure their right to enforce it as a trading currency with China. Indeed, opium was then a commonly available household drug, most frequently used as laudanum: a tincture of opium dissolved in alcohol. (One goldfields recipe for infant croup consisted of a syrup of opium dissolved in sweetened gin.) Despite the fashion for smoking opium among Europeans, Asian addiction to its use was stereotyped as particularly reprehensible, associated in the popular mind with other 'Asian' vices such as gambling and lechery.

One anonymous contributor to the Western Australian newspaper, the *Inquirer*, tried to stir up feeling against the Chinese immigrants. 'A.S.O.W.A.' (a son of Western Australia), in a poem titled 'John Chinaman My Jo',[9] admitted that 'the character I give you/ I must say is second-hand', but that did not stop him from stereotyping the Chinese who, he predicted, would one day return home 'Leaving nothing but your vices here':

> *Wherever you have been*
> *There is nought but immorality*
> *Has ever yet been seen.*

And the worst of all the vices are the opium dens:

> *John Chinaman my Jo John,*
> *I've seen your loathsome dens,*
> *Where you've enticed your victims,*
> *Like sheep going from the pens.*
> *But better were they killed like sheep*
> *Than live to know the woe*
> *Your opium-smoking dens have caused,*
> *John Chinaman my Jo.*

Despite its reasoned response to *The Chinese Question*, the *Melbourne Punch* was no less guilty than other periodicals of the pastime of inflammatory stereotyping. The poem 'Only Thirteen'[10] appeared in 1870, following newspaper reports of a white girl having been found living in an opium den. Like the *Inquirer* piece, it paints a picture of white victims lured to their doom by oriental vice:

> *Coaxed to the Chinamen's Camp, ere I knew*
> *There I was drugged by that merciless crew.*
>
> *Tempted to taste their foul opium smoke,*
> *Fancy my feelings at length when I woke.*
> *No one looked after me, so from that hour*
> *Here I've remained in the aliens' power.*

Not content with sensationalising the second-hand report, the poem generalises it to an image of widespread exploitation and entrapment:

> *Sisters in misery many I have –*
> *Each one a victim, and each one a slave:*
> *Each one by Chinamen's cunning beguiled –*
> *Each one demoralised – each one a child.*

The reality behind this tabloid journalism was, of course, much less clear-cut. Another commentary in *Melbourne Punch* in 1873 reflects the double standards of both the legal system and contemporary social attitudes. It also hints at the stereotype of the Chinese males as unable to control their desire for white women (or girls):

> *Decency must be at a low ebb at Bowman's Forest, near Beechworth, when the farmers' daughters of that locality are accustomed to associate with the Chinese, even going so far as to habitually romp and play kiss-in-the-ring with them. After this, no one can wonder at a John Chinaman being beguiled by one of these degraded beings into carrying his attentions to such an extent, that his playmate gave him in charge, and got him sentenced to a month in jail.*[11]

It is easy to see the ways in which anti-Chinese sentiment grew in a white European community that felt itself to be under threat. This feeling, which originated in the goldfields, was compounded in other areas when successive commercial interests used cheap Chinese labour as a handy means of breaking strikes by white workers – as occurred, for example, in the Shearers' Strikes of the 1890s. The resentment and frustration that finds expression in anti-Chinese sentiment permeates through the literature of the time in infinite small ways. For example, in one brief collection of satirical prose pieces with the lengthy title, *The "Fireflash," four oars and a coxswain: where they went – how they went – and why they went: and the stories they told last Christmas Eve*, by the enormously successful Melbourne dramatist and humourist Garnet Walch, for example, it is revealed in passing that a five year old has been taught to recite 'Chinkey Chow-Chow' in the original Chinese as a party trick to impress visitors.[12]

Such things persisted in folklore, turning up, for example, in twentieth-century children's playground rhymes, like:

> *Ching chong Chinaman*
> *lookee velly sad*
> *All him vegetables*
> *all gone bad.*[13]

As always, there were writers who opposed popular sentiment. Henry Lawson, ever the champion of the underdog, wrote in his story 'Ah Soon': 'I never knew a Chinaman who didn't pay his debts, who did a dishonest action, or who forgot a kindness to him or his, or was not charitable when he had the opportunity'.[14]

It was, however, in the popular novels that xenophobic sentiment found its strongest expression. Colonists felt betrayed by Britain's support for the Chinese immigrants – the Imperial Government had rejected the 1876 *Queensland Goldfields Amendment Act*, which sought to discriminate against Chinese diggers – and local literature began to explore the dangers for Australia of placing its trust in Imperial policies of racial tolerance. Federation of the colonies under a central government which would be granted the final say over internal policy became, for many Australians, the only way to free themselves of British interference in local affairs, without giving up the benefits of Imperial defence strategies. The line between the fiction and the politics is very blurred in such novels: not only were they vehicles for unashamed political agendas, many of them were written by politicians and party leaders to popularise their manifestos.

Fear of invasion by barbarous, ravening and homicidal hordes really took off after the Franco-Prussian war of 1870-71. In England, Sir George Tompkins Chesney had leapt to the defence of his country with the publication, just after the fall of Paris, of *The Battle of Dorking*, a dire prediction of Britain's similar fate. This book provoked a host of imitators, not just in Britain itself, but throughout Europe and the colonies. Writers in Germany stoked the fires of anti-French and anti-British hysteria. In France they thundered their condemnations of perfidious Albion just across the Channel.

In Australia, the *Sydney Quarterly Magazine* carried in 1885 an anonymous novella: *The Fall of Melbourne*.[15] The French were the villains in this first local invasion tale, first strengthening their New Caledonia garrison, then cutting the telegraph link between Australia and Britain and sending a naval squadron to attack Port Jackson. This is the prelude to the real action: the invasion of Victoria. In a foretaste of the racist xenophobia to come, the real horror of the attack lies in the troops used – the *Chasseurs D'Afrique*, Arab horsemen with a fearsome reputation.

The pride of the Victorian navy, the ironclad monitor HMVS *Cerberus*, proves no match for the larger French squadron, and Melbourne falls – a warning against colonial complacency.

The Fall of Melbourne is, however, measured in tone compared with what was to follow. The real popular fear was of invasion by 'Mongol hordes' – a fear given impetus in May 1887 by the visit of a team of Chinese Commissioners sent to investigate the condition of Chinese living in Australia. This visit was a tardy and grudging response by the Imperial Government in Peking to British and American pressure for China to take an interest in those overseas citizens who had emigrated under the terms of the various treaties that had forcibly opened China to the West. In many parts of Australia, however, the visit was interpreted as a mission to spy out the Northern Territory for colonisation and to prepare reports of Australian mistreatment of the Chinese. It was feared that retaliatory punitive action would be taken.

This fear was rapidly reflected in the fiction of the time. In 1888 the anonymous novella *The Battle of Mordialloc or How We Lost Australia*[16] reflected concerns amongst conservatives that independence from Britain would leave Australia vulnerable to invasion – concerns fuelled by the recent advances in the technology of communications:

> *The friendly seas which surround us are no longer a protection. Every advance in science tends to shorten the distance which one time separated us from the old world. We live in the iron age; not, as our smooth-tongued orators would seek to persuade us, in the age of gold. The questions which agitate the nations are solved not by the frothy rant of upstart demagogues, but, as Bismarck says, 'by blood and iron.' The most forcible arguments are now those which are backed by the strongest battalions – the most convincing eloquence that which proceeds from the cannon's mouth. The moment we cease to be a part of the British Empire, that moment the German, the Russ, the Frenchman will be thundering at our gates.*

In the novella's scenario, Australian prosperity leads to an unbounded national confidence. It also leads to the rise of a generation ignorant of the lessons of European history and unwilling to be guided by a better-educated conservative social elite. The conservative voice of the narrator sketches in the background to 'the Chinese question':

> *The Orientals had domiciled among us by the thousand. They were, upon the whole, an inoffensive and law-abiding race. They lived on little, toiled like beavers, and carefully hoarded their modest gains, in the hope of one day returning to their native land. Some few of them occupied high positions as merchants, and were held in general esteem for their probity and benevolence. The great majority, however, were content to engage in the humblest occupations. They cooked and washed, they grew vegetables and hawked them about the country, they searched for gold in old and abandoned claims. In the tropics, under conditions which rendered white labour impossible, they toiled hard in the construction of railways and other public works.*

This comfortable view of peaceful co-existence is, however, disrupted by widespread unreasoning prejudice among the lower classes. The narrator has no sympathy with their outright racism:

> *By certain sections of the community they were regarded with suspicion and repugnance. With the lowest, or 'larrikin,' class it was enough that they were strangers in a strange land; that their skins were yellow, and their eyes set in their heads at an angle which did not altogether square with the 'larrikin' notion of the fitness of things.*

But when it comes to economic arguments, even the apparently liberal voice of the narrator regards prejudice as both understandable and reasonable:

> *The distrust with which they were regarded by the artisans and labouring classes rested, it must be admitted, on more tangible grounds.*

> They were charged with lowering the rate of wages; with
> ousting white labour in certain employments, and with
> showing signs of steady encroachment in others. This they
> were enabled to do by their style of living, so much beneath
> the ordinary European standard of comfort and decency.

The greatest danger to all levels of society, though, comes from the threat of inundation by unstoppable Chinese hordes. And it is a danger exploited for short-term political gain, according to the narrator, by 'Ambitious, time-serving politicians, and irresponsible agitators – the curse of democracies':

> The ever-smouldering fire of anti-Chinese feeling was blown
> by them into a perfect flame. An anti-Chinese literature
> sprang up in rank profusion. The organs of the press 'run' in
> the interests of Liberty, Fraternity, Equality, and the rights
> of man, were conspicuous for their hostility towards the
> unfortunate Mongols, and increasing in their demands for
> the expulsion of the entire race from Australian soil.
>
> As the Chinese spectre loomed more and more portentous
> on the horizon, the public alarm increased. The anti-
> Chinese agitations spread like wildfire. meetings were held
> all over the country. In every city, in every town and
> township, the question – whether the Chinese were desirable
> immigrants – was keenly debated, and everywhere answered
> in the negative by overwhelming majorities.

This popular hysteria climaxes in 1897, with the passage of colonial legislation ending all Chinese immigration and imposing heavy residential taxes. The legislation is rejected by the Imperial Government in London and when war breaks out immediately afterwards between Britain and Russia, the colonies seize the moment to declare their independence. And the inevitable happens:

> A Sydney telegram had come in announcing that the
> steamship Cathay had just arrived from Hong Kong, having
> narrowly escaped capture by the way. Her captain reported
> that the long-standing difficulty between Russia and China

> about Manchooria had been patched up, and that a secret treaty had existed for some time between the two powers for the invasion and partition of Australia.
>
> The Chinese government and people had long resented the treatment of their countrymen in the colonies, and had determined to exact vengeance at the earliest possible opportunity...
>
> With the Australian Declaration of Independence, and the outbreak of war between England and Russia, had come the golden opportunity.
>
> The Chinese fleet, officered for the most part by Europeans, had at once effected a junction with the Russian Pacific Squadron, which had recently been greatly strengthened, and the whole were steaming rapidly southwards, under the command of a Russian Archduke.

The book was published in Melbourne, so quite naturally the force bypasses Brisbane and Sydney and heads straight for Mordialloc, on Port Phillip Bay, where the rapidly assembled might of the Victorian Defence Force Volunteers awaits them. The problem they face is largely logistical. 'Given 6000 Victorians, how to dispose of a force backed by half the human race? That's the problem we have got to solve.'

Bad enough of course to be absorbed by the Russian Empire, but this was as nothing compared with the contemplated horrors of invasion by the avenging yellow hordes:

> It was expected that the Russians would occupy the town on the following day, and proceed at once to restore some sort of order, but there were terrible misgivings that at any moment the Chinese troops, bent on massacre and pillage, might pour into the town before the former arrived on the scene.

Like most of these invasion fictions, *The Battle of Mordialloc* has its theory of conspiracy and political mismanagement, which in this case have combined to threaten the future of Australia by departure from the imperial ideal:

> 'Those fellows in there,' he said, pointing with flashing eye in the direction of the House, where Parliament was at that moment sitting, 'have brought the country to a fine pass with their clap-trap about independence.'

The book offers a stern warning of the dangers, not of racism as such, but of governments which give way to the stirrings of democratic populism:

> It may be that in the days to come another Australia shall arise to take the place of the old, clearer of vision than we, and wiser through our mistakes. But, however that may be, I can never recall to mind the closing scenes in our national history without the most bitter and unavailing regrets, that a career so brilliant, and a future so full of promise, should have thus been wantonly flung away.

In the same year that the Melbourne suburb of Mordialloc was lost to Victoria, Brisbane was also in danger. William Lane arrived in Australia in 1885, two years before the publication of *The Battle of Mordialloc*, and was rapidly embroiled in local politics on the other side of the fence from the author of that work.

Lane is probably best known as the social idealist who tried to found a 'New Australia' in Paraguay – an experiment described by Vance Palmer as 'the substance of the Australian dream'.[17] If the dream was a white-only Australia, then indeed this was the case. 'New Australia' put into direct action Lane's ideal of a racially purified future: like Australia's wider labour movement, in which he was influential, Lane's utopia drew its strength from the vision of a nation of unmixed blood.

Lane's particular brand of strident socialism, combined with a virulent racism, made him a leading and controversial figure in Queensland political debate, and ensured his fame outside the colony too. Lane was almost certainly one of the main targets of the conservative narrator of *The Battle of Mordialloc* who attacked the 'irresponsible agitators – the curse of democracies' who fanned the flames of anti-Chinese feeling with calls for the 'expulsion of the entire race from Australian soil'. *The Battle of*

Mordialloc was also scathing of the popular link between 'Liberty, Fraternity, Equality, and the rights of man' and 'hostility towards the unfortunate Mongols'. 'Rights', in this context, being of course confined to the white working man.

In Brisbane, Lane edited the weekly periodical *The Boomerang*, in which he took every opportunity to advance both his social and his racial views. He made no secret of his intense dislike of both the Kanaka and the Chinese presence in Brisbane, and encouraged the most active prejudice against them. He himself wrote both editorials and at least one long piece of racist fiction: *White or Yellow?: A Story of the Race War of A.D. 1908*.[18] This was serialised in weekly episodes between 18th February and 5th May 1888, and called for the expulsion of the Chinese. Writing under the pseudonym 'The Sketcher', Lane painted a picture of an Australia sold out by its legislators to British interests, at the mercy of misguided imperial tolerance:

> *...the Imperialistic traitors of the Salisbury era had triumphed. The naval defence scheme had been but the first of persistent moves all aimed at the emasculation of the national spirit. With ribbons and titles and false promises Australia had been bought and sold. British troops garrisoned her ports. British ships watched her coast. British interests dominated her Parliaments. British diplomacy fanned the local jealousies that kept the colonies apart.*

In Lane's projected future, the imperial government overrides the colonies' anti-Chinese legislation and actively encourages Chinese immigration. By the end of the first decade of the twentieth century, Australia's population of 42 million is more than a quarter Chinese – a proportion that would have been higher had it not been for a tightening of American immigration laws that redirected the mass of European migration to Australia.

But this battle of the numbers is tipped in favour of the industrious Chinese, who 'monopolised a score of important industries and had long ceased to be hewers of wood and drawers of water only...they sat in Parliament, directed State departments, and one even had place upon the bench'. Clearly, in Lane's eyes, a single Chinese magistrate threatened the very fabric of White Australian society.

A small group of 'plutocracy and landocracy' benefits from the changes, but the vast majority of the European population ekes out an existence on the margins as 'white trash', 'sinking to a condition beside which that of the European masses was comfortable'. 'When our story opens in the winter of 1908, it only needed a leader to light the flames of racial war'.

In this future nightmare the Queensland premier, Lord Stibbins (a member of the newly established Australian aristocracy), plots to establish a celestial dynasty of his own, by marrying his daughter to Sir Wong Hung Foo, 'the new Chinese capitalist, the Queensland-born son of the prosperous Chinese merchant, the man in whose brain the wondrous patience of the Mongols had been fermented by the leaven of Caucasian knowledge'.

For Lane, the accident of being born in Australia confers no special claim to Australian status on the Chinese community. They remain stubbornly alien or, in conforming themselves to local culture, adopt only its worst aspects, combining these with the inherent malignancy of their racial origins:

> *Sir Wong spoke English like a native. He dressed in the Australian fashion, except that he retained the pig-tail and wore it coiled round his pate. He read English Literature and owned half-a-dozen newspapers. He had all the English vices and his own as well. They told frightful stories of his evil ways in the Valley, which the whites held as a citadel in opposition to the yellow-ridden North Brisbane,* [ironically, the Fortitude Valley area of inner Brisbane is today occupied by 'Chinatown'] *and up around his country seat at Toowoomba it was hardly safe for Sir Wong to walk at night unaccompanied by the big bloodhounds that were always unloosed at sunset. Sensuality was stamped upon his heavy lids and drooping eyelids and upon*

> *the expressionless mask wherewith, Mongol-like, he veiled his face.*

The reason that an Australian-born Chinese could not be considered Australian was, of course, the inherent racial difference which – in Lane's eyes – would always lead to separate development and the struggle for supremacy. This is an attitude that persisted in political debate. In her 1996 maiden speech to Parliament, Pauline Hanson asserted that Australia was in danger of being 'swamped' by Asians. According to Hanson: 'They have their own culture and religion, form ghettoes and do not assimilate'.[19]

Even those characteristics which are seen as desirable in white Australians become, in Lane's view, marks of Chinese depravity. The European virtue of patience becomes in the Chinese the mark of inscrutable oriental cunning, by which the drive to dominate can be transmitted from generation to generation, carefully guarded until the moment is right to strike.

Of course, transmission of racial intolerance applies equally to the Whites, in whom it is a genetic defence system. Even Stella, the daughter Lord Stibbins has bred for dynastic purposes, is not immune to an inherited revulsion:

> *...within her leapt up the instinct of race that all her surroundings tended to smother – involuntarily she felt repelled by the tawny skin and rounded forehead and flattened nose, even while the glittering eyes and brutal mouth possessed for her a strange fascination.*

To that fascination is added the lure of power promised by Lord Stibbins and Sir Wong. The promise draws on its own form of social Darwinism: rule by a self-selected elite, which the socialist Lane clearly rejects in favour of the 'true' Darwinism of racial struggle:

> *Your father bade me tell you that it is his plan, and he has spent his life in working for it; that if we two, he and I, cast our weight together Queensland will be ours in six months and Australia ours in a year. It is time that we rooted out*

> the 'white trash,' this braggart mob which is at once
> unreasoning and uncontrollable, which is puffed up with
> ideas of equality and incapable of accepting the rule of the
> fittest.

Their dastardly plan is based on the popular stereotype of the fanatical and almost impossibly disciplined Asian horde, combining oriental cunning with western aristocratic duplicity:

> At my bidding 12,000,000 men will move as one. We are
> organised and the whites are not. Your father can depend
> upon the heads of departments and upon all who hold
> places of trust. The imperial government can be
> hoodwinked until we get aid from the cruisers of China.
> Your father will be viceroy for China first. When we have
> Australia in our hands we will declare independence and
> establish a dynasty that in the future will rule the world.

Returning from an afternoon ride, Sir Wong and Stella have a stand-off over right of way with a white farmer in his cart. The farmer is John Saxby, secretary of the anti-Chinese League, whose dead wife was so anti-Chinese that 'when they were younger and before John took to farming, [she] had persisted in going for months without vegetables rather than buy from the Chinkie pedlars'. Saxby's son-in-law-to-be, Bob Flynn, is 'a brawny sailor-lad' who asserts with fierce pride that '"It is ours, this land"' (there is no Aboriginal presence to challenge such an assertion in this fiction). He and Saxby have been instrumental in creating a secret white force which includes 'four naval brigades and nearly forty Volunteer companies' throughout Queensland.

Lane's description of Sir Wong's manner in meeting Saxby is a masterpiece of ironic resonances, conveying all Lane's loathing for the Chinese, and for aristocratic behaviour. The wealthy and well-connected Chinaman speaks to the sturdy and unresponsive farmer 'in the insolent way wherewith he addressed his "inferiors"'. The incident ends with success for the farmer when he produces his rifle and threatens Sir Wong:

> *It was a mere chance that a rifle lay in the farmer's cart, and [Sir Wong] inwardly vowed to get Lord Stibbins's docile Parliament to forbid the possession of weapons without a special permit.*

Saxby's use of arms against Wong gives Lane a chance to slip in an argument against gun control by suggesting that the ruling elite would profit from removing firearms from 'the common man', who might otherwise take the law into his own hands. This argument is an uncanny foreshadowing of the 'conspiracy' theories of more extreme members of the modern gun lobby, whose claims that a new 'class elite' of 'gun banners' are planning to disarm ordinary citizens in preparation for an unspecified 'internationalist takeover' of white Australia are echoed in one of those sections of *Pauline Hanson: The Truth* which has subsequently been disclaimed by Hanson herself.

In another passage reminiscent of the wilder statistical predictions of *The Truth*, Lane's Saxby predicts that a generation after the marriage of Stella and Sir Wong, 'there won't be a pure-blooded white man in Australia'. For Lane's purposes, however, the catalyst for a white 'rising' must come from some dreadful deed of the Chinese and not from the racial hatred of the whites themselves. There must be immediate moral justification to support the racial imperative.

The catalyst taps into all the worst popular stereotypes of Chinese behaviour. On the eve of his wedding, Wong Hung Foo inexplicably rapes and murders Saxby's daughter – something of a lapse from his former good judgement, and one which Lane makes no further attempt to explain. What follows is a revolution of the battlers against established colonial interests which support the alien Chinese presence. The outraged whites rise in rebellion, attacking Lord Stibbins' home and attempting to lynch Sir Wong. Lane ducks the direct issue of legality, seeking a 'justification' of the action. Sir Wong is 'tried' in a kangaroo court for the murder of Saxby's daughter, but a counter-attack by government troops means he survives the noose. He is eventually shot by Lady Stibbins herself, whose better nature has come to the fore, and alerted her to 'the degradation of this unholy wedlock' between Sir Wong and her daughter.

The attempt by Chinese government troops to return Lady Stibbins's fire unites every white man, government or revolutionary, against them – white men defending the lives and honour of their women. Stella reveals her father's plot to establish an imperial dynasty, and the white forces rally with the battle cry 'Australia for the Australians!' White Australia, that is.

In the end, Lord Stibbins is slaughtered by revengeful Chinese, allowing Lane once more to evade the darker implications of class-based revolution in favour of the clear-cut issues of a race war that unites all true Australians. The Queensland parliament falls to the forces of the League, and is quickly joined by the other colonies. Together they drive the Chinese hordes from Australia and throw off the shackles of British domination. 'Australia was true to her destiny. In spite of white Chinamen, she stayed white'.

Lane's political rhetoric in *White or Yellow?* echoes the revolutionary principles that underpinned both the American War of Independence, and the French Revolution of 1789:

> For 'Law and Order!' It is hardly necessary to mention that
> these were the principles which Lord Stibbins stood for on the
> evening of the memorable day when the Anti-Chinese
> League unfurled the Australian flag, and when the whole
> continent rang with the signal that called the whites to
> arms. It is always of Law and Order that tyrants prate
> when men move for Freedom, their law being ever the unjust
> statutes which conserve their interest...

This slightly old-fashioned view of popular uprising is updated by Lane's theory of imperial conspiracy and colonial self-interest (the populist interpretation of the conservative political position adopted by the narrator of *The Battle of Mordialloc*):

> ...upon the side of Law and Order gathered the tinsel
> knighthood with which the Imperial Government had

> *attempted to debauch the colonial spirit, the squatocracy of the country side and the landocrats of the towns, with those who had fond remembrances of the black labour days and who loved the Chinaman as the brutal English squire loved his horse, as a thing which ministered to their pleasure and was therefore of more value to them than nationality or racial ties... Wherever there was a monopolist, there Law and Order found defenders; wherever luxury and idleness were the reward of social wrong, there were found white men who cast in their lot with the Chinese.*

Against this unholy alliance are ranged 'the pick-and-shovel men of the Australian fields', with the support of the merchants whose business interests have been damaged by Chinese competition, and a few right-minded members of the plutocracy:

> *...it was gladdening to see that here and there blood proved stronger than self-interest. Here and there a squatter galloped to the nearest town with his rifle on his saddle-bow and the white-and-yellow cockade, which betokened racial distinction, mounted on his hat.*

It is here that Lane's enthusiasm for socialist ideals really comes to the fore, pointing the way ahead to the popular risings of 1905 and 1917 in Imperial Russia:

> *Poverty was forgotten. The misery to which the white poor had been reduced was swallowed up by the excitement of the moment. It had never been patiently endured, this poverty and misery; the Australians had year by year grown more turbulent and rebellious under its pressure; but now it seemed almost forgotten in the overshadowing presence of this great upheaval. 'Flour and beef for all who need it; the nearest tree for the thief caught red-handed;' was the terse code which replaced in the emergency the Law and Order for which the Plutocrats were rallying.*

In Russia, chaotic popular enthusiasm was rapidly supplanted by the efficient authoritarianism of Bolshevism; in Lane's Australia, it is immediately channelled by absolutism:

> ...an absolutism to which men yielded unhesitating
> obedience; the absolutism of the perilous times when the
> whole heart of a nation is concentrated on one single end;
> an absolutism backed by an organisation which had staked
> all on this rising and had prepared for its coming for years.

This is the rhetoric of an idealised socialism, before it has been tempered by the twentieth-century realities of totalitarian state communism. It is also the rhetoric of organised racism, targeting a racially identifiable group as scapegoats for the economic disadvantages of working-class whites. And finally, it is the rhetoric of nationalism, in which the nation state is racially *exclusive*, not inclusive of all its members. It is, in effect, national socialism – what became in its later German manifestation the *Nationalsozialistische Deutsche Arbeiterpartei*, or Nazi party, with its ideology based on racism, nationalism, and the supremacy of the state over the individual. In one respect only does the Anti-Chinese League differ from the Nazis, though this seems more a matter of practicality than of morality. Lane's Australia lacks the resources of the Nazi state for genocide:

> ...if we crush them what can we do with them or where can
> we crush them to? We can't kill 12,000,000 people and we
> can't have them in Australia.

Lane's answer, however, is little different from the early form of the Nazi solution, before the concentration camps and the poison gas. It is a chilling foretaste of the burning of the synagogues, the destruction of Jewish shops, the murders in the streets of Germany in the 1930s:

> Let us strike while the iron is hot and before they are ready.
> Let us terrorize them so that they will never recover. Let us
> convince them that we are desperate and that their only
> chance is to obey. We can fire Chinatown within an hour.
> We can burn down every Chinese store and house and
> plough up every Chinese garden. We can hang every white
> man who is a traitor to the whites in this war.

And, like the pre-war European negotiators who briefly toyed with the idea of creating a home for the Jews in Madagascar, Lane's white League is prepared with its own plan of mass deportation. In the League's final solution there echoes a chilling reminder of the quiescence of ordinary people in the face of terror – the quiescence on which the Nazis would later rely for their mass extermination of the Jews:

> *They can be sent to the north-coast ports; we can put every truck and engine in the country on those lines and can keep running until they have every one gone north. We can send every steamer and every sailing vessel round to those ports and ship them across to the East Indies. It will take a year or two to ship the last and until they are shipped we'll have to feed them, but we can manage them so that they'll do anything to get away, even wait quietly.*

The justification for this ethnic cleansing?

> *...gentlemen, it must be either them or us, remember, and they have no right to expect consideration for they will use us like dogs if they get the chance.*

In other words, this is a pre-emptive strike against the untrustworthy Chinese – another chilling foretaste of the Nazi propaganda which 'justified' extermination of the Jews.

The real political power of works such as these cannot be underestimated in a social climate of doubt and suspicion. During the serial publication of William Lane's *White or Yellow?*, the citizens of Brisbane took the story to heart and the city erupted into its own mini race war. *The Brisbane Courier* said of the riot:

> *The real reason of the demonstration is hard to tell, but it is generally believed to have been at least encouraged by persons whose social position should have placed them above such behaviour.*[20]

Like *Pauline Hanson: The Truth*, Lane's *White or Yellow?* supports an extremist political position, blaming Chinese immigration for all the ills that beset the working class. In response, *The Battle of Mordialloc* has a bet each way, asserting the inoffensiveness of the Chinese in Australia, but accepting the argument of economic disadvantage and the peril of unchecked immigration. In this it foreshadowed the uncomfortable position of John Howard's Liberal government, caught between its desire to respond to Hanson's One Nation Party and its fear of alienating wavering conservative voters.

The popular invasion fictions were always very closely tied to political thinking, especially as many of them were written by politicians. Another such scaremongering text, *The Yellow Wave: A Romance of the Asiatic Invasion of Australia* (1895),[21] was written by Kenneth Mackay, member for the New South Wales Legislative Assembly seat of Boorowa (and member of the Legislative Council for 34 years). Mackay combined politics and a distinguished military career in white Australia: he raised the 1st Australian Horse in 1897, commanded the New South Wales Imperial Bushmen's Contingent in the Boer War, and was director-general of the Australian Army Reserve in the First World War.

For *The Yellow Wave*, Mackay drew on his experience of foreign and domestic policy issues to construct a plausible fiction. In 1879 the 3,400 Chinese in the Northern Territory outnumbered Europeans by seven to one. In the late 1880s rumours abounded that the visit by the Chinese Commissioners was laying the groundwork for the establishment of a Chinese colony in the 'empty' North (this fear became a recurrent theme in subsequent invasion fictions). Speaking to the New South Wales Parliament on the subject of the Coloured Race Restriction Bill (1896), Mackay reiterated the beliefs expressed in his novel when he declared that: 'I believe that unless some step is taken, racial troubles will take place in Northern Queensland. Unless some step is taken to prevent an invasion of coolies and aliens into that territory, it will be a very poor buffer to put against an invasion of Asiatics in the future'.[22]

In *The Yellow Wave*, the Russians are in alliance with the 'sub-human Mongol hordes'. The idea in this novel is that both India and Australia will be simultaneously attacked, thus tying up the British fleet and allowing Russia to capture Constantinople. As in later Asian invasion stories, Mackay portrays a British command turning away from Australia's defence in order to protect its other possessions. For Russia, the Australian conflict is to be a strategic part of an overall European plan; but for China, blocked from expansion in Asia by both Russia and Japan, it is a serious territorial grab for colonial land.

In the section called 'The Wave Breaks', chapter two, 'The Coming of the Mongols', the sleeping dragon of Chinese imperial expansion awakes. There can be no doubt about the evil intent of the invaders, who are specifically linked with the legendary atrocities of Ghengis Khan before they ever arrive in Australia:

> At intervals a sharp command rang out, spoken in a tongue that was old before the Western world rose out of chaos, and in response men with the broad yellow faces and coarse black hair of those fierce nomads who followed Genghis Khan sprang to obey. The lights, falling on them as they worked, lit up their features with ghastly distinctness. From their cruel lips flowed a song, discordant, fear-compelling, which, as it floated out over the sea, filled the air with its awful cadences.

The language and the song may be old, but these invaders are armed with the latest in technology. The character Jansen, hearing them, muses that:

> ...silken-sailed galleys, with glittering shields and triple banks of oars, were not for demons such as these. Such a song should only come from betwixt the folds of bat-like sails, and up out of the bowels of dragon-prowed junks. Tonight it rose above the decks of swift, low-lying, smoke-less cruisers, armed with the latest weapons of the Western world. It was the battle-cry of Tamerlane shouted by warriors such as his; but, in place of the bow and spear, they held in their relentless, clawlike hands the weapons of a

> civilization which had risen and marched on while his race
> stood still. The Mongols, after a sleep of centuries, had
> awoke at last.

The Mongol monsters are deliberately described in terms of dangerous animals roused to attack by their treatment at the hands of Imperialists:

> Still brave as lions, enduring as dogs, and rapacious as
> wolves, they had shaken off their death-like stupor and
> again taken up the glorious traditions of the past. Cunning
> as foxes and far-sighted as ravens, they had learned by
> defeat, and now, following out their policy of making use of
> their enemies, were led by a renegade, who could be
> destroyed when he had fulfilled their purpose.

And, once again, the Darwinian question of survival of the fittest resurfaces, with the Mongols seeing themselves in the ascendancy:

> Strong as ever in their belief in their absolute superiority to
> all mankind, and armed with the very weapons which in the
> past had brought about their humiliations, they were coming
> under the old banners of blood and fire to avenge past
> insults and win new possessions.

The leader of the invaders, General Leroy, is 'outwardly an American soldier of fortune, in reality...a servant of the Czar', who has undertaken the reorganisation of the Chinese army. Described as being 'not only born to command men, but savages', he is:

> Broad-shouldered, and deep-chested, with dark eyes that
> never flinched, either at the ping of bullets or the frown of
> another, with lips devoid of sensuality, but almost cruel in
> their firm, close lines, and with a large though delicately-cut
> nose, he looked essentially a leader of war-like men. His age
> was always a subject of dispute among his comrades. For
> while his close-cropped hair was white, his heavy moustache
> and strongly-marked brow remained black. The lines about

> his mouth and under his eyes were those of a man who had
> either lived hard for years or else long in a short space of
> time; but in all matters of endurance he was still in his
> prime.

The traitorous plotters on the Australian mainland put their faith in Leroy, assuming that the superior white general can indeed control the Mongol savages. Count Zenski's subordinate, Bourouskie, mutters 'God help us if these savages get out of hand!', to which the Count replies 'we are between the devil and the deep blue sea if they do; but fear not, Leroy is an admirable wild-beast tamer'.

But they have seriously underestimated the effect of the arrival of the Chinese fleet and the depth of feeling among Chinese colonists. On the streets or on the battlefield, the Chinese have no mercy:

> *Staggering through the press, a half-drunken planter pushed aside a powerful coolie with an impatient curse. Suddenly drawing his knife, the Chinaman drove it into his assailant's chest. As the man fell back, a stream of blood spurted out of the wound into the face of his murderer, and, moved by one common impulse of slaughter, the hybrid, down-trodden slaves became brutal avengers.*
>
> *Rushing back into the streets, they began to kill with the indiscriminate hate of wild beasts, and, drunk with slaughter, dared to stain with their bloody feet the piazza of the Mitylene Palace.*

Unfortunately, the Russians are hard pressed to restrain the bloodthirsty hordes, and Leroy, ever the soldier of fortune, has alliances with Chinese Commissioner Wang as well as with Count Zenski. The Mongols are out of control, slaughtering women and children:

> *'There are women and children running in front of them!... One has fallen; now she's kneeling over her child. My God! the wretches are butchering her! They've caught up to the*

rest. Ah!' and the strong man winced as if beneath a blow.
'The devils are cutting them to pieces!'

The true horror of the Mongol savagery slowly becomes apparent to the dismayed soldiers:

> For a little while they were puzzled by the standard carried
> by the leading trooper. Then with a thrill of horror they
> realized that it was a girl's head stuck on the point of his
> spear! Her long hair, streaming in the breeze, glittered
> fitfully in the dying sunlight as the ruffian waved his lance
> with a gesture of defiance. Behind him raced a yelling
> horde, some bearing trophies such as his, others with human
> heads dangling from their stirrups. Splashed with blood and
> drunk with slaughter, on they came, their broad, squat
> features, tangled elf locks, gleaming eyes, and shark-like
> jaws, combining to make up a picture worthy of the hell they
> were sent to create.

In an extraordinary conflation of distorted Darwinism and gothic excess, the glittering hair on the girl's head invokes the violation of a blonde-haired Australian ideal by the nightmare forces of Asian evil.

Even General Leroy is appalled at the results of the Chinese invasion he has let loose upon the white colony:

> He had looked on many such a scene unmoved in Asia, but
> then the prisoners there were only having meted out such
> treatment as they had often meted out to others. Here they
> were beings born under the same skies as himself; perhaps
> among them slaved men who had been schoolmates of his
> own. One old man had looked into his eyes with a glance of
> half-recognition that very afternoon as he struck up the arm
> off a Kalmuck who was cutting the bent, weary back with a
> bloody quirt.
>
> Now he remembered where he had seen the face; it was
> years ago in his father's house; the old man had patted him
> on the head and given him some trifling present. God! It
> was awful! He was a modern Attila without the old

> barbarian's excuse, the wielder of a scourge wet with the blood of men who had called him friend, and blasted by the dishonour of women who belonged to the same race as his own dead mother. Appalled by the recognition of his own baseness, Leroy moved on through the deserted, ruined street...

He faces further terrible scenes of destruction and violation of white women and children at the hands of the yellow savages:

> ...a man lay on the floor, his head split almost to the chin, and across his body a middle-aged woman reclined in a huddled mass. Stretched across the tumbled bed lay two young girls, their white limbs bruised and bloody – in their eyes the print of that despair which flashed through their scarce-opened lids into the faces of their destroyers.
>
> One child's poor fingers still clutched fragments of white drapery; from the other the spoilers' lustful hands had torn aside all covering, and now naked and dead they lay before his eyes.

Despite a heroic defence of Brisbane by a vigilante band of white Australian rangers, led by the brave Dick Hatten, broken but still fighting against the odds to protect their homes and sweethearts, *The Yellow Wave* ends inconclusively.

The novel was intended, like *White or Yellow?* and *The Battle of Mordialloc*, as a cautionary tale. The ordinary people are shown as having been betrayed by their leaders on all levels. Australian interests have been sold out to foreign owners by government officials obsessed by Imperial honours and careless of the well-being of their constituents. When the invasion comes, the members of the New South Wales Parliament are depicted wasting precious time in debating whether or not they have the right to send troops across the colonial border to defend Queensland – a problem solved only by the men themselves, who volunteer *en masse*.

Mackay's story sought to remind Australians that failure to stay armed with the latest technology and/or lack of vigilance could lead to destruction at the hands of the yellow hordes of Asia. The underlying fear of 'colonisation' which it tapped proved very persistent. As late as 1909, Randolph Bedford's play *White Australia: Or, The Empty North*, premiered in Melbourne. It took a socialist, republican and racist position similar to the more extreme William Lane. And, like so many other of these writers, Bedford took an active political stance to which the fiction contributed. A former journalist, wealthy speculator, novelist and travel writer for the *Bulletin*, Bedford became a member of the Queensland Legislative Council from 1917-22, and a member of the Legislative Assembly from 1923 until his death in 1941.

The basic scenario in these tales, of infiltration followed by invasion, seems to have been based in part on remarks by Sir Henry Parkes, the 'Father of Federation', made in his Presidential address to the first Federation Convention in 1891, when he suggested that China was 'awakening to all the power which immense population gives them in the art of war, in the art of acquisition, and all the other arts known to a European civilisation'.[23] Parkes predicted that the 'Asian invasion' would be by way of 'effecting a lodgement in some thinly peopled portion of the country, where it will take immense loss of life and immense loss of wealth to dislodge the invader'.

Parkes, the Premier of New South Wales, relied heavily on the fear of Chinese invasion in making his appeal to the other colonial governments to federate Australia. When Federation finally came in 1901, it was driven as much by the popular racism and xenophobia that were fed by these political fictions, as by any burning desire for nationhood.

And, as the newly federated Australia set about developing its collective identity, the widespread dystopian fictions of anti-Asian sentiment continued to play an important part in manipulating popular opinion.

5

Federation and Exclusion

William Lane's *White or Yellow?* (1888) and Kenneth Mackay's *The Yellow Wave* (1895) both explored the destruction of white Australian civilisation and the marginalisation of European settlers by Chinese victors whose aggression was largely a retaliatory response to the ways in which their countrymen had been treated in the colony. At about the same time, Nellie S. Clerk, the English-born wife of a Gippsland farmer, and organist at the local church, published her only book of verse, *Songs from the Gippsland Forest*. It included the prophetic poem 'Federation',[1] which appeals to the conservative desire for colonial federation within a federated British Empire:

> Ye Britons of these Austral lands,
> Ye Britons spread o'er every zone,
> The time has come to join your hands,
> And link your Mother's with your own.

The impetus for this union is the same as that highlighted by Sir Henry Parkes, by Kenneth Mackay, and by the author of *The Battle of Mordialloc* – the growing external threat from China:

> Behold black storm-clouds in the North,
> Their gathering, threatening progress see;
> Brittania's sons, prove now your worth,
> Fulfil your glorious destiny.
> Arise, unite, show all creation
> Your great and glorious Federation.

Clerk's vision is not at all modest in its ambition:

> *'Tis yours to make the deserts bloom;*
> *The ends of all the earth to gain;*
> *To give your thronging peoples room;*
> *To guard the freedom of the main.*
> *All they that strive with you shall fall;*
> *To you the nations all shall bend*
> *If you but heed the Almighty's call,*
> *Truth, honour, justice to defend.*
> *Thus shall you show to all creation*
> *How great your glorious Federation.*

The voice of the poem is old-fashioned in its echoes of early neo-classical Australian verse which celebrated the God-given inheritance of Australia by the English. It is disturbingly forward-looking in its imperial theme of 'living room' for the British – a sentiment that was echoed in the German Nazi Party's call for *Lebensraum*, their rationale for the invasion of Poland in 1939.

Like *The Battle of Mordialloc*, Clerk's vision of a worldwide British hegemony is not explicitly racist. 'Federation' looks forward to a time when the British imperium spans the globe, uniting the whole world in a common civilisation and a common language. This will be a union of consent and harmony, respecting difference while it incorporates it:

> *Of every land hold ye the keys,*
> *Until despotic power shall break;*
> *Until the oppressed shall dwell at ease;*
> *And every tongue your language speak.*
> *A company of nations! You*
> *Like the unconquered main shall roll,*
> *Your waves of separate form and hue,*
> *United still from pole to pole.*

Imperial federation was never to occur. But Parkes played a key role in the Federation Conventions of 1890-91, and was so successful in his drive to federate the Australian colonies under the British crown that he is often called the 'Father of Federation'. The federalists were successful, too, in their further aim of passing the unified anti-Chinese legislation which the Imperial Government had so far largely blocked.

The first Act passed by the new Federal Government meeting in Melbourne in 1901 was the *Immigration Restriction Act*, seen as a model of diplomatic resolution of the conflicting political interests of Australia and Britain. Rather than block immigration from particular countries or racial groups (which might offend China, and so upset British foreign policy), it imposed the language test, by which a potential migrant could be asked to demonstrate their competency in any European language. When an individual was to be excluded, they were simply tested in a language they did not speak (Welsh and Swedish were among the languages variously pressed into service when necessary).

Following Federation and the passage of the *Immigration Restriction Act*, attention shifted away from the Chinese and Russian Empires as the most immediate threats and focused instead upon a rapidly-developing Japan. This fear was heightened when, in 1905, the Japanese navy unexpectedly annihilated the Russian imperial navy, proving that they were more than a match for one of the more technologically advanced and largest nations in the world.

Two Australian scientific romances, *The Coloured Conquest* (1904), by 'Rata', and the enormously popular anti-Japanese dystopia, *The Australian Crisis* (1909), by C. H. Kirmess, both dealt with the new fear, of an Asian people armed with the benefits of European technology, bent on southward expansion. The defeat of the Russian fleet by Japan in 1905 increased these alarms.

In *The Coloured Conquest*,[2] the ultimate nightmare of 'coloured' domination of the world is played out. Written by 'Rata', a pseudonym for the elusive Thomas Roydhouse, this 1904 novel is set in the future of 1913. It is narrated by Danton, the last 'free Britisher' left after Japan's takeover of the world. In this scenario, Japan has emerged as leader of the 'Coloured Races', largely in response to the appalling treatment of those races at the hands of white imperialists. China has developed an aggressive navy, and the Negroes are taking over America. As the story unfolds, Australia's leaders have refused to spend money on defence and the country is about to be attacked by the superior Japanese fleet.

As in *The Battle of Mordialloc*, *The Coloured Conquest* presents an alliance between forces hostile to White Australia – but this time, it is the Japanese fleet that has joined with the Chinese navy to attack Australia. The British navy has already been routed, having fallen prey to superior naval might combined with a communications trap, 'one of the things that the Oriental mind rejoices in'. The vulnerablility of the world to control of cable communications networks is emphasised here: the cable stations have been seized and infiltrated by 'trained Japanese and Chinese cable operators', who were substituted for the original workers so that 'the outside world was deluded until the blow fell'.

Australia's vulnerability to international news services is again prominent here. The infiltrated cable operators are also spreading propaganda. The morning after the Japanese landings in Sydney, Melbourne, Adelaide, Brisbane, Fremantle 'and elsewhere', the morning papers print the cable news report:

> ...and the story that came over them – from the Japanese senders in London – was that India and Africa were now under Coloured rule. Europe was being invaded by a Yellow and Brown army that was just eating it up, like a plague of locusts, and the Japanese flag was flying over the British Isles.
>
> America and Canada were as yet untouched, but there could be no question as to their fate. The eight million Negroes included in the population of the United States were already holding camp meetings and singing songs welcoming the approaching new era, when the long despised Coloured man would rule. Criminal assaults upon White women had increased...

The cable news also reveals that the small Japanese force that occupies the British Isles has brought with it:

> A cruel feature of the investment – an interesting one, the
> Japanese cable described it – [which] was that the Japanese
> brought a large number of Indian troops with them, all in
> their British uniforms.
>
> There were two or more Indian regiments in all the great
> cities of Britain, and they lorded it over the White people as
> (so they said) the Whites had lorded it over them in India.

The outcome for defenceless Australia is a foregone conclusion. Before the invaders arrive, Sydney erupts in chaos, resulting in a frightening conflagration. As usual the politicians are seen as dangerously useless: '"Give the Japs a Moscow to come to," shouted a loud-mouthed politician. And the sentiment appeared to be greatly appreciated.' So, like Moscow, burnt to deny Napoleon's army a base in Russia, Sydney is destroyed. The city burns but the Japanese are undeterred, landing ten thousand troops the next day.

Australia surrenders and is occupied by Japanese forces. 'The Mikado's Australian Government' enslaves the white population and sets it to work to develop the interior. Schools are abolished; no white children will be educated. As the Japanese officer points out: 'In two or three generations the White people will become accustomed to their position, and will not, what you call, buck up'. The methodology is straightforward: 'The White man understood...the Brown rulers were taking the surest step to crush nationality. The Whites alive fifty years hence would know nothing of the grand past of the nation to which they belonged'. Most Whites are, furthermore, refused the right to reproduce, but selected individuals (mostly women) are placed in 'Fair Lily Colonies' to form breeding stock whose purpose is to produce beautiful consorts for their Japanese masters.

The position of the narrator Danton appears, on the one hand, more liberal than most, since he points out the hypocrisy of white claims to superiority of behaviour in their dealings with 'the coloureds'. His response, however, is the usual one: to strengthen Australian defences, particularly naval defences, against the inevitable Asian backlash. And like many of our other writers of invasion fiction, 'Rata' argues that Australia cannot afford to stand alone: to survive in a hostile region, it will need strong naval ties with Britain.

Another less violent vision of future decline was posited in a book by C. H. Kirmess, *The Australian Crisis* (1909).[3] *The Australian Crisis* predicts the infiltration of northern Australia by a Japanese colony: the invaders have butchered the male Aborigines and bred with the 'lubras', their children having all the rights and protections of Australian-born citizens. Like the endangered whites of *Pauline Hanson:The Truth*'s extrapolated twenty-first century Australia, the European population is rapidly outbred and marginalised.

Kirmess's only apparent contribution to Australian public life was this book, which was serialised in *The Lone Hand* as 'The Commonwealth Crisis' before its later publication as *The Australian Crisis*. Kirmess's real identity is obscure. At various times it has been speculated that he was Frank Fox, editor of *The Lone Hand*, writing under a pseudonym (though this now appears unlikely), or that he was a German national, living in Australia, who returned home prior to the First World War.[4] Whatever the facts may be, *The Australian Crisis* represents a major contribution to the literature of Australian xenophobia. Its vision of 'underpopulated' and 'undeveloped' Australian land being developed by insidious Japanese colonists reads like a direct attack on the very arguments advanced by *The Chinese Question* in favour of Asian immigration.

The events of *The Australian Crisis* – set in 1912 – are told in 1922. Kirmess writes that the central idea of the book is 'the possibility of a coloured invasion of Australian territory, organised on such lines that the Australians would be unable to persuade the heart of the Empire that there was any invasion'.

Interestingly, Kirmess is very sensitive both to the effect of popular grass-roots action and to the power of the press in bringing about the crisis. The trouble starts with advertising slogans:

> The storm broke in Melbourne. A pushing Emporium there, famous for topical advertisements, alluded in one of these to the universal brotherhood of man. It also exhibited in one of its show windows a white and a yellow figure shaking hands over a conciliatory motto. Of course commercial men might wish for a relaxation of the tension, but a more ridiculous blunder could not have been made just then. Crowds assembled in front of the shop and soon became threatening. The window was smashed and the whole concern on the point of being sacked. Only the valour of the police and the presence of mind of the proprietor saved the situation. Big posters were made hurriedly and pasted everywhere, reading: 'Down with the Japs,' 'No quarter for Mongolians,' 'White Australia for ever,' a change of mind which satisfied the besiegers and proved a sound stroke of business as well. From that moment onward nearly all shops displayed signs: 'No coloured people served.' The boycott had begun.

The trouble soon spreads to Sydney, where similar popular sentiment comes to the fore:

> The immediate cause [of the 'Sydney Riots'] was a quarrel on board a ferry steamer on Saturday afternoon (July 13). A couple of Chinamen were accused of having annoyed...some white girls. In the end, the alleged offenders were thrown into the harbour.

The crowd prevents the white ringleaders from being arrested at Circular Quay; Japanese seamen are jeered at, as are other coloured marines, and jeers soon become action when some boys throw mud at the sailors and are beaten by them in return. This incites a full-scale riot:

> ...the noise attracted comrades of the seamen on the ships nearby. They brought iron bars and other heavy weapons as means of defence. The opposing forces soon came to blows and a pitched battle raged between the white riff-raff on the one hand and a yelling multitude of maddened Lascars, Chinamen, Japanese and other Asiatics on the other.

Crowds continue to gather:

> *Crazy with the sight and scent of blood, the masses surged up town, amidst cries of revenge. Their numbers were continually swelled by fresh recruits. A huge mob assembled around the Belmore Markets,...the Chinese quarter.*

Violence leads to a fire, which threatens the city with destruction. The conflagration rages, with great loss of life, described as 'Sydney's delirious night of colour riots'. News of this breaks in Melbourne, with 'Sunday papers breaking the local laws against Sunday publications' in their rush to sensationalise the events 'exaggerated beyond their hideous reality'. Further violence flares in that city: Little Bourke Street is invaded by larrikins, and again there are riots and loss of life.

Inflamed by journalistic excesses, the pattern of violence is repeated across Australia:

> *The example set by the two sea-capitals was emulated all over the interior of the Continent wherever the hated aliens dwelt. A long list of deeds of violence against a helpless minority stains the fair record of Australia here... Ingrained contempt changed to sullen suspicion; some imprudence or impudence committed by a yellow man followed by a white blaze of indignation quenched only by the trickling of the red blood of the maimed offender or his unfortunate kinsfolk.*

Maritime trade unions take the opportunity to boycott all ships carrying coloured crews, with White Australia extremists declaring 'that the Ocean should be white as well', with the result that there is a shortage of imported goods.

But the worst violence is reserved for Queensland, where local outrage at Japanese-run brothels has feelings running high, to the extent that: 'The disgust which had accumulated against them had become at least equal to the ferocity which burned negroes at the stake on the other side of the Pacific'. The local outrage is encouraged by the arrival of racist Americans, who stir up more trouble:

> *Upon this poisonous ground Western Americans, with all their traditions of race violence, set foot in quest of the White Guard. ....in poured the reports of how the South had dealt with the Asiatics... It seems that a secret league was formed...[and]...extended to all the picturesque townships scattered along the blue Pacific and round the Gulf of Carpentaria. One evening...an end was made with one accord right over North Queensland (July 27). The brothels were entered, the inmates seized. Of the subsequent proceedings no official version exists...too many influential persons are still alive who were deeply implicated in the conspiracy. Apparently the culprits were not only exterminated, but exterminated in the most degrading fashion. In towns where only a few were taken, they were burnt at the stake. Where the numbers were larger, they were hanged and made targets of. So far it is hardly possible to pity the victims much. But there is one blot. The coloured trade goods disappeared for ever. These unfortunates, brought up to a life of infamy, perhaps sold into it by fond parents, were irresponsible. Some say they were shot and buried quietly; others, that they were drowned. As a fitting termination, the Asiatics who plied less contemptible callings received warning that their safety could be guaranteed only until after the departure of the next few steamers bound north.*

Kirmess is accurate about the response of the international press to such activities – it is very little different from the reaction that would occur today:

> *The first news of anti-colour riots was served up to the British public as Sunday reading. Several up-to-date preachers referred to it in their sermons, likening the misguided Antipodeans unto Assyrian wolves. On Monday the London Stock Exchange marked its disapproval in a more practical manner by depressing Australian State funds several points more. And they fell lower when the meaning of the boycott was realized. There never was a*

> worse dislocation of trade. The leading shipping companies met boycott with boycott... The stoppage sent up the prices for meat, butter and fruit in the markets of the United Kingdom...

Naturally, Continental shipping lines quickly discover a method of turning the state of affairs to advantage, by using all-European crews and driving up the freight rates, with the result that the counterboycott is broken, and 'the foreigners had established still more firmly their hold on Pacific trade'.

But the result of sensationalism in the press is still more dangerous for Australia's right to self-determination:

> The disgust of classes and masses alike in the United Kingdom against the Commonwealth had had time to become deep-rooted when the first rumour of the Queensland atrocities – so called by the London Press – leaked out. Public opinion was emphatic in condemnation. The effect was electric and transformed the existing bitterness into a dead set against Australia which nothing could overcome. Should Britannia bare her righteous sword in defence of such brutal, bloody deeds? The thing was not to be thought of. Several sensational journals demanded bombardment of the guilty ports and a blockade of the Commonwealth until all the perpetrators of the outrage should be punished, and until satisfaction should be given to the insulted nations. There can be no doubt that the series of violent outbreaks, and particularly this culmination, did immense harm to the Australian cause.

The lack of support from other colonies is also predictable:

> Above all, weak-kneed adherents in the sister dependencies who were peering around anxiously for a chance to conciliate the financial over-lords, were supplied with a pretext to recant their former implicit applause under the plea of horrified humanity. From this period may be dated the ascendency of the Moderates in the other autonomous colonies.

As a direct result of all this, when the Japanese establish a colony in the Northern Territory, white Australians are unable to convince Britain that there is any threat to the Commonwealth. On the contrary, visiting British dignitaries report that 'these industrious [Japanese] settlers have done a great service by their careful cultivation and methodical penetration of the wilderness'.

One sinister fact that soon becomes apparent is that, while the Japanese villages are full of native women, there is a 'complete absence of any male aboriginals'. The narrator comments that:

> *It is not difficult to imagine why the presence of the male*
> *natives must have been inconvenient to the immigrants.*
> *The fellows had seen too much and might begin to boast of it*
> *to the British as soon as they should have discovered, with*
> *natural cunning, that the white and yellow races were really*
> *opposed to each other in spite of momentary friendliness.*
> *Moreover, the blacks were no longer useful as guides, since*
> *the country had been explored thoroughly, nor as*
> *subsidiaries, now that no further attacks were apprehended.*
> *On the other hand, they might have become troublesome*
> *enemies in the bush. That possibility had to be guarded*
> *against. Probably the Japanese copied the example of the*
> *White Guard and butchered the male aboriginals.*

Whatever the local animosities, the result of international opinion is that the Japanese colony enjoys the rights of British imperial citizenship, and the White Guard, which attacks the settlements, is eventually forced to retreat and watch helplessly as the Northern Territory becomes an independent entity through stealth rather than conquest. While the white garrison is forbidden to fraternise with the local women, the Japanese colonists are engendering a new race:

> *The soothing influence of womanhood, of motherhood, was*
> *now penetrating the whole settlement. Numbers of children*
> *were born there daily. Perhaps no other fact did more to*
> *deepen the coolness between the two races into revengeful*

> *estrangement. For the Australians, who keenly missed appropriate sex partnership of their own race, watched helplessly the rapid progress of the despised Asiatics from a mere horde of invading nomads into a settled nation bound to the conquered soil by the most sacred ties – by little brown babies quite unconscious of their own significance, all young Australians – Austral-Mongoloids. And the white heirs to the continent had to stand by impassively, condemned to look on and record the event.*

It is, once again, the power of the international press that brings matters to a head. Unwilling to offend Japan by defending the actions of an Australian, Colonel Ireton, who had ordered the flogging of eleven 'Asiatic assassins', Britain caves in to Japanese demands for action against the Commonwealth. The British Navy blockades the Australian coastline to protect the fledgling Japanese colony against Australia's righteous anger, adding insult to injury by making sure that 'Australia's subsidised navy was employed to coerce Australia'.

The narrator comments, bitterly, that:

> *That very influential section of the English Press which preaches Imperialism from a capitalistic point of view, and which would have smiled at the flogging of Asiatics if it had happened in India or in some other colony with approved conservative principles, had nothing to say to the Commonwealth... Its readers, the wealthy classes of the United Kingdom and their hangers-on, had become so accustomed to the thought that Communism – as they termed it – must run its full course in Australia.*

He also points out the economic basis of the Imperial actions: 'Great Britain feared one thing – the repudiation of the public debt by Australia'. Britain, it appears, cares far more for the security of her investment in the colony than for the plight of the colonists themselves.

Australian attempts to reclaim the lost land are doomed. In the final chapter, 'Black Christmas', set in 1922, there is a breathing space, but it is clear that 'The White Continent had become a thing of the past'. There is faint hope for the 'White Commonwealth', but a very blunt warning is spelled out in capital letters:

> A great deal depends on successful white settlement in the North...it is the problem which in vital importance overshadows all others. For the alienated extreme Northern corner – Australia Irredenta – is flourishing with a hostile civilization. Under lenient British rule a new Japanese empire is in the making. Already it is said to contain, if the second generation is counted in, an Asiatic population of 200,000 souls. It is constructing railways and ports. A truce has been cried until 1940 A.D. Till then the Commonwealth must get ready for its relentless march to the North to save the purity of the race by sweeping the brown invaders back over the coral sea. The alternative is the irretrievable conquest of tropical Australia by the hordes of the Orient. In this struggle the still larger issue is bound up whether the White or the Yellow Race shall gain final supremacy. Christian civilization cannot afford the loss of this Continent, FOR AUSTRALIA IS THE PRECIOUS FRONT BUCKLE IN THE WHITE GIRDLE OF POWER AND PROGRESS ENCIRCLING THE GLOBE.

As always, there is a very fine dividing line between political fiction and political fact. In *The Australian Crisis*, Kirmess's insistence on the complicity of the international press is of great interest, particularly since Frank Fox, editor of the *Lone Hand* periodical, used *The Australian Crisis* as a political lever to foment anti-Chinese feeling. Frank (later Sir Frank) Fox began his career as editor of the *Australian Workingman* and the *Bathurst National Advocate*, then joined *The Age* as chief of reporting staff. He joined the *Bulletin* in 1901, and became first editor of *Lone Hand* in 1907. In 1909 he returned to England.

It was Fox who published Kirmess's work. So convinced was he of its importance that he used his political contacts to arrange discussion of *The Australian Crisis* in Federal Parliament. Prime

Minister Alfred Deakin had already made his views on the need for a White Australia policy clear when, in 1901, he described it as 'the profoundest instinct of individual or nation – the instinct for self-preservation' and added that 'nothing less than the national manhood, the national character, and the national future...are at stake'.[5] The debate, however, did not happen: Prime Minister Alfred Deakin fell from power before it could take place.

In a series of short stories titled 'The Secrets of a Prime Minister', published in *The Lone Hand* from June to August 1907, Fox represents the political problems of the day in fictional form. Secret 'No. 1. – The Incident of the Microphone'[6] deals with an Asian threat to Australian security that arises from Australia's deportation of 'Beluchistan' residents of the Northern Territory. The Prime Minister, Uling, recounts the situation to his journalist-biographer:

> *The British Government has got what is practically an ultimatum from Beluchistan about our Northern Territory Deportation Act. You recollect the difficulty we had in getting the Royal Assent to the Act – how it was represented that the deportation of that colony of Asiatics, which had established itself on the Roper in defiance of our laws, was almost certain to cause trouble. Well, it has. Worse trouble than we anticipated. The Pan-Asiatic Council has taken up the gauge for Beluchistan, and talks war.*

Once again, Australia's naive reliance on the British navy is at issue:

> *What's more, they're ready for war right now. And the whole Empire hasn't a single first-class battleship in these waters.*

What is needed is time for the great powers to complete their treaty arrangements:

> *Three months' delay...would make things right. Great Britain is just on the point of completing a convention with France, the United States, Russia, Italy and Austria, to the*

effect that all the Powers make war together in the event of one being attacked by any combination of Asiatic nations. When that Convention is signed the Pan-Asiatic Council will look at things differently.

The solution? As the journalist suggests, Australia should:

Give Beluchistan a little slack. Play with her a bit. Hang up things for three months. Promise anything, everything, until we're safe. All is fair in a game like that.

Uling responds that this is 'Spoken like a journalist, who in the cause of freedom and democracy runs that most absolute of despotisms – a newspaper office!'. He points out that the real difficulty lies in domestic politics. The Prime Minister cannot announce that his government will not interfere with the Beluchistan colony, which is popularly believed to be a tacit invasion of the Northern Territory – to do so would be political suicide. Nor does he feel able to trust either the Third Party or the Leader of the Opposition as confidants – they have their own political positions to maintain. So, in a Machiavellian sequence that is all too familiar today, Prime Minister and journalist indulge in a little campaign of misinformation and leaked confidences, designed to manouevre the members of the opposition into a position where they will not oppose the government. The ploy is successful, with Uling bringing down a resolution giving himself full powers of negotiation, and then immediately proroguing Parliament. A postscript announces that:

The Beluchistan difficulty was settled most satisfactorily. The Prime Minister, unhampered by Parliament, played the position splendidly, pretending hopeless funk and holding out all sorts of promises of a complete recognition of Beluchistan's cheeky claims. When the Convention of St Petersburg, which lifted from Europe for all time the fear of Asiatic attack, was announced, the Australian hand was declared with the forcible expulsion of 'our friend the enemy'; and neither Beluchistan nor the Pan-Asiatic Council said a word.

The role of the press in providing 'edited' information or colluding with political figures, together with the pettiness of local politics in inhibiting issues of national importance, are continuing themes in the Asian invasion literature of the time.

Fox further makes his own support for a White Australia clear in a volume of articles, originally published in the *Bulletin* and the *Lone Hand* and collected under the title *From the Old Dog: 'Being the Letters of the Hon. – –, ex Prime Minister to his Nephew...'* (1908).[7] In chapter XI, 'Foreign Politics and a White Australia', he advises that:

> *...as an Australian, I'd say that there are two principles on which you should never make a concession.*
>
> *Domestically – A White Australia.*
>
> *Abroad – The hegemony of the White Races.*
>
> *You'll hear fools talking often of the 'White Australia' principle as a selfish fad of the working classes. It was some Conservative, eager for cheap, reliable household slaves, or some capitalist, anxious to make profits out of servile labour, who, knowing his own selfish motive, invented the lie that the White Australia aspiration represents 'the selfishness of the working classes.'*

Fox goes on to appeal to the principles of social Darwinism to argue for the purity of the race, citing:

> *...the instinct against race-mixture which Nature has implanted to promote her work of evolution. Our white race, having developed on certain lines to a position which promises, if it does not fulfil, the evolution of a higher human type, has an instinctive repugnance to mixing its blood with peoples in other stages of evolution... Once a type has got a step up it must be jealous and 'selfish' in its scorn of lower types, or climb down again. This may not be good ethics. But it is Nature.*
>
> *The question doesn't necessarily involve any issue of individual superiority, or even of race superiority in any but*

> the ethnological sense... But our race, as a race, has taken up the white man's burden of struggling on towards the 'upward path,' of striving at a higher stage of evolution. It would certainly be more pleasant for us if we took to the lotus-eating life of the Kanaka, or the submissive, passive life of the Asiatic. But the choice has been made by Nature rather than by man. The Caucasian, with his passion for Liberty, for individuality, bears the standard in the van of humanity. If we were to stop to dally with races which would enervate us, or infect us with servile submissiveness, the scheme of human evolution would be frustrated. And that's why the sane, right-thinking man instinctively objects to all mixture with the coloured races.

So there you have it. Fox doesn't pull any punches. Like Kirmess, he uses the example of racial violence in America as a warning of what Australia might become without the White Australia Policy he is advocating:

> We're always hearing from the United States of America of some unhappy nigger being kerosene-soaked and grilled at the stake by the whites. That is a warning to our country to beware of mixing the black man and the white, and of cultivating a servile alien class with which our own people cannot mingle on even terms. It is the existence of the black elements which has led the Southern United States to become the scorn and loathing and disgust of civilised nations. That region is the only white man's country on earth where burning alive is still a common and frequent form of punishment. Utter disregard of law is added to utter disregard of decency and humanity. At one horror special trains were run to bring crowds to see the nigger burned, and front seats at the loathsome iniquity were 'reserved for the ladies.' All this is done to preserve the purity of the white race – burning is the punishment reserved for the nigger who is accused, on good evidence or otherwise, of an outrage on one of the women of the dominant race.

Fox has more to say in a similar social Darwinist vein, before he concludes that:

> *If we don't keep Australia White, we must one day grill our black or brown brother, to keep him in order, unless it so happens that he grills us. It isn't worth incurring that future, even if we could make millions out of coloured labour.*

He extends his arguments to the similarly inherent racial problems of dealing with 'Asiatics'. His response to arguments about the value of Asiatic trade is 'Damn the tuppence worth of trade!' – it's not worth the problems it will cause:

> *Keep the Asiatic out. He is the worst of alien dangers, because the most powerful, the most pertinacious, the most arrogant... The essential arrogance of Asia is the fact which you, accustomed to the fawning humility of the well-kicked Cantonese Chinaman, may find it difficult to comprehend. But Asia has ever nurtured an insolence beside which any white-race pride is insignificant.*

Fox cites the arrogance of the Persians, the Huns and the Turks in their treatment of European races, and reminds the reader that:

> *In his secret heart...the Asiatic, whether he be Japanese, Chinese, or Indian, holds a deep disdain for the white. The contempt we feel for them is returned more than one hundred fold... Still in his heart the Asiatic keeps his arrogance.*

These arguments are hardly new – they are being restated here to reinforce the perceptions of Fox's readers, and to keep the main argument for a White Australia in the forefront of the public consciousness.

Fox's own contribution to the invasion literature of Australia, *Beneath an Ardent Sun* (1923),[8] was published in London. It reworks the ideas of *The Australian Crisis*, with its fear of an expansionist Asian power armed with new European technology, but this time the Asian enemy is less controversially 'Cambodian' (replacing Japan, which had been an ally of Britain in the First World War). Fox had moved on by the time he wrote this slight romance, and invasion scare novels were so well established that readers could be expected not to need too many details. The outcome of Fox's story is more upbeat than in Kirmess's book, and the majority of the plot is devoted to a story of love and politics, to which the events of the crisis serve as a backdrop.

In *Beneath an Ardent Sun*, the crisis this time results from the settlement of 'an island, half within, half without, the mouth of the Gulf of Carpentaria, on which was a little colony of, let us say, "Cambodians"'. The 'Cambodians' react truculently when disturbed in their small Arcadia by the crew of an Australian warship. Exponents of the White Australia policy set about removing the enclave and a crisis in international law results:

> *Cambodia made significant preparations. The great*
> *European Power, which was not fully appreciative of the*
> *Divine right of England to empire, began to take an open, as*
> *well as a secret interest in Cambodian affairs. In Australia*
> *the Feverish Party sang songs and shouted. The Stupid*
> *Party followed in their steps helplessly.*

The Prime Minister, Trent, had come to office 'pledged to maintain White Australia but without any heedless breaking of china'. But once a British minister gains international publicity by scoffing at 'Australian Jingoism and urging Britain not to support Trent's political solution to the problem of the island, the Australian situation flares again: 'there was a new Fever in Australia. The British Government was against White Australia! Trent was secretly conspiring with the British Cabinet to abandon the cause of White Australia at the bidding of Cambodia! A meeting was held to collect money to send a delegation to seek help in the United States', and so on. The behaviour of the press is familiar enough to modern readers accustomed to seeing political 'beat-ups' occur on a regular basis. Trent's political reaction is also familiar in its strategy:

> *Before the end of November, we shut up Parliament. December we do nothing. Absolutely nothing. We go into summer quarters and let the journalists do the talking, and our friend the enemy do the blundering... We have declared what we are going to do and we are doing it. But the enemy talks...talks all the more furiously because we are silent...commits a thousand extravagances.... We move out suddenly from our summer quarters...we cry up the flag and beg for a policy of reason and true patriotism. Then, afterwards, with foot, horse and artillery, an attack all along the line. And perhaps we can hasten the arrangements to deport a few Cambodians...*

This time, the politics go to plan, and things come out in favour of the white Australians – a rather less paranoid conclusion which may perhaps reflect some cautious sense of improved security in the establishment of an Australian Federation.

Beneath an Ardent Sun was in some ways an anachronism. Japan's support for the Allies in the First World War helped temporarily to take the sting out of its increasing military power. 'The enemy' immediately after the end of the war, in 1918, was once more a European power (albeit a defeated one). But like Roydhouse and Kirmess, Fox used his fiction to urge on complacent white Australians a continued preparedness for what he saw as the real possibility of invasion. The old, pre-Federation sense of being entirely at the mercy of imperial diplomacy and foreign interests might have receded a little, but fear of being overwhelmed by the Asian hordes on Australia's doorstep remained.

6

Austral-Asia?

After the First World War, Australia settled comfortably into its new role as an exclusively British dominion. Japan had fought on the side of Britain and, for a while, the Turks and the Huns displaced the yellow hordes of Asia as the popular fictional bogey men. But by the end of the Great Depression (1929 – mid-1930s), the yellow peril was back as fictional public enemy number one, the looming threat to our national wellbeing.

A. J. Pullar's *Celestalia: A Fantasy A.D. 1975* (1933)[1] revives the cautionary Asiatic invasion story in grand xenophobic style. Originally written as a serial for *The Argus*, and reprinted in book form with two additional chapters, its acknowledgement page states that: 'Its intention was to awaken the people of Australia to the tragic possibilities of apathy towards adequate defence measures'. The title refers to the country's change of name to 'Celestalia', a conflation of Celestial China with Australia. This renaming is a common fictional device to indicate the loss of cultural and political autonomy. It turned up in *Pauline Hanson: The Truth*, with the renaming of Australia as 'Australasia' to emphasise the threat of future Asianisation.

In *Celestalia*, Australia is no longer autonomous; it is revealed at the end of the novel that 'we lost the bloody place'. A system of resolving conflicts by 'Olympiads', based on the ancient model of combat between selected champions, has replaced warfare as the accepted means of solving disputes between nations:

> The powers had really had enough of war after 1952, and at a conference at Lausanne, and as a direct result of the

> successful manner in which the U.S. and England had
> terminated their differences, had put their seal...to a pact to
> disarm, and also test the practicability of substituting
> Olympic contests for war, combined with an international
> naval force to enforce obedience of its findings.

The question of our national identity is debated at length in a courtroom scene. Talia, a Chinese-born, white, part-Italian girl skilled in the use of weapons, is defending her right to represent China by casting doubts upon the legitimacy of white Australian claims to citizenship of their continent. Her own claim to Chinese citizenship is straightforward:

> [Quong] testified to her having been born in China... She
> had been rescued from drowning in the Yangtze Kiang, in
> the far west of China. She spoke the Chinese of the Province
> of Szechuen, and this appeared to be her native tongue.

Her opponent, Robert Armstrong, has more difficulty in satisfying the court of his Australian nationality, exposing a mass of contradictions and prejudices in his explanation:

> 'My grandfather "made good", as we call it, in Australia,
> and took his family home for a trip. On returning to
> Australia he left my father, who had been born in England,
> with his brother, a childless man, who brought him up,
> educated him, and eventually he married in England.
> Subsequently, on a visit to his father (my grandfather), I was
> born in Australia and remained with my grandfather, he
> having lost his other sons in the wars.'

> 'So your parents were English?' said Talia...

> The judge said: 'Let us get this clear. I understand from my
> notes that your grandfather was an Australian. Why do
> you claim this?'

> 'Because,' said Bob, with pride, 'he was the son of a pioneer
> family.'

> 'Now I am confused,' said Talia. 'This pioneer family, by
> that I presume you mean Aboriginal?'

> 'No abo in my crowd,' said Bob indignantly. 'No, the pioneers were mostly English or Scotch or Irish – British, you know.'

The confusion continues, coming down to the question of country of birth and the nature of the British Empire:

> 'What is Australian? Must you be born there?'
>
> 'No,' said Bob. 'Residence there is necessary for a certain period; it is not laid down how long you must remain to be an Australian. In six months, I think it is, you can vote; that is, of course, if you are a Britisher.'
>
> 'Nationalization is not necessary if you are British?' asked Talia.
>
> 'Oh, no,' said Bob.
>
> 'Well... Your great grandfather was English, your grandfather Australian, your father was English, and you are an Australian because you were born there... But if you pleased, you could call yourself English?' asked Talia.
>
> 'Yes,' said Bob. 'Or, no: rather British would be more correct, I suppose.'
>
> 'Oh, I know that,' said Talia. 'You are British because Australia belongs to the British Empire. How does it belong?'
>
> 'It acknowledges the King of England, who is the head of the British Empire.'
>
> 'Apart from his majesty, then, you are an independent people?'
>
> 'Yes,' said Bob.

The question of a country's ability to maintain its national identity through force of arms now becomes a vital question – how can Australia claim to have exercised genuine autonomy if it could not enforce its borders?

'Then, if the Olympiads did not exist, and quarrels were settled in the old way, by war, instead, it would have been the Australian Army and Navy which would have been fighting the Chinese. Is that so?'

'At the time to which you now refer, we could not have fought anybody,' said Bob, trying to recall his history. 'Forty years ago, in '32, before the Olympiads, we were practically unarmed. We had a small but efficient navy – three or four ships – no submarines. We had only the nucleus of an army.'

'So that if you had been attacked...' said Talia expressively.

'Oh, in that case,' broke in Bob, 'England would have, of course, defended us. We could not have waged an offensive war ourselves. I mean the Australian people. As was so disastrously demonstrated a few years later, when England was engaged in a war and could not help us, we suffered humiliation,' and Bob flushed to the roots of his hair.

Once again, the question of white Australia's right to the continent comes to the fore:

'When did you first claim this country of Australia as your own, and why did you?' asked Talia. 'Did you acquire it by conquest?'

'No,' said Bob. 'The Aborigines were not very dangerous. A few settlers got speared, but we could not claim to have acquired the country by overcoming any resistance they put up. It was more a peaceful penetration, and the overcoming of natural forces and difficulties, I suppose.'

'By the English pioneers, you mean? But why did their descendants claim Australia for their own?' asked Talia. 'Was any injustice meted out to them by the government of Britain?'

'Never heard of any,' said Bob... 'In my own mind, I always associated our independence with the time we first began to beat them at cricket!'

Talia's conclusion is that:

> '*I claim to legally represent China, because I was born there, and in spite of my father being Italian. And, furthermore, I claim that this gentleman...is an Englishman living in Australia; that, in fact, there are no such people as Australians other than the aborigines... If he is a bona fide Australian, I am a bona fide Chinese.*'

But we later learn that Old Australia cannot make an Olympiad claim by combat, the '*piece de resistance* [of which] was a game in which a thousand a side took part...based on the American game of football, with certain minor alterations and improvements, derived from English Rugby Union rules', because 'We [the world powers] have barred by mutual consent the entering of any country of mixed blood', which is what Australia has become.

As usual in such fictions, *Celestalia* lays the blame for its current plight on inept politicians, whose economic mismanagement and concomitant failure to maintain adequate defence forces have led to national disaster. Following a period of National Party rule (1932-35), during which there was a massive increase in unemployment, and the country was on the verge of bankruptcy, the 'Socialists and those other wreckers of that day... swept the country in the elections of 1935'.

The new Socialist government, described as 'well meaning ignoramuses', set about radical reform:

> *[They] chucked out the governor, abolished the Oath, in fact, cut the painter with the old country, and started with a clean sheet (as they thought), no debts, private or public. A self-contained country, no money, barter, everybody taking in everybody else's washing, and all trying to dodge their turn at driving and emptying the various municipal tip-carts.*

The national self-image also comes in for ridicule in *Celestalia*:

> *Hadn't they proved themselves in 1914-18? Didn't they continue to win at cricket? Weren't their youth, both male*

> and female, the finest physical beings on the earth? What
> had they to fear? War? No! America, the U.S., stood
> between them and their only potential danger. She couldn't
> afford to let another race, and a yellow one, flourish on such
> a hot-bed. No, Australia was safe to work out her own
> destiny and development. There would be plenty of time to
> think of defence when the signs pointed that way.

Following major earthquakes around the world, which had resulted in the collapse of population centres such as Tokyo, and the displacement of millions, a great exodus of Japanese citizens into China had strained the latter's resources, and Australia became a tempting prize. The self-centred Australian population is all unaware:

> As for the question of menace to the security of the country
> developing, this was occasionally mentioned, but could not
> have been thought in the remotest degree probable, because
> the country was literally defenceless. I really believe that
> they thought that it was better not to mention it too much in
> public in case other nations needing an outlet for their
> swarming populations, should notice it. As if they hadn't a
> better knowledge probably than anybody in Australia, or
> England, for that matter, both of the country's potentialities,
> and its vulnerability.

Once again, the culpability of the press in failing to alert the populace is noticeable. News from Japan is relegated to the inner pages, in small type, while sporting events dominate the reports:

> We had a team of English footballers over, and the Test
> games were on; golf was in full swing; the Davis Cup team
> were doing well at Wimbledon, and we were pretty busy
> summing up the promising ones for the Melbourne Cup.
> Oh, yes, we were pretty busy one way and another... How we
> were led, and our minds moulded by the newspapers of that
> day; we weren't allowed to think for ourselves; the largeness
> of type was our guide and mentor. Largest type meant a
> murder, certainly, but all the lessening degrees of type were

> meant, and did make a less and less impression on our
> minds; many never got beyond the largest type, only very few
> read the smallest.

Similarly, the tendency of the Australian press to emulate American practices is attacked:

> About the end of the nineteenth century...the editors thought
> they could not create an Australian tradition without
> destroying another...their chief weapon was a cheap form of
> raillery at everything English. They got their cue from
> American journalism, where for half a century a large
> portion of the press was bitterly anti-English. It was a trivial
> matter, possibly...but more serious was the fact that it...
> prepared the grounds for influences...that the American
> screen invasion accentuated. Everything American was to
> be copied and emulated...

Britain is blamed for not recognizing the gravity of the situation, for not instigating a migration scheme to populate Australia with suitable white settlers. But whoever was to blame, it is clear that Australia cannot return to its former, white state.

Celestalia ends with this enigmatic remark from the departing Lord Haredale:

> 'If,' he said, 'they [the Australians] would entirely forget their
> English ancestry and so lose their failings, or always
> remembering it cherish their virtues, they would have the
> makings of the finest people on God's earth.'

This, however, seems unlikely. The Australian population is still characterised as being poorly led, under-defended, and ill-informed, with its interests represented by a media far more inquiring in matters of sport and gossip than international politics. In Pullar's view, this is a recipe for disaster and Australia remains a tempting prize for our potentially expansionist Asian neighbours.

In a similar vein, Erle Cox's novel, *Fool's Harvest* (1939),[2] warns of the dangers of complacency. In this cautionary tale, an Australian guerilla movement in the bush resists the cruel and exploitative Asian invaders by systematic sabotage. The book's publicity page, captioned 'Shells on Sydney; Massacre in Melbourne', describes it as:

> ...an exciting and possibly prophetic novel...in which the author sounds the warning to Australians that the protective isolation of our Commonwealth exists no longer... Erle Cox shows how readily a Fool's Paradise may become a Fool's Harvest of national humiliation and defeat.
>
> Military possibilities are not greatly exaggerated and this story of Australia's peril from a predatory power, shows on what slender support our present possession rests.

The book acknowledges that the 'War of the Future has been used previously as the medium for sensational fiction', but nevertheless asserts its claim to prophecy in this case.

Cox is an enigmatic writer. After the success of *Out of the Silence*, he waited over twenty years before publishing *Fool's Harvest*. The 'War of the Future' had indeed become a standard form for cautionary tales of this nature, and in this version Cox uses the tradition of the eye-witness account, presenting the story as a true journal account of the 'Australian debacle of 1939, written in secret by one Walter Burton, who began his narrative as 'an inmate of the notorious concentration camp at Carrington, the suburb of Newcastle, in 1948'.

The scenario of *Fool's Harvest* is that Australia has been defeated by the Asian 'Paramount Power', which has reduced the white population to slavery in concentration camps and is systematically stripping Australia of its resources, from wool and wheat and timber to mineral reserves. The great foreign powers have not defended us:

> In the world without there was no hand raised to help us. We were the spoils of war to an arrogant power. Europe was one vast battleground. Britain...was barely holding her own against overwhelming odds. India was in flames...

Despite 'The Treaty of Berlin', which later gave the Paramount Power a limited 'twenty years' right of occupation', there is no sense in the journal that the promised Australian evacuation will take place after the twenty years has elapsed. An interpolated editor's note tells us that America did eventually enforce it, in 1966, thus enabling this 'historical account' to be written.

As the story begins, the Paramount Power has hoodwinked the American Commission of Inspection into believing that 'They are treating us with kindness and generosity, and we are repaying them with savage hostility, and are totally unfitted to govern ourselves'. Burton is part of the underground resistance, valiantly opposing the depredations of the Paramount Power. As always there are spies and counter-spies and conspiracies. The Paramount Power is in the habit of torturing the wives and children of suspected conspirators. Pointing out that 'No man knows how he will behave until the moment of choice comes to himself, and the agents of the Paramount Power had made a science of creating traitors', the narrator goes on to detail some of the unpalatable methods of interrogation:

> *A favourite method of trying to make a man betray his friends was to capture a wife or daughter, and use her as a form of torture, as they did Hill's wife a few months ago, here in Newcastle.*

The system is simple:

> *When their police found they could not obtain information by tormenting a man or woman, they used 'indirect interrogation.' This euphemism for scientific savagery meant that the victims, men or women, were given the alternatives of watching wife, husband or child treated with barbarity, or answering questions put to them.*

The response is defiant: Burton's sister tells her husband that 'if you ever bought my life at that price I would spit in your face before I died of shame for my husband'. But the problem is very real, and the guerillas have finally 'checkmated them by excluding all married men from all subversive societies'.

Traitors and spies for the Paramount Power are grouped under the descriptive title 'Blowflies', and 'sooner or later they were discovered and unpleasant things happened to them under the guise of accidents'. Burton has been 'tailed' to his sister's place, but is well aware of the dangers and the ability of the resistance to deal with them: 'I...walked off slowly towards the camp to give my follower time to sight me. It is a remarkable coincidence that four evenings later he was accidentally run down and killed by a motor lorry on the Maitland Road'.

Once again, the power of the press and of deliberate propaganda is identified as a major factor in the continued subjugation of Australia. After the collapse, Australians 'were a conquered race...leaderless and helpless'. This enabled the 'Cambasians' to claim that 'there was no authority from whom they could accept surrender, or to whom they could dictate terms'. They declined to recognise the remaining 'real' Australian leadership, and simply enforced martial law by Proclamation. They followed up with a massive public disinformation campaign:

> *Then...our conquerors had begun to put into effect that policy of preventing news of what was being done here from being spread around.*
>
> *They set in motion that propaganda machine that spread round the world, when it was quiet enough to hear, that vile tradition of the anarchy, cruelty and treachery that we never lived down. They understood thoroughly the psychological value of the saying that a lie will go halfway round the world while the truth is pulling on its boots. With devilish ingenuity they filled the American press with sensational stories of Australian cowardice, cruelty and treachery. They told of their necessity to take over its Government for the sake of humanity, because they found the Commonwealth in a state of utter anarchy. They told how their kindly and considerate rule had been met with barbaric murders and tortures of their people that would shame a savage. They told these stories with a wealth of circumstantial detail, and inventive genius, that was as brilliant as it was foul.*

> *Their half truths were worse than their pure mendacity.*
> *They alleged that at the battle of Seymour 100,000*
> *Australians had broken and fled with scarcely any*
> *casualties, before 10,000 Cambasians.*

An editor's note reminds us that this was not the case; that the numbers were more or less reversed, and that the story was a coverup for the sinister killings of wounded on the field by the Paramount Power.

The position of the Australian guerillas is most difficult in the cities, where the Paramount Power is most able to control its subjects, to the extent that:

> *...the slightest infringement of a regulation was punished*
> *summarily by death without trial, and on the spot. Men, for*
> *not raising their hats to Cambasian officers, were shot dead*
> *in the streets. The whole aim of the policy was to terrorise*
> *the people into abject submission.*

Resistance is more effective in the country. Livestock had been turned loose during the invasion, and:

> *...the bush and ranges were full of stock that had, perforce,*
> *been abandoned to run wild because they were either*
> *ownerless or their owners had no means of using them or*
> *profiting from them. It was these that provided the guerrilla*
> *bands with food and, in the end, clothing.*

Forced by necessity, both men and women have honed their bushcraft, establishing contact with other groups, evading capture and harrying the forces of the Paramount Power. There are tales of great bravery, and great deprivation.

But eventually, in 1942, the Paramount Power is triumphant and more than 40,000 men are forced to surrender their weapons. Life in the prison camps is barbaric: prisoners who had taken up arms are marked for hard labour, their heads shaven to mark them out from others, their food 'boiled wheat and treacle, with the coarsest meat twice a week.' Once a few men had escaped, a system of hostages was instituted: 'Each man had to nominate two comrades as hostages. If he escaped, his hostages were shot after 24 hours.' The ex-guerillas respond with sabotage and theft, but the Australian experience is miserable indeed.

As it becomes clear to the prisoners that they will not be reprieved by the Berlin Treaty, the situation deteriorates:

> *Slowly the exactions and oppressions of the Paramount Power have become more inhuman and pitiless, and our silent underground resistance has become more vindictive... Hopelessness has bred a recklessness of life that would be unbelievable to people differently circumstanced.*

The narrative breaks off mid-sentence, describing reprisal killings in 1941. The closest thing to a formal ending is the narrator's statement that:

> *I can feel neither regret nor self reproach for what I have done during these past nine years. I set out to tell the whole story... But my courage has not been equal to the task. But no-one, I believe, could do so. I have killed bound men without pity or compunction. It has all been part of our harvest.*

And a bitter harvest it is. Like his predecessors, Cox warns Australia against lack of preparation. As the frontispiece has it, *Fool's Harvest* demonstrates that an ounce of preparedness is worth tons of belated courage and heroic self-sacrifice; and that safety consists in being forearmed.

It is interesting that in *Fool's Harvest*, written in the period of anxiety leading up to the Second World War, the 'Paramount Power' is a generalized Asian force rather than a specific Asian nation. Like Frank Fox in *Under an Ardent Sun*, Cox used Cambodians – here, the 'Cambasians' – as the aggressors. The real attack, when it finally came, was Japanese.

The pre-Second World War xenophobic fictions were both wrong and right in their predictions of Asian invasion. Although the writers had concentrated solely on discussion of Australia's position, in 1941 the Japanese plan was far more sweeping. It was certainly not a war of retaliation for white Australian treatment of Chinese gold diggers or settlers. Those who had been predicting that Britain, for one reason or another, would not or could not defend Australia were closest to the mark. After the combined British forces had suffered years of heavy attrition in fighting in Europe and the Middle East, and were struggling in Burma, Japan's military command, under Emperor Hirohito, responded to Britain's perceived inability to defend its far-flung territories – particularly Hong Kong, Malaya, Singapore, New Guinea and, ultimately, Australia. The situation was more extreme than those predicted in the fictions: not only was Britain engaged elsewhere, it had also drained its Dominions, including Australia and New Zealand, of what fighting men and equipment they had possessed, leaving them vulnerable to attack.

When Hong Kong surrendered on 26th December 1941, there were already rumours of Japanese plans to invade the Australian coast. Labour Prime Minister John Curtin's New Year Speech to Australia made our defence position very plain when he said: 'I make it quite clear that Australia looks to America, free of any pangs as to our traditional links or kinship with Britain'.[3] In 1942 Curtin defied the wrath of English leader Winston Churchill when, after the bombing of Port Moresby on 3rd February and the surrender of Singapore on 15th February, his war cabinet refused to send the Australian 7th Division, then sailing in the Pacific, to Burma, recalling them and further troops to defend New Guinea and Australia's Northern Territory. Four days after the fall of Singapore, both Darwin and Broome were bombed, and by 8th March, the Japanese had landed in New Guinea. America had indeed entered the war after the Japanese bombing of Pearl Harbor in December 1941. On 7th-8th May 1942 the Battle of the Coral Sea was fought and, by July – which marked the closest Japanese advance to Port Moresby – the Australian forces had started to win. There were submarine attacks on Brisbane, Newcastle and Sydney, but no Japanese landings there.

Writers such as Kirmess, whose *The Australian Crisis* (1909) had posited a scenario of British partition of Australia with Japan, also saw a partial vindication of their prognostications. It had been rumoured that Churchill's military plan had been to draw a line across the Australian continent, and to defend only the more heavily populated areas, a position which may have appeared reasonable to Westminster but looked like treachery to patriotic Australians who had seen their country stripped of manpower and resources in the defence of Britain. Those writers who had argued that America would defend White Australia against coloured conquest were only partly vindicated, as the question of how the United States would have responded had Pearl Harbor not been bombed has been the subject of much debate. Nevertheless, American troops – described by Australian men with whom they competed for the attention of local girls as 'overpaid, over-sexed, and over here' – were involved in the defence of Australia, and the country has since retained a strong strategic alliance with the United States.

Although Japanese forces won no Australian territory, a great many of our troops found themselves under Japanese control as prisoners of war in other arenas. The atrocities committed against white prisoners of war by the Japanese were far more extreme than anything the fiction writers had dared imagine. Australian feelings were running high and the Japanese once more replaced the Huns as monsters in popular fiction, featuring largely in comic books and cartoons. The White Australia policy remained in force, and was one of the main planks in the political platform of pro-British post-war Prime Minister, (Sir) Robert Menzies, who was fond of reminding his Australian constituents of the dangers of the yellow peril to our North.

In later years, it was inevitable that Australia's Second World War experiences against Japan spilled over into xenophobic fiction, but given the comprehensive defeat of the Japanese Empire it is hardly surprising that invasion paranoia receded for a while. It resurfaced in 1968 in an apocalyptic novel by John Hay (the pen name of farmer John Warwick Dalrymple-Hay). His book, *The Invasion*,[4] was published at the height of the Vietnam War, when protests in America and Australia were gathering strength. Like its nineteenth- and earlier twentieth-century counterparts it is, in this sense, a warning. It draws on Nevil Shute's famous book, *On the Beach* (1957), which was set in an imaginative future aftermath of a nuclear war. Hay adds images clearly based on the experiences of former PoWs, and combines these with a generalised fear of communism. There is no very clear political scenario, but an underlying presumption that President Nixon's 'domino theory' of the spread of communism through South East Asia has proved to be correct. The invader is a communist state occupying the Indonesian archipelago. It has run out of living room for its expanding population, even after occupying New Guinea and the Melanesian islands, and seizes the opportunity provided by the accidental outbreak of nuclear war to launch its invasion of Australia.

The cover of the book features a mushroom cloud over Sydney Harbour Bridge, and title details in oriental characters. In an updating of the traditional nightmare of Asian hordes descending on the vast empty spaces of Australia in search of food, the comfortable rural existence of John Stanley-Harris, station owner, is disturbed by the nuclear annihilation of Australia's cities by Chinese satellite weapons, followed by the invasion of the Armada of the South-East Asian Republic.

Despite its more sophisticated characterisations and plot, *The Invasion* still displays many of the features of its predecessors. Chapter Two describes the bombing of Australia that precedes the coming of Asian settlers:

> *Extinction came from the high-flying satellite bombers that orbited, unheard by man... Specks, capsules, holding death in their spherical bellies. This death was for the capitals, the heavy centres of population, for the people cluttered in their tenements, high in the air of their concrete and glass nests...*
>
> *A single bomb, no larger than a football, dropped soundlessly out of an innocent blue sky... streets trembled and crashed and the ashphalt vomited upwards in giant mushroom clouds... long after an eternity of silence came the*

> whispering howl of the fighters, the Armada of the South
> East Asian Republic.
>
> Resistance was slight, as it is when countries are still old-
> fashioned enough to put their faith in treaties...
>
> Then...came the bulky shapes of the low flying skycraft
> transports...heavy with troops and equipment. A long
> moving picture of invasion...
>
> Where the skycraft transports landed on a roadway, they
> would spawn lorries and troops...their steel-helmeted cargo,
> hard-eyed and trigger-conscious, searched the road and
> countryside for the enemy.

Policies of integration and trade with Asian nations are blamed for Australia's lack of preparation and inability to defend itself, but the narrator also takes a swipe at policies of Aboriginal reconciliation:

> The townspeople still talked of assimilation, though, and for
> one Aborigine Week in the year there would be a half-
> hearted activity to do the 'right thing for the abo' under
> pressure from people in groups in the cities who did not have
> to live with them.

The invasion itself is motivated by the drive for expansion: 'the Kommando Tinggi, the High Command, had circled the areas of the country that could be made fertile through water'. But like *The Battle of Mordialloc* and *The Yellow Wave*, *The Invasion* paints a scenario of Asian retaliation for all the accumulated racial insults of the social Darwinist past. Captain Atmadi, commander of the Third Assault Group, recalls the Japanese overthrow of European dominance in Asia with a kind of grim satisfaction:

> The Captain had been surprised to see dark people living
> near the whites. In his own country it had been different
> until the Japanese occupation, when the whole world of
> values had changed. The white man was no longer a
> 'Tuan'. Atmadi had seen him existing as a slave, a white

> *coolie working in the paddy fields and on the railways. He had felt pity but it had quickly been buried like the life before World War II. Remembering their superiority and the barriers the Europeans had placed between themselves and the Atmadis, he felt that the white man had received what he considered his just dues.*

Even in the hardships of leading a military occupation, Atmadi can find time to reflect on the reversal of fortune and where it will lead:

> *And to think that twenty years ago Europeans had sneered at them, called them 'polished apes', and their country a 'boong republic'!*
>
> *Within months, families would be brought down by giant hundred ton skycraft and settled in the irrigated areas. The islands were already at bursting point with population, and special pioneer brigades had been formed to cultivate and make this dry continent yield up its store of life.*

Nevertheless, *The Invasion* is not a straightforward cautionary tale of racial war. Its cast of Australian characters includes: Chee, the station's Chinese cook; Lucas, the half-caste Aborigine (and member of the Australian Communist Party); Polish trucker Stefan Bezjak (married to a Dutch woman, best friends with a German); and Sydneysider Eddie Burke and his family. This is the later twentieth century, and Australia has been changed by post-war immigration. Bezjak recalls his early encounters with Australians:

> *They classified you straight away as a Pole, a German, an Eyetie, a Yugoslav. They had almost a genius for simplifying. Once you became a German Australian or an Italian Australian they became bewildered – almost hostile. You should stay in your box where they had put you.*

And it is Burke, the naive city man fleeing the homestead into unfamiliar country, who rejects the assistance of bushman Chee in hunting food, preferring hunger to giving arms to a Chinese:

> ...the old suspicions and dislikes returned, smudging his thoughts. 'The Chink!' he shouted. 'Give him the gun? I'm a wake-up to that yellow bastard. Next thing he'd be marching us back to old Harris to gloat over. No thanks.'

Curiously, Hay's book appeals to both nostalgia for a better past and the desire for a better future. Stanley-Harris muses on what has gone wrong:

> Here was the generation after him, a brash, materialistic generation who were now paying the cost of their negative thinking with human suffering.

But the reversion of Lucas to his 'savage' antecedents is just as unattractive as the self-centred intolerance of Burke. *The Invasion* is not a 'back-to-nature' tract. It laments the lost opportunities for further development of the Australian land:

> Mi-Yan never ceased to be amazed at the quiet New Australian's knowledge, and was just as amazed at him not being allowed to practise his profession in his new country. In most developing countries, men or women with Bezjak's qualifications would be snapped up.

There is suspicion, too, of the possibility for reconstruction from the ruins of squandered opportunity:

> Start again in the caves of Four Hills. Start again with the Chinese woman. And there'll be Burke and Shirl, Stefan and Lucas, the raw ingredients of a new primitive post-bomb society and the South East Asian Republic will leave you alone because there's nothing to take any more. And will the rest of the survivors have learned to live together with tolerance?

The book is equally cautious about an unquestioning acceptance of racial intermarriage as a solution:

> What would Atmadi's or Corporal Kali's children be like if they stayed in Australia? Would they become more like Australians? He shook the thoughts from his head. But they lingered on. There is no reason, he thought, why when

> we escape we should not continue the race. Race? Black?
> Yellow? White? No more ancestors looking down their noses
> in cold breakfast rooms, but a group struggling for survival
> in a harsh environment. Like Neanderthal man. And their
> ancestors would be brown, with slanting eyes on an Asian
> continent.
>
> Stanley-Harris shuddered at the thought. It was like joining
> up his pure Merinos with Crossbred rams. Hybrid vigour
> but no purity.

It seems, briefly, that there is hope, represented by the defection of Major Sui Mi-Yan, the Chinese engineer sent to supervise development of the station for food production. Her disillusionment with the random nuclear destruction brought about by cold war is reflected in a rejection of the doctrines of Chairman Mao, doctrines that remind us of the extraordinary universality and persistence of social Darwinism to the present day:

> The dogma of Mao stamped through her tired brain.
> 'Whether it be a struggle between individual and
> individual, or race and race, the outcome is that the unfit is
> defeated and perishes while the superior who is equal to the
> situation flourishes. In this movement of evolution there
> must be a sacrifice of the individual for society, of the
> present for the future'... Now, in the context of her
> disillusionment, it all seemed a giant hoax.

In the end, however, it is not the individuals who succeed in this impossible situation. In an echo of H. G. Wells' microbial end to the Martian invaders in The War of the Worlds, the Australian climate brings destruction to the settlement in the form of massive flooding. Riots and clashes between the soldiers of the South-East Asian Republic and workers from China wipe out the invading presence almost as suddenly and arbitrarily as nuclear weapons had wiped out the cities. And the handful of mixed-race survivors retreats to the caves, where Lucas hunts the food for them all. Only in the final collapse of civilisation does prejudice at last cease to matter – a far from positive view of the return to 'stone age' ways:

> *The watchers saw the children now as they came closer.*
> *They were dusty and their stomachs jutted. They were dusty*
> *with the extent of the hunt. Burke's Marcia was with them,*
> *but the watchers could not see their colour.*

Though it lacks the overt and brutal racism of its nineteenth-century antecedents, Hay's apocalyptic vision of Asian invasion still stands as a grim fictional warning: against complacency; against under-development of the continent; against petty bureaucracy and political incompetence which fail to take advantage of the human resources of post-war migration. It is not an unqualified appeal for racial tolerance; rather it condemns the mindless racism that was the hangover of the White Australia policy. It asks for considered exploitation of the wealth of new potential to be found in selective immigration.

Despite some of the more reasonable aspects of Hay's novel, it remains an alarmist text. Like its nineteenth-century counterparts it warns of the potential threat to complacent Australians from the dangerous combination of ignorance and over-population among our land-hungry Asian peasant neighbours. Above all, it appeals to what it sees as the essentially humane values of Western civilisation, threatened by materialism and militarism.

Exploitation of the fear of 'Asian invasion' has proved remarkably persistent in Australian writing. *Pauline Hanson: The Truth* (1997)[5] was merely another instalment in a long line of xenophobic tracts. It represented a reversion to the more scaremongering forms of political fiction. Its publication was staged as a media event. The 'limited edition' book was very limited indeed, since it had a tiny print run and was not generally available to the public. The stated intention of this book was 'the defence of Pauline Hanson' against her critics, especially those in the media. It is not a coherent text, but rather a series of unconnected sections. The first part reproduces three of Hanson's speeches, an extract from *The Australian Shooters Journal*, and a media release on Aboriginal benefits. The second part, produced collectively by anonymous members of the 'Pauline Hanson Support Movement', addresses issues such as gun control and native title under inflammatory headings that employ phrases like 'Betrayal of Australia'. Part II offers a mixture of political opinion, polemic and sensationalized 'discussion' of highly dramatic topics such as 'Aboriginal cannibalism'. It ends with an equally inflammatory 'conclusion' by Bruce R. Whiteside, who ends his harangue with what appears to be a 1946 poem by a namesake, William Whiteside, called 'I Am Fear', a poem that echoes the paranoia of earlier texts in its assertion that statesmen, members of the media and all those in positions of public office are guilty of political and ideological cowardice, which in turn leads to social mismanagement that is only to be overcome by those in 'the brotherhood' of true faith and unity.

In *The Truth*, Part 2, Chapter 8, we discover just where political mismanagement of immigration will lead. Under the heading 'Political Correctness and the Assault on Traditional Australia', there is a remarkably derivative future fiction in the style of the early texts. The scenario in *The Truth* is close to C. H. Kirmess's infiltration theory in *The Australian Crisis*, but with a homophobic elaboration unfamiliar to earlier sensationalists. It combines racist paranoia, xenophobia and conspiracy theory in a tale of a disenfranchised and Asianised future Australia, where a 'World Court' has punished the country for past racism under the White Australia Policy and for genocide against Asians and Aboriginals. Australia has been made the home for the world's polluting industries and its name changed to Australasia. Its president, Poona Li Hung, is a Chinese-Indian cyborg lesbian with neuro-circuits developed by a Korean-Indian-Chinese research team.

The Truth is not alone in this reversion to the paranoias of the previous century. In 1992, Ronald E. Henderson self-published his revised edition of *The Last White Rose? The White Race, Survival or Oblivion?*[6] It was dedicated:

> To the memory of our Ancestors, and the founding fathers of this nation, who understood the necessity for a White Australia Policy. Also to those loyal Australians who, at this present time, are prepared to fight for our heritage and the survival of the White Race.

Chapter titles include 'The Threat to our Survival', 'The Betrayal of Traditional Australia' and 'Treason'. Like its predecessors, and *The Truth*, this book combines various muddled conservative political and social positions with an overarching conspiracy theory that foreshadows the rise of social media. Unlike the works of Hanson, Lane or Mackay, however, Henderson's text is not a blueprint for serious political organisation. Bewildered, disappointed, threatened by change in all he sees, Henderson represents instead the kind of constituency all too easily exploited by political demagogues.

It has a familiar ring to it.

This, then, is the literature of Asiatic invasion. When *Aliens & Savages* was first published in 1998, it appeared remarkable that sensible readers could be influenced by such writing. But we are the inheritors of a political and social system that was shaped by the biases of its time. To an average nineteenth-century Western reader, racism appeared as natural a way of seeing the world as humanitarianism would appear to most Western readers in the later twentieth century. Today, however, multiplying conspiracy theories and divisive public rhetoric have shattered the comforting illusion of overarching humanitarian values. It is all too clear that the 'fair go for all' to which Australia is traditionally dedicated – an extension of the 'fair go' once afforded only to white, English-speaking Australians – is under attack.

Part Three
Towards Reconciliation?

7

Federation and Empire

In the twenty-first century, federation is accepted as an obvious expression of Australian nationhood. In the late nineteenth century, however, debates about colonial federation were far more divisive and acrimonious than any current discussion of an Aboriginal and Torres Strait Islander Voice to Parliament. Although people of all political persuasions were in favour of some form of political union, ideas on how this might be achieved varied widely. Many conservative members of the new Australian establishment favoured a colonial federation that would lead to a larger imperial union; but many socialists, for example, saw Australian union as the first step to a complete break with Britain.

The politics of racism were never far from the surface in this debate. Popular fear of the 'yellow peril' was exploited in the press, as nervous demagogues sought to follow America's example of controlling immigration by excluding Asians. The American *Chinese Exclusion Act* of 1882 had denied entry to Chinese immigrants and excluded those already resident from American citizenship. In Australia there was, until relatively recently, no such thing as Australian – as distinct from British – citizenship from which to exclude anyone. Nevertheless, Federation in 1901 was closely bound up with the Australian desire to restrict further Asian immigration.

There was another, less well-known, form of exclusion that came into operation with the new Federation: despite the general neglect of Aborigines throughout the nineteenth century, in some states, at least, adult Aboriginal males did have the right to vote. Under the new constitution, relations with Aborigines and Torres Strait Islanders were formally administered by the new federal government, which adopted a benevolently paternalistic approach. In a conflation of the 'noble savage' representation of Aborigines as children of nature with the social Darwinist positioning of them at the bottom of the ladder of human evolution, the new Australian Commonwealth excluded the indigenous people from all rights and responsibilities, effectively assigning them the status of permanent minors.

As a result of the active exclusion of non-white immigrants, in conjunction with the denial of civic involvement to Aborigines, when the new nation began self-consciously to define what it meant to be 'Australian', the terms of reference were exclusive, rather than inclusive.

From the earliest days of settlement there had, of course, been individual white voices dissenting from the general strategies of violent displacement and neglect. In 1832 one anonymous author, using the pen-name of 'Hugo', roundly criticised the damage caused to Aboriginal society on the margins of Sydney. 'The Gin',[1] like Eliza Dunlop's equally critical 1838 poem, 'The Aboriginal Mother (from Myall's Creek)', was written from a female and Aboriginal perspective:

'But where is Bian? – where is he? –
My husband comes not to my meal:
Why does he not the white man flee,
Nor let their god his senses steal?'

The poetic voice of the Aboriginal woman lays the blame for the man's failure to return on the dangerously seductive pleasures of Sydney Town: '"Lingers he yet in Sydney Streets?"'; and looks back nostalgically to a paradisal age before the British came:

'Oh! for the days my mother tells,
Ere yet the white man knew our land;
When silent all our hills and dells,
The game was at the huntsman's hand.'

The alternative solutions – withdrawal of the colony, or government-sponsored assistance to the Aboriginal community – seem equally unlikely:

> *'Avaunt ye from our merry land!*
> *Ye that so boast our souls to save,*
> *Yet treat us with such niggard hand:*
> *We have no hope but in the grave.'*

In the end, the white voice of the poem takes over from the Aboriginal mother's point of view, as though such mediation is the only way to find a sympathetic hearing. The invocation of religion as a solution sounds ironic today, given the role played by well-intentioned religious groups in the separation of Aboriginal children from their parents in the twentieth century: a role highlighted by the 1997 Human Rights Commission report, *Bringing Them Home*, on what has come to be known as 'the stolen generation' of Aboriginal children. But the appeal was clearly well-intentioned:

> *Their health destroyed – their senses depraved –*
> *The game, their food, for ever gone;*
> *Let me invoke religion's aid*
> *To shield them from this double storm*
> *Of physical and moral ill;*

Unlike grudging official response to the 1997 Wik decision, which coloured debate on both the stolen children report and on native title, this writer uncompromisingly acknowledges the responsibility that arises from dispossession of one culture by another. Simply to ignore the problems, Hugo states, is just as bad as active discrimination:

> *We owe them all that we possess –*
> *The forest, plain, the glen, the hill,*
> *Were theirs; – to slight is to oppress.*

A decade later, another anonymous contributor in the Port Phillip settlement also adopted an Aboriginal voice to criticise the behaviour of the colonists. 'H. L' wrote 'The Aborigine's

Complaint'[2] in a rather clumsy ballad form (the editor of the *Port Phillip Gazette*, in which it appeared on 10 August 1844, called it 'second or third rate' poetry). Unlike Hugo, H. L. savages the role of religion in the displacement and killing of Aborigines:

> *Remorselessly slaughtered by those who expound us*
> *Their Gospel of 'mercy,' of 'good will' and 'peace;'*

Noting in passing the prior Aboriginal ownership of land, the poet also attacks the settlers' propaganda of denigration:

> *The oppressors have wronged us, and now we are dubbed*
> *(As we tread o'er the ground which to us doth belong,)*
> *A lawless banditti, though we are the robbed –*
> *Crushed and trampled upon by the feet of the strong.*

Where Hugo saw only a future of decline or white intervention, H. L. expresses a startling sympathy for more direct Aboriginal action:

> *And we – we have nought but extinction to hope for,*
> *And soon in the forests our race will not range;*
> *Our rights, nay, our freedom, 'twere madness to cope for,*
> *And the course we'll pursue is deep, deadly revenge!*

It is worth noting the apparent agreement of the editor of the *Gazette* who, in explaining his reasons for printing this second-rate poem, states that 'the sentiments are good'.

The warnings were ignored. In the face of the economic imperatives of colonisation, attempts at sympathetic understanding, or even active reconciliation, were widely regarded as something of an indulgence. With the advent of social Darwinism to justify both direct action against Aborigines, and the often equally damaging indirect effects of neglect, the great majority of the population was happy to slip into a comfortable position of innate superiority. Possession of the continent by its white colonists and elimination of the Aboriginal inhabitants seemed to most of the settlers clearly justified, whether by divine or by natural law.

The 'justification' for this position now appears inherently racist. It is important to bear in mind, though, that such a dominant world view as Darwinism was bound to colour every aspect of life. It was not necessary to take a radical position like William Lane's overt attacks on the Chinese, for example, to appear racist to a modern reader. People who regarded themselves as compassionate, moral and humane, and who expressed every sympathy for the plight of Aborigines – like Mrs Aeneas Gunn, whose books, such as *The Little Black Princess* (1905) and *We of the Never-Never* (1908) were extremely popular – often adopted an attitude towards the older culture that to our eyes appears offensively patronising and discriminatory.

It is also important to remember that the Australian position was part of a worldwide understanding of human development. Social Darwinism seemed to justify the Anglocentric world view that arose from military and economic dominance. In this context, Australia's white inhabitants saw themselves as part of a natural process of human evolution that was going on all over the globe. Eventually the whole world would be governed by the European (especially British) type, either absorbing other races and cultures or displacing and replacing them. In these circumstances, to suggest that Aboriginal culture should be guarded and valued for its own sake was an eccentricity.

Similarly, Anglocentric social Darwinists could not accept the suggestion that expansion of the 'inferior' Chinese race was merely a matter of politics. For a white person to espouse the idea that the Asiatic masses were legitimate competitors with white civilisation was not merely misguided, but was regarded by many as a betrayal of the natural evolution of the whole human species.

Belief in the future of a crowning white civilisation also came to colour issues of Australian nationality and independence. Federation of the colonies was on the agenda almost immediately after the 1850s achievement of colonial self-government in Victoria, New South Wales, South Australia and Tasmania. All the new governments except New South Wales sent delegates to a Federation Convention. In an article called 'Australian Federation' which he wrote for the *Southern Cross* in 1860, Daniel Deniehy, a well-known literary figure and member of the New South Wales Parliament at the time, argued strongly in favour of the move.

In a post-Darwinian world, however, relatively simple arguments about political and strategic necessity were complicated by the sense of the shared imperatives of race – the belief in the common future of all 'British' peoples. In Australia, the multiplying range of interests produced such paradoxes as the Asian invasion fictions which appealed to common British race goals by decrying the British government. Writers argued equally fervently for and against independence on very similar grounds.

One connection made in some parts of the popular imagination (particularly among the pro-British lobby) was a kind of natural progress from colonial federation to a larger imperial federation. In April 1877, for example, the *Melbourne Review*, examining a Royal Colonial Institute pamphlet entitled 'On the Benefits to the Colonies of being Members of the British Empire', sketched the arguments for representation at Westminster versus the creation of an Imperial Parliament. The *Review* pointed out the fatal flaws in both arguments: that no British government would willingly surrender power to another body; and that, given the degree of independence they had already established, the Australian colonies were almost equally unlikely to accept mere representation at Westminster.[3]

Despite this discouragement, I. B. Watson, writing in the *Queensland Review* in 1885 called colonial federation 'the stepping-stone towards Imperial Federation and the unity of the great Colonial Empire of Queen Victoria';[4] and the *Publisher*, in 1886, foreshadowed actual outcomes when it suggested that federation of Australia was a patriotic duty which would allow the creation of a strong southern nation capable of defending itself and supplying troops for England when called upon.[5]

It was not just conservatives who supported worldwide federation. The potential social and economic benefits of a united empire – an imperial counterpart of today's European Union –

encouraged socialist supporters of labour reform, who favoured the strengthened protection this union would provide for internal trade. In fact, arguments between protectionists and free traders offer a close parallel with similar positions today, when the dominance of the World Trade Organization in a 'free' global economy arouses the suspicion of many, including some national industry lobby groups and 'old fashioned' socialists. Many early socialists were also protectionists, opposed to the free trade policies of the Imperial government, which seemed to them to increase the wealth of the privileged by the use of cheap foreign labour at the expense of British wage-earners within the Empire. This suspicion explains much of the Australian socialist resistance to Britain's open-handed treatment of Chinese immigrants, and recurs in many of the racist fictions of the time.

One socialist commentator who remarked on this tension at an early stage was the British writer and politician Sir Charles Dilke. In the 1860s the young Dilke travelled extensively around the world and spent some time in Australia. On his return to Britain he published a highly successful account of his travels, in which he argued strongly for a federated Empire. *Greater Britain: A Record of Travel in English-Speaking Countries*[6] was first published in 1868, going through multiple printings and several editions. It was still in print shortly before the First World War.

Dilke, who inherited a baronetcy on his father's death in 1869, might have been expected to be a confirmed supporter of the status quo. When in 1868 he entered parliament as MP for Chelsea, however, it was as one of the most radical members of Gladstone's reformist Liberal Party. He served as Under-Secretary for Foreign Affairs and President of the Local Government Board, and for a time was a supporter of British republicanism. He was defeated in 1886 (after a divorce scandal) but returned to Parliament in 1892 as a leading labour figure, and organised the labour members into a party. He was an ardent supporter of reform, saying firmly in *Greater Britain* that 'The existing system of labour is anti-democratic'. He was also not an English supremacist, writing in explanation of the title of his book that: 'the development of the England of Elizabeth is to be found, not in the Britain of Victoria, but in half the habitable globe. If two small islands are by courtesy styled "Great," America, Australia, India, must form a "Greater Britain"'.

Dilke's visit to Australia convinced him that the unrestricted movement of Chinese labour into the colonies, supported by British and colonial capitalists, was counter-productive:

> *The burthen of proof lies upon those who propose to destroy the rising nationality by assisting in the importation of a mixed multitude of negroes, Chinamen, Hill coolies, Irish and Germans, in order that the imports and exports of Victoria and New South Wales may be increased, and that there may be a larger number of so-called Victorians and New South Welsh to live in misery.*

Dilke accepted the conventional rank-ordering of races by intelligence, but was less certain of the conclusions to be drawn. Though his racism is far less overt than William Lane's, he expressed a similar fear for the future of British culture in direct competition with other races:

> *It would almost seem as though we were wrong in our common scales of preference; far from right in our use of the terms 'superior' and 'inferior' races.*
>
> *A well-taught white man can out reason or overreach a well-taught Chinaman or negro. But under some climatic conditions, the negro can outwork the white man; under almost all conditions, the Chinaman can outwork him.*
>
> *Where this is the case, is it not the Chinaman or the negro that should be called the better man? Call him what we may, will he not prove his superiority by working the Englishman off the soil?*

As did *The Chinese Question* a decade later, Dilke wrote of the forcible opening up of China under 'free trade' agreements. The intention of teaching the Chinese Empire the benefits of free trade, he suggested, might have been less successful than the lesson of the need for exclusion of foreigners which the Chinese experience had taught the colonies:

> Many Victorians, even those who respect and admire the Chinese, are in favour of the imposition of a tax upon the yellow immigrants, in order to prevent the destruction of the rising Australian nationality. They fear that otherwise they will live to see the English element swamped in the Asiatic throughout Australia. It is not certain that we may not some day have to encounter a similar danger in Old England.

The solution for Dilke is imperial federation, within which the 'silent revolution' of socialist reform can take place, with the wages-for-hire system 'giving place to ... a perfect marriage, in which the labourer and the capitalist shall be one'.

Another influential supporter of the ideal of a federated, reformed and protective Empire was the novelist Sir Walter Besant. Besant wrote a number of fictions aimed at provoking social reform (this led directly to the 1887 creation of the People's Palace in London – a place of affordable popular recreation). He also became the first chair of the Incorporated Society of Authors in 1884. His 1897 book, *The Rise of the Empire*,[7] was published as part of the 'Story of the Empire' series: a democratic project which aimed at educating the general public about the Empire so that voters at the imperial centre might make informed decisions on major issues.

Besant's contribution takes an overview of the formation of the Empire and the future of its inhabitants. He takes a sympathetic position in relation to such groups as the Aborigines: 'It is in our dealings with the native races whom we are dispossessing that we feel most compunctions of conscience...Nor can we justify a wrong thing because it happened to be done in pursuance of a right end'; but is firm in his belief in the ultimate rightness of colonisation, saying firmly that: 'The land should be occupied by those who can make the most and the best use of it'.

Like Dilke, Besant argues for a 'permanent Union' of sovereign states, 'not one being before or behind the other'. This union would, according to Besant, rely on 'common ancestry... common love of the Mother Country... possession of the same institutions, liberties, history, literature and art' and prevalence of religion. He also wanted to include the United States in 'a united Federation of the English-speaking States' in which 'no one country will have authority over another'. And again like Dilke, he gave no special preference to England, suggesting that the capital of such a federation would be somewhere convenient – perhaps London, perhaps Cape Town. Although his Darwinism is more convinced than Dilke's, Besant goes further than Dilke in his arguments for political and social change within the Empire, suggesting that the colonies and the United States had all refused to create aristocracies and – more optimistically – that England had already 'swept away all but the shreds of aristocratic privilege'. The six Anglo-Saxon nations, he asserted, 'are already, and will always remain, republics'.

Despite this optimism, the radical reformers at the heart of the Empire were heavily outnumbered by the conservatives. Even the colonial reformers were not proof against some of the tactics by which these people held the line. Banjo Paterson satirised one republican figure, George Richard Dibbs, Premier of New South Wales in the 1890s, who on a visit to England went over to the imperial side, accepting a knighthood from Queen Victoria:

> *This G. R. Dibbs was a stalwart man*
> *Who was built on a most extensive plan,*
> *And a regular staunch Republican.*
>
> *But he fell in the hands of the Tory crew*
> *Who said, 'It's a shame that a man like you*
> *Should teach Australia this nasty view.*
>
> *'From her mother's side she should ne'er be gone...'*[8]

Paterson's choice of words echoed William Lane's savage 1888 attack in *White or Yellow?* on the establishment figures who supported Chinese immigration. Lane had called them 'the tinsel knighthood with which the Imperial Government had attempted to debauch the colonial spirit'.⁹ In Paterson's 'The Ballad of G. R. Dibbs', the Tories offer to buy all the Australian leaders:

> 'With a tinsel title, a tawdry star
> Of a lower grade than our titles are,
> And a puff at a Prince's big cigar.'

The sense of betrayal was deep at a time of major economic depression in the colonies. Henry Lawson had mounted a more serious attack on Australian complacency just a few years earlier, addressing the savage treatment of the working class poor by a new class of industrial capitalists. 'Faces in the Street' brooked no compromise:

> *They lie, the men who tell us in a loud decisive tone*
> *That want is here a stranger, and that misery's unknown...*¹⁰

The poem is a scathing reminder of just how bad conditions could be for the marginalised underclass in a capitalist society: for the 'wan and weary' workers hurrying past 'like a pallid river' to jobs 'Yielding scarce enough to eat; for the city's unemployed upon his weary beat'; for the 'Woman of the Street' with her 'dreadful, thankless trade'; for the inhabitants of 'the filthy dens and slums...Where human forms shall rot away in sties for swine unmeet'.

Lawson intended 'Faces in the Street' as a serious warning for the Australian establishment. In its own way the poem is as radical as Lane's *White or Yellow?*. Lawson, however, did not rely on scapegoating; his vision of uprising is straightforward class warfare, a necessary cleansing by 'Red Revolution' like the Russian revolution thirty years later:

> *And, like a swollen river that has broken bank and wall,*
> *The human flood came pouring with the red flags over all,*
> *And kindled eyes all blazing bright with revolution's heat,*
> *And flashing swords reflecting rigid faces in the street –*
> *Pouring on, pouring on,*
> *To a drum's loud threatening beat,*

> *And the war-hymns and the cheering of the people in the street.*

Lawson was not alone in his dire predictions. Sydneysider Samuel Rosa, born in 1866, was Lawson's contemporary. Educated in Britain, Rosa worked as a journalist in the United States before returning to write for the Sydney periodicals, the *Truth* and the *Labor Daily*. Like William Lane, Rosa was an advocate of revolutionary socialism and was in fact expelled from the New South Wales Labor Party for his extreme views (he briefly formed his own socialist party). At a time when Australia's economy was severely shaken by the 1890s depression, Rosa produced a fictional projection of the possible revolutionary outcomes entitled *The Coming Terror: A Romance of the Twentieth Century*.[11] He paid for its publication in 1894, intending it as a warning of what Australia would face if it continued to pursue its capitalist course:

> *Crash! Crash!! Crash!!! went the falling timbers of the Austral Bank, while a furious and ferocious mob, drunken with wine and victory, shrieked, fought, and swore in front of the burning edifice.*

The mob is 'rendered savage by want, suffering, and oppression', caused by the domination of the economy by the Austral Bank. Currency depreciation, which does not affect institutions and wealthy individuals with transnational interests and is positively beneficial in boosting profits on exports, has ruined the middle classes. They are finally driven to the desperation of joining the working-class revolution. Rosa's new Australian order is led by Oliver Spence, who introduces a planned economy of fixed prices, equal wages for men and women, maximum hours and minimum weekly wages. So successful are his measures that Spence is appointed dictator. Rosa's idealism is tempered for us by knowledge of what happened to the Soviet Union under Josef Stalin; unlike Stalin, however, it would appear that Spence does not let power go to his head and remains a benevolent despot, working for the common good:

> ...the people had been swindled, plundered, and oppressed by corrupt ruling gangs called Parliaments. They would now see what could be done by the rule of one good, wise, and capable man.

Warnings of violent revolution by writers such as Rosa and Lawson were to be proved right elsewhere: the parallels with the advent of European communist dictatorships are clear. In the event, however, the predicted Australian revolution did not come. Nor did invasion, colonisation or the collapse of an Australian-British identity under the pressure of Chinese immigration. What came was Federation, under the imperial defence umbrella, and White Australia.

Wherever we turn, Federation in 1901 appears as the significant defining moment in the creation of a unified popular Australian identity. Not because it marked the shift from a 'colonial' to a 'post-colonial' mindset (support for republicanism declined after Federation), nor because it allowed the development of a distinctive cultural industry (the vigorous literary industry of the 1880s and '90s actually declined significantly in the twentieth century, swamped by British publishing), but because Federation provided for the popular consciousness the sense of a safe haven reached at last, a secure White berth within the protective enclosure of the British Empire's naval defences. Australians felt themselves protected both from the overly open-handed imperial policies that had encouraged Chinese immigration, and from external retribution for their anti-Chinese policies. It was possible, it seemed, to have the cake of imperial ties and, at the same time, to eat the cake of protectionism and isolation. The British Empire was the defensive bulwark behind which the exclusive new Australian Federation could develop its own policies of social equality and improved living standards for its white inhabitants. The significance of the moment was recognised and marked by the shapers of cultural identity.

Nettie Palmer was already sixteen years old at the time of Federation. Like many Australians of the period, she extended her education overseas in Britain and Europe. In 1914 she married journalist and writer Vance Palmer. Both were active workers for refugees from the Spanish Civil War and both became well-known voices on ABC radio. Together, they were instrumental in developing and defining the canon of Australian Literature.

In 1924 Nettie Palmer's Lothian Prize Essay, *Modern Australian Literature (1900-1923)*[12] boldly asserted that the new century was a 'milestone' for Australia, a turning point 'recognised by poets, politicians and patriots'. 'A sense of expectancy was in the air', wrote Palmer, an expectation that the combination of the new century and the new national status spelt a new psychological beginning: 'Perhaps the chief possession of Australian writers in the year 1901 was this consciousness of nationhood'.

Of course, the concept of a national literature was not new. In 1856 German immigrant Frederick Sinnett published the first extended critical account of Australian writing: 'The Fiction Fields of Australia'.[13] Sinnett came to Australia to escape the ravages of tuberculosis (a common and lethal disease in nineteenth-century Europe), helped found the *Melbourne Punch* and was lead writer for the *Argus* for three years from 1857-60. Dismissive of attempts to create a national identity by the appropriation of Aboriginal themes and local colour, Sinnett's analogy of landscape painting is striking for the detached, 'scientific' equivalence given to local flora and fauna, including the Aboriginal people themselves:

> *If Australian characteristics are too abundant – if blackfellows, kangaroos, emus, stringy barks, gums, and wattles, and any quantity of other things illustrative of the ethnology, zoology, and botany, of the country are crowded together, a greater amount of detailed information may be conveyed upon a given number of square inches of canvas than would otherwise be possible, but the picture loses character proportionately as a work of art.*

Equally, however, he recognised the difficulty of establishing a distinctive local voice in the absence of some historical sense of local culture:

> Unless we go into the Aboriginal market for 'associations',
> there is not a single local one, of a century old, to be
> obtained in Australia...

There were many further attempts at some kind of definition of a national literary culture, particularly in the numerous magazines and periodicals of the later part of the nineteenth century. In fact, Australia had a remarkably flourishing collection of such publications (though many were short-lived). The most significant was undoubtedly the Sydney publication, the *Bulletin*, founded in 1880. With its policy of actively encouraging local writers and themes, the *Bulletin* was central to the development of Australia's modern literary identity, and its cultural chauvinism made it the periodical most closely associated with Australian nationalism and the myths of Australian identity. Its early roll call of names reads like a *Who's Who* of the canon of early Australian literature, including figures like Banjo Paterson, Henry Lawson, Steele Rudd, Joseph Furphy and Norman Lindsay. Its cartoons too became famous, including work by artists such as Norman and Lionel Lindsay and David Low. The *Bulletin* supported the federation of the Australian colonies, an Australian republic and universal democracy, and proudly carried the masthead 'Australia for the Australians'. It also strenuously opposed imperial federation and Chinese immigration (or even the continued residence of Chinese in Australia). After the success of Australian Federation, it replaced its nationalistic masthead in 1908 with the uncompromisingly racist slogan: 'Australia for the White Man'.

There is no paradox here. Australia, in the modern sense, was founded on principles of egalitarianism and 'a fair go', but only for the White population. It was equally founded on officially sanctioned racism and defensive xenophobia, which amounted, initially, to a kind of collective paranoia about the Asian nations to the north. Once Federation was achieved and the principles of exclusion established, the paranoia began to recede. But it was a long, slow – and still far from complete – process. The initial decline of invasion fears that followed Federation can be traced in the reduced numbers of invasion fictions published. *The Coloured Conquest* (Rata, 1904) and *The Australian Crisis* (Kirmess, 1909) were both published prior to the First World War, but when Samuel Rosa published his book-length study, *The Invasion of Australia*,[14] in 1920 after the War, he was not predicting fearful outcomes for an undefended Australia. Instead, his book was a reasoned rebuttal of what he called the 'popular delusion': the 'Invasion Imposture' promoted by politicians like wartime Prime Minister Billy Hughes. Hughes had argued in 1916 that Australia's independent future was dependent on Britain's victory in the First World War. If Germany won, Hughes said, then Australia would be handed over as part of the prize.

Rosa drew on a wide range of technical studies of modern warfare and strategic analyses to argue that, regardless of the outcome of any conflict between Britain and Germany, such a handover could never have happened. He pointed to the logistical difficulty of transporting large numbers of troops and ancillaries by sea, even when an attacker had full control of the sea lanes. If, he argued, an enemy reached Australia in sufficient numbers to invade, the problems of getting ashore would be almost insurmountable. He pointed to Australia's own experience at Gallipoli, where Turkish defensive positions could not be taken by vastly superior invading forces, and where sixteen-inch naval guns were effectively outclassed by six-inch shore batteries with the advantage of height and defensive earthworks. The timber-decked battleship of the time was, he argued, vulnerable to shellfire from above (a theory amply demonstrated in the Second World War when the timber-decked, veteran battle cruiser, HMS *Hood*, was utterly destroyed by a direct hit from the German ship, *Bismarck*). The Gallipoli experience had also demonstrated the fighting spirit of Australian troops. Operating on home soil, Rosa believed, they would be undefeatable. And even if a landing could be made, the Australian environment was so hostile that an enemy force could not long survive and operate effectively against the co-ordinated guerrilla defences of Federated Australia.

Although Australian foreign policy continued to be dominated for many years by a nervous official reliance on Britain, the increased sense of security imparted by Federation would encourage writers to look beyond the narrowly exclusive confines of White Australia for their definitions of a national identity. Nettie Palmer's sense of 1901 as a psychological turning point would be amply borne out in the work of the first post-Federation generation of writers.

8

Stories of a White Australia

Change came slowly to the new Australian Federation. In 1908 the *Bulletin* affirmed its anti-Chinese principles when it replaced an earlier masthead with the uncompromisingly racist slogan: 'Australia for the White Man'. It would not be removed until 1960, the same year that the Labor party finally abandoned its use of the term 'White Australia'. Nevertheless, the very fact that an exclusive white Federation gave the nervous colonies a sense of increased security also meant that writers could afford to be less strident in their racism. With some of the larger threat of Asian invasion removed, the lesser irritant of the Aboriginal presence could be addressed in more moderate terms. A degree of concern for the Aborigines and the grosser abuses of simple humanity in relations between the cultures could even be expressed.

Historian W. K. (later Sir Keith) Hancock was born in 1898 and grew up in the new Australia. His reputation was founded on his book, *Australia*,[1] published in 1930. Its opening chapter, 'The Invasion of Australia', deals not with a European invasion of Aboriginal territory but with a metaphorical invasion of the land, in which 'adventurous pastoralists skirmished with drought and raided the desert'.

Hancock's Australia is 'British' in the generic sense promoted by the federalists: 'Many nations adventured for the discovery of Australia, but the British peoples alone have possessed her'. It is also a country in which 'occupation' is equated with the benefits of economic development: 'if to this day one-fifth of Australia remains completely unoccupied, that is because it is scarcely worth occupying'.

Hancock is thoroughly sympathetic to the Aborigines, but his positive description of their culture retains the essential social Darwinism that was a key feature of the White Australia policy. In Hancock's Australia, Aborigines, 'cut off from co-operative intelligence', have 'never imagined that first decisive step from the economy of the chase' which would have made them 'masters of the soil'. He continues:

> Instead they fitted themselves to the soil, modelling a complex civilisation of intelligent artificiality, which yet was pathetically helpless when assailed by the acquisitive society of Europe. The advance of British civilisation made inevitable 'the natural progress of the aboriginal race towards extinction' – it is the soothing phrase of an Australian Governor. In truth, a hunting and a pastoral economy cannot co-exist within the same bounds.

Hancock's sympathy is made possible in part by the psychological distancing of the Australian nation from the 'mother country', realised at Federation. For the new generation of Australians, to be 'British' in the generic sense was not the same as being British colonists. Hancock actually uses the term 'British' in two different ways: one that acknowledges common race; and one that recognises a separate nation. When he condemns early atrocities against the Aborigines, it is not his White Australia that bears the blame: 'sometimes the invading British did their wreckers' work with the unnecessary brutality of stupid children'. This sense of separateness from colonialism has proved a potent force in the slippage of Australian national memory about the historical appropriation of the continent. So effective was it that Hancock viewed white supremacy as an accomplished fact. He is quite able to regard the 'remnant' of the Aboriginal race as having, effectively, an alien status. Discussing their plight, he remarks that 'Australian democracy is genuinely benevolent, but is preoccupied with its own affairs'. He wonders whether remaining Aborigines might be 'saved' in 'well-policed local reserves in Central and Northern Australia', but immediately notes the economic unlikelihood of such expensive provision for an 'alien' people.

Then as now, Australian governments were reluctant to spend money on Aboriginal welfare. Hancock noted with some irony the prevailing cynicism of a political system which 'From time to time...remembers the primitive people whom it has dispossessed, and sheds over their predestined passing an economical tear'.

Revision of the past by nationalist commentators included revision of the literary canon. Writers who seemed to represent the colonialism of the nineteenth century were excised. Henry Kingsley's novel, *The Recollections of Geoffry Hamlyn* (1859) had been hailed at the time of publication as the best novel written about Australia. Rolf Boldrewood drew heavily on it when he wrote *Robbery Under Arms*, and the only real criticism of it in Australian journals was that its mention of shipwrecks on the Victorian coast might discourage potential immigrants. Even the *Bulletin* approved of *Geoffry Hamlyn*. But the fact that the novel dealt with the pre-gold rush world of the squatters, and was representative of its time in that its middle-class English central characters came to Australia to make their fortunes, was enough to blacken it for literary revisionists. Worse still, according to Joseph Furphy's attack on the novel in *Such is Life*, Kingsley's characters were 'English' in their cultural attitudes and behaviour. Such a picture of Australian identity did not suit the post-Federation image of commitment to a new nation built on egalitarian labour, and it was easy enough to dismiss Kingsley on the ground that he had spent 'only' five years in the colonies.

The process of revision continued apace. Rex Ingamells (1913-55) was born just before the First World War, and published his first book of verse, *Gumtops*, in 1935, more than a decade after Nettie Palmer's influential essay. His literary nationalism was complemented by his membership of the Australia First movement, founded in 1941 by the cultural commentator P. R. Stephensen. Ingamells' literary manifesto, *Conditional Culture*,[2] was published in 1938, and explained his use of the term 'Jindyworobaks' as a label for what he hoped would become a new national literary movement. According to Ingamells, who borrowed the term from the glossary entry 'Jindy-worabak' in James Devaney's short story collection *The Vanished Tribes* (1929), 'Jindyworobak' was an Aboriginal word meaning 'to annex, to join'. Ingamells saw it as representative of those who 'are endeavouring to free Australian art from whatever alien influences trammel it'. His intention was to give Australians 'a suitable thought-idiom' for nature, so that they could develop their 'spiritual and emotional' potential. He claimed (somewhat immodestly) that from this start 'Australian culture will grow'.

The culture that Ingamells planned was, however, an essentially artificial construct, a White Australian literary culture that was connected with its 'roots' only by that central act of appropriation of Aboriginal terms. Ingamells' cultural annexation paralleled the wider appropriation of Aboriginal lands by white settlers, but he seems to have been unaware of the irony of adopting the anglicised form of an Aboriginal word – 'Jindyworobak' – the translation of which ('to annex') carried undertones of violent action by one nation against another. In his children's book, *Aranda Boy: An Aboriginal Story* (1952),[3] Ingamells offers a sympathetic portrait of Aborigines in their first contact with pastoralists, but resolves the clash by incorporating the displaced tribe into the pastoral industry.

P. R. ('Inky') Stephensen was another of the post-Federation writers who helped shape the new culture, with the 1936 publication of *The Foundations of Culture in Australia: An Essay Towards National Self-Respect*.[4] He was a Rhodes scholar at Oxford University, where his early communist sympathies nearly led to the termination of his studies. He became business manager for the Fanfrolico Press, which published work by the Lindsay brothers, and founded the Mandrake Press, which published D. H. Lawrence. He was part of the artistic scene in London, but after severe financial difficulties he returned to Australia in 1932. He set up his own company in Australia, publishing a number of authors, including 'Henry Handel Richardson' (pen name of the writer Eleanor Dark), and was instrumental in the revisions to Xavier Herbert's first novel, *Capricornia* (1938).

Despite his previous communist sympathies, in the 1930s Stephensen's politics moved towards a form of right-wing nationalism. As foundation President of Australia First in 1941, he espoused Australian isolation and extreme nationalism. Australia First was anti-English, anti-semitic and anti-communist, and even expressed sympathy for imperial Japan and Nazi Germany. The movement was later satirised by Xavier Herbert in his novel, *Poor Fellow My Country* (1975). Sixteen members of Australia First, including Stephensen, were arrested and interned in 1942, and Stephensen himself was considered such a threat to national security that he remained interned until 1945.

Australia First and the Jindyworobaks sought to create a national identity by deliberately alienating many of the major international influences of the period and appropriating some of the forms of Aboriginal culture. At the same time, however, other writers were less concerned with defining the boundaries of a possible 'Australian' identity than with the harsh realities of the interaction between White Australia and its marginalised indigenous inhabitants.

The sexual use of indigenous women by white men had long been a problem, with significant social stigma being attached to white men who chose to 'go black'. The predominant white excuse that such relationships could be dismissed as merely physical and devoid of real emotional attachment was challenged in the early twentieth century by a number of writers. In 1913, English biologist and writer E. L. G. Watson published his first story, 'Out There', in the *English Review*.[5] Watson had travelled during 1910-11, with anthropologist Radcliffe Brown and Daisy Bates, among the Kimberley Aborigines and was deeply concerned by the way whites treated them. 'Out There' portrays an eternal triangle – white man, black woman, white woman – in which the black-white relationship is affirmed and the harmony of Aboriginal life with the land is endorsed. Watson went on to write a good many more works of various kinds, including six novels with Australian settings. In *The Desert Horizon* (1923), Watson addresses the problems of accommodation between isolated white settlers and indigenous peoples in the North West, while *Where Bonds Are Loosed* (1914) concentrates more on relationships between the white settlers themselves in remote areas. One of the first white writers to represent indigenous culture in an unprejudiced way, Watson's position remained one of support for Aboriginal culture and outrage at its continued debasement at the hands of whites.

Discussion of pastoral expansion and the comcomitant issue of black-white miscegenation in the far north was later continued by novelist Jessie Litchfield, whose *Far North Memories* (1930)[6] places the blame for most murders in the North squarely on 'unauthorised interference with gins'. This socially sensitive issue of black-white sexual interaction was further developed in the fiction of the 1920s by two prominent Australian writers, Vance Palmer and Katharine Susannah Prichard, both of whom rejected the dismissive 'black velvet' stereotype (a common description for a liking by white men for sex with Aboriginal women) and offered more sensitive accounts of such relationships. In Palmer's 1928 novel, *The Man Hamilton*,[7] the white Hamilton of the title rejects a white governess in favour of his Aboriginal 'wife' and son; while in his next book, *Men Are Human*,[8] the situation is reversed, and the white man Boyd rejects the pregnant 'half-caste' Josie for a white woman, Barbara.

But perhaps the best known of early twentieth-century works sympathetic to the Aboriginal perspective is Katharine Susannah Prichard's *Coonardoo*,[9] which shared the 1928 *Bulletin* novel prize. Prichard (1883-1969) was a colourful character. She was born in Fiji, the daughter of the editor of the *Fiji Times*. She grew up in Tasmania, then Melbourne. She worked as a governess, then as a freelance journalist for the Melbourne *Herald*, before leaving for England to pursue her career as a novelist. Her first book, *The Pioneers* (1915), won the Hodder & Stoughton novel prize and was made into an Australian film (twice, once in 1916 and again in 1926). Prichard returned to Australia in 1916, married Hugo Throssell in 1919, and moved to Western Australia. She was deeply involved in politics, becoming a founding member of the Communist Party in 1920. A tireless worker for women's rights, she co-founded the Perth Unemployed Women and Girls' Association and, when the Labor Party excluded women from the movement against war and fascism, she founded the Modern Women's Club in 1938. She held numerous posts, notably as president of the Australian Writers' League, and was nominated by the Fellowship of Australian Writers for the Nobel prize.

Prichard combined politics with fiction in works such as *Black Opal* (1921) and *Working Bullocks* (1926), then in *Coonardoo* she tackled the vexed question of black-white relationships. The novel is a beautiful evocation of bush life in the north-west of Western Australia and tells the tragedy of a love story marred by cultural taboos. The Coonardoo of the title is an Aboriginal girl, raised on a cattle station, and has fallen in love with the station owner, Hugh Watt, a proud man who suppresses his own reciprocal love for her. Coonardoo, described as 'his dark soul', is always associated with the land itself, with the spirit of the station, Wytaliba. She is bound to Hugh all her life through ties of land and duty. She nurses Hugh through his delirium after his mother's death, bears his child, acts as servant to his new wife. She stands by him through the years, until Hugh learns by accident that she has been raped by his enemy Geary. He assaults her and bans her from the station – actions which result in her death.

The prejudices of the time are still at work here: in the Foreword to the first edition, Prichard asserts her novel's verisimilitude through an appeal to authority, telling her readers that, before publication, the manuscript was checked by 'Mr Ernest Mitchell...Chief Inspector of Aborigines for Western Australia'. She goes on to refer to the Aborigines Department and various regulations, such as one 'to prevent white men from taking rooms for a gin, or half-caste, in a hotel'. The reader is warned that:

> People who see the blacks only along the transcontinental line, or when they have become poor, degraded and degenerate creatures, as a result of contact with towns and the vices of white people, cannot understand how different they are in their natural state, or on isolated stations of the Nor'-West where they are treated with consideration and kindness.

But, curiously, she also refers to social Darwinism as a justification for writing about them:

> Basedow in The Australian Aboriginal says, 'Anthropological relationship connects the Australian (including the proto-Australian) with the Veddahs and Dravidians of India and with the fossil men of Europe, from whom the Caucasian element has sprung.' They are only a few generations removed, after all, Coonardoo and Andromache. 'In other words, the Australian aboriginal stands somewhere near the bottom rung of the great evolutional ladder we have ascended.' His and our 'racial development was very early dissassociated from the Mongoloid and Negroid lines'.

With this statement comes commentary about the innate value of the Aboriginal corroboree songs, some of which are 'in a dead language', while others have meanings which Aborigines 'are reluctant to give'. It is a combination that suggests that Prichard, like so many white Australians, shares the belief that Aboriginal people are a doomed race, existing beyond their time. And yet the novel is at pains to point out that the 'blacks' have true cause for complaint against the white settlers who dispossessed them. As old-timer Saul points out in conversation with Hugh and his citified wife Mollie: 'No black ever did to a white man what white men have done to the blacks'.

Mollie, who came from one of the coastal towns, 'had acquired the belief that it was a divine right of white men to ride roughshod over anything aboriginal which stood in their way'. She protests that 'the abos are filthy and treacherous'. Hugh is horrified, and responds: 'No, girl...they're not treacherous – except when they've been treacherously dealt with. And filthy? You never saw a wild black look as dirty as a native about the towns'. The abuses of Aborigines by white settlers are detailed here, ending with Saul's descriptions of some of the more infamous instances:

> 'You can't help seein' the blacks' point of view. White men came, jumped their hunting grounds, went kangaroo shooting for fun. The blacks speared cattle. White men got shootin' blacks to learn 'em. Blacks speared a white man or two – police rode out on a punishing expedition. They still ride out on punishin' expeditions...'
>
> 'Didn't police in the coastal towns get one and sixpence a head for abos they brought in?' Hugh asked.
>
> 'Reduced to a shilling after a bit... The police was makin' a good thing out of 'punitive expeditions'. Used to bring the niggers in, in chains, leather straps round the neck, fastened to their stirrup irons. Twenty or thirty like that, and I've seen the soles of a boy's feet raw when he came in. Never spend eighteen pence a nob on 'em either. Police'd let one or two men hunt for the rest, bring in kangaroo.
>
> 'And there was black-birding, too... I've seen blacks brought in, in chains for the pearlers' crews...'

Although it is now considered an Australian classic, *Coonardoo* had a stormy reception. The *Bulletin*, supporter of the White Australia policy, was unprepared for the backlash from readers outraged at the inter-racial material – so much so that it rejected Vance Palmer's 1929 work, *Men Are Human*, because it could not risk a second outcry. The editor of the time wrote to Palmer:

> On reconsideration, we have decided that we can't print Men Are Human – *at any rate in its present form. I am sorry, because it is so well done, but our disastrous experience with* Coonardoo *shows us that the Australian public will not stand stories based on a white man's relation*

with an Australian Aborigine... There is no chance, I suppose, of you whitewashing the girl?[10]

The *Bulletin*'s decision not to publish Palmer's work was an incidence of covert censorship in response to public opinion. But public opinion was equally shaped by official censorship. The *Commonwealth Customs Act*, passed at the time of Federation, banned the import of 'blasphemous, indecent or obscene' materials. It was supplemented by State legislation covering such key areas as defamation.

Such interlocking laws could be used to great effect by governments keen to suppress debate or restrict the flow of information to the public. The conservative 1930s federal administration of Joseph Lyons was particularly zealous in its application of import controls. In 1936, for instance, when the *Bulletin* tried to discover which titles were on the list of banned materials, its reporter was told that even the list was banned. In the same year, an anti-Nazi play by American playwright Clifford Odets, *Till the Day I Die*, was banned by the New South Wales Chief Secretary, after a protest by the German consul in Sydney. The ban was not lifted until 1941, two years after the outbreak of war, when the State government was quite sure that Germany could no longer be regarded as a 'friendly power' which should not be offended by literary attacks.

Political censorship of general Australian publications increased during the Second World War and stayed firmly in place in the period that followed. This interventionist policy is evident in the censorship of works such as M. Barnard Eldershaw's *Tomorrow and Tomorrow*,[11] which was cut heavily before its original publication on the grounds that it was politically subversive – thus ironically demonstrating the power of the pervasive forces of heavy-handed government described within the text. 'M. Barnard Eldershaw' was the collaborative pseudonym of Marjorie Faith Barnard (1897-1987) and Flora Sydney Patricia Eldershaw (1897-1956), a partnership that had Barnard doing most of the writing and Eldershaw being more active in planning and critical functions.

Tomorrow and Tomorrow, the fifth of their novels, was by Barnard alone; the censored 1947 edition was restored and reissued by Virago in 1983, as *Tomorrow and Tomorrow and Tomorrow*. The book is an extrapolative fiction of the future, in which the twenty-fourth century narrator, Knarf, resident of the Tenth Commune (formerly the Riverina), is writing an historical novel based on Australian life from 1920 to the 1950s. The opening sequence looks back from the dreary Asiatic utopian socialist civilisation that Australia has become, to discuss its political and social antecedents. Knarf's description of the lost Aboriginal race is an elegiac confirmation of the fate of the tribes as projected by nineteenth-century writers: total extinction. Knarf writes that the Aboriginals, the 'First People', had lived in the land:

> ...according to its terms without changing it or penetrating it. The pattern of their lives wound, like a kabbalistic sign traced in water, through the bush. Their apparently free roaming had followed a set tide. Their food supply, since they did not intervene in nature save in the spearing of game, was bound upon the seasons. Within this cycle of nature was the human cycle, the pattern of contacts, the linking invisible trade routes, the crossing and recrossing of tribe with tribe, the circulation of thought and knowledge as natural and primitive as the circulation of blood within the body. Within the human cycle was a mystic cycle, the linking of rites and places, of ceremonies that were symbols of symbols forgotten even in the beginning of time but that continued to draw men through old, remembered ways.

This is not a view of the vanished tribespeople as noble savages, but rather as peaceable earlier inhabitants, whose nomadic lifestyle could not withstand the onslaught of 'progress' when the white settlers arrived. From the twenty-fourth century perspective, the Aboriginal people are:

> Far away, reduced by distance of time to outline, theirs was only another arrangement of the eternal pattern, of eating,

*communicating, and reaching out into the unknown. They
were gone. Completely and utterly, nothing was left of them
but a few rock drawings, a few spearheads in rosy quartz,
some patterns incised on wood, the words of some songs, soft,
melancholy, their meaning forever sealed.*

In M. Barnard Eldershaw's extrapolation, the white settlers, the Second People, have not fared any better. In a passage that echoes some of the socialist fictions of the late nineteenth century, the causes for the decline of the Second People are spelt out. Although they conquered the land, their foolish policies left them vulnerable and they too are now extinct:

*The Australians, of whom the Pioneers were part, had been
the second people. They had been so few, never more than
eight or nine million in the whole continent. They had been
a very strange people, full of contradictions, adaptable and
obstinate. With courage and endurance they had pioneered
the land, only to ruin it with greed and lack of forethought.
They had drawn a hardy independence from the soil and
had maintained it with pride and yet they had allowed
themselves to be dispossessed by the most fantastic tyranny
the world had ever known, money in the hands of the few,
an unreal, an imaginary system driving out reality. They
had their hardbitten realism and yet they co-operated in the
suicidal fiction of production for profit instead of for use.
They thought of Australia as a land of plenty and yet they
consented to starve among the plenty. They lost the reality
of their land to the fantasy of the Banks. They looked
always to Government for redress and assistance but they
were always scornful of their governments and with a
persistent lawless streak in them.*

The 'Second People' are thought of as having been 'Tough, sardonic, humorous, they were romantics the like of which the world had never seen. Crusaders without a crusade, they fought for any cause that offered...fighting throughout the world...for brave words and a coloured rag'. Their loyalty to Britain proved fruitless and destructive. The narrator Knarf 'could think of the Australians as living in a perpetual high gale of unreason', divided and helpless in their cities when competition merged into monopoly and they were sold out by their institutions. When the 'dark age' came, many of the descendants of the Pioneers chose migration from their mortgaged farms, heading beyond the Murrumbidgee into the wilderness beyond, thinking to start again with their cattle and their sheep. But they were exiles, barred from commerce, unable to sell their wool, unable to keep their flocks alive, eking out a meagre existence until they:

> ...were as tough, as thin, and almost as black from the sun, as the First People had been, but, unlike the First People, they had no festivals, no corroborees, no old rites. They were scaled down to something below that. It is said that as a people they stopped breeding.

In the twenty-fourth century of the novel, they have become part of folklore, their ghosts haunting solitary lands, with their ghost dogs and ghost flocks.

In this future world the remnants of the white Australian race still exist inland, where 'blood mingles slowly' and the men are taller, less compact, less Asiatic in appearance. The parallels with the situation of people of mixed Aboriginal-white blood in twentieth-century Australia are clear. The book uses a tried and tested fictional device, forcing the comfortable reader into the position of a marginalised people, disturbing the certainties of racial and cultural dominance.

Where *Tomorrow and Tomorrow* relies on the impact of a speculative future to makes its point, Xavier Herbert's first novel, *Capricornia*,[12] is set firmly in the uncomfortable realities of the present. Xavier Herbert (1901-1984) was another major writer who grew up in the immediate post-Federation period. He trained as a pharmacist, but later wandered around northern Australia working in various jobs. The experiences of this time formed the basis for *Capricornia*. Perhaps his best-known work, which returns to some of the difficult Aboriginal themes raised in *Capricornia*, is *Poor Fellow My Country*, published in 1975 (and the longest novel ever published in Australia).

Capricornia adopts from the start a heavily ironic tone about relations between settlers and Aborigines. In the opening chapter, 'The Coming of the Dingoes', Herbert describes how the first settlement in Capricornia (the Northern Territory) 'was set up on what was perhaps the most fertile and pleasant part of the coast and on the bones of half the Karrapillua Tribe'. The place that eventually became the only real town on the coast was originally 'a Corroboree Ground of the Larrapuna Tribe, who left the bones of most of their number to manure it'.

Herbert uses an entirely Australian metaphor to acknowledge the power of social Darwinism in the colonising process. But the picture created has none of the sanitised 'objectivity' of so much of the earlier writing, nor the romanticisation of the image of doomed tribes. Herbert's vision of 'natural' extinction is red in tooth and claw: 'When dingoes come to a waterhole, the ancient kangaroos, not having teeth or ferocity sharp enough to defend their heritage, must relinquish it or die'.

He is equally uncompromising in his description of the aftermath, when the Aboriginal survivors eke out an existence on the margins of white society:

> [T]he civilizing was so complete that the survivors of the original inhabitants numbered seven, of whom two were dying of consumption in the Native Compound, three confined in the Native Lazaret with leprosy, the rest, a man and a woman, living in a gunyah at the remote end of Devilfish Bay, subsisting on what they could get from the bush and the sea and what they could buy with the pennies the man earned by doing odd jobs and the woman by prostitution.

But where Xavier Herbert took an uncompromising stand on the destructive and degrading results of white Australia's successful occupation of the continent, most popular writers were content to offer a less confrontational view. Mary Grant Bruce

(1878-1958), like Nettie Palmer, was born long enough before Federation to bring to the new era some of the attitudes of the nineteenth century. Like so many of the writers of this period, Bruce began her publishing career as a journalist, with the Melbourne *Age* and the *Leader*. She went to London in 1912 and married her second cousin, Major George Evans Bruce. They divided the remainder of their lives between Ireland and Australia.

Bruce was a phenomenally successful and prolific writer of children's books. She wrote thirty-seven novels between 1910 and 1946, and is probably best known for the 'Billabong' books. Set on a Victorian station called 'Billabong', these books created an idealised type of the pastoral world in the new White Australia and were extremely influential in fixing popular perceptions of what it meant to be 'Australian'. Stock characters include Lee Wing, the vegetable gardener, Black Billy, the rouseabout, Brownie, the housekeeper, and Murty O'Toole, the stockman. The family, too, is stereotyped into its gender roles.

Bruce's portrayal of Chinese and Aboriginal characters is fully aware of relative status, based on those rankings of the races developed by social Darwinists. Aborigines remain potentially threatening and unreliable savages, but are childlike and amenable when brought within the influence of station life. In *Billabong Riders*,[13] for example, Rob encounters an Aborigine and initially holds back: 'He was not very big, and strange blackfellows might not be friendly'. Even when the 'blackfellow' is identified as Jacky, Rob remains suspicious: 'they had no proof that he was really a station hand. He certainly looked dirty and ugly enough for anything'.

The Chinese are treated rather better. In *Billabong Adventurers*,[14] the motivation of the young Li Chang is explained in terms of parental obedience, honour and duty. But when he is rescued from kidnappers who have starved and tortured him, Li Chang's picture of his rescuers reflects Bruce's rather hazy understanding of Chinese religion. Bruce cannot resist privileging the European characters through Li Chang's eyes: 'They were, he felt sure, gods who had come to his rescue, so tall and strong they seemed, so full of quiet authority'.

In the adult field of crime fiction, Arthur Upfield (1890-1964) was best-known for his series of mysteries featuring the part-Aboriginal Detective-Inspector Napoleon Bonaparte. Upfield arrived in Australia from Britain in 1910 and, like Herbert, worked at a variety of outback occupations. His first novel was published in 1928 and was followed a year later by *The Barrakee Mystery*,[15] which introduced the figure of Bonaparte, or 'Bony', who combined the mysterious intuition of his Aboriginal mother with the reasoning powers of his white father to solve crimes. The introduction of an Aborigine as the central character of a popular fiction was a bold move, and certainly intended by Upfield as a positive representation. The stereotyping of the qualities belonging to each race is, however, a reminder of the much older nineteenth-century division between rational adult males and their inferior emotional counterparts – women, children and savages (who were regarded as honorary children).

A.E. Martin (1885-1955) worked in advertising and publicity for the publishing industry, but did not begin his writing career until he won a *Women's Weekly* competition for new novels in 1942. His books included a range of crime mysteries, and his short story, 'The Power of the Leaf',[16] revisits a first contact incident. Set in 1847, the bulk of the story is told from the point of view of an Aboriginal 'detective' who tries to understand what has actually caused the death of a young man of another tribe. The man's companion has confessed, but no-one can offer a reasoned explanation of how a small hole in the forehead could have killed someone. The clues are strange tracks, branches broken at a height that could only be reached by a man on another's shoulders, and so on. The reader is left to work out the significance of these clues, which are finally tied together by a second, much shorter account of the same incident, in a diary entry that records a brief visit by a group of Europeans, during which a 'native' is accidentally shot.

Again, Martin's intention is entirely positive. But again, the 'Aboriginal' voice of the story suffers from its positioning within a European genre. Like historical detective tales which almost inevitably suffer from the anachronism of trying to introduce individual deductive reasoning into periods when it was simply not usual, 'The Power of the Leaf' cannot really overcome the difficulty of pitting deductive logic against 'superstition' within a single culture that does not recognise either concept. The resolution, which provides the ordering conclusion of the tale, is entirely European. Nevertheless, Martin's story is a remarkable attempt to 'think' the reader into the perspective of another culture at a time when, despite a hundred and fifty years of contact, few white Australians knew much at all about indigenous culture.

Treatment of Aboriginal themes was on the increase in the 1950s, but the majority of works adopted an essentially white point of view. One of the better-known examples is *Walkabout*,[17] first published in 1959 under the title *The Children*. It was made into a film in 1971, and in this form became an icon of the Australian rejection of the city – part of a world-wide back-to-nature movement that followed on from 1960s 'flower power'. *Walkabout*'s author, James Vance Marshall (1887-1964), was a union organiser, a radical associate of Henry Lawson and an anti-conscription agitator who was jailed in the First World War. He, too, was a journalist and worked in a range of outback jobs, travelling the world from post to post. He eventually became an administrative officer with the Australian Immigration Office in the 1950s.

Walkabout features a relationship between an adolescent white girl and her brother, who are rescued in the outback by an Aboriginal boy. The book's representation of Aboriginal culture is highly romanticised, harking back to the early days of the 'noble savage'. The girl's naïve rejection of the boy's advances leads to his death, but he forgives her at the end, in an act of reconciliation that bears little relation to actual black-white interaction of the period.

Ion Idriess (1889-1979) was another writer who romanticised Aboriginal life. Idriess began work in the mining industry, and then worked in many and various jobs around Australia, including deckhand, rabbit-catcher, boundary-rider, opal-miner, pearler, station-hand, gold fossicker, surveyor and crocodile hunter. He worked in Queensland, the Northern Territory, Papua and the Torres Strait Islands, and in the First World War served in the Australian Light Horse. Before the War he began contributing to the *Bulletin*, but his first real writing success came in 1931 with *Lasseter's Last Ride*,[18] which told the story of the fabulous gold reef that Harold Lasseter claimed to have discovered in central Australia. The book went through seventeen print runs in four years and set Idriess on a writing career that saw him produce more than forty books.

Idriess' work drew heavily on his own experiences but, like Mary Grant Bruce, he offered an idealised picture of the outback Australia he loved. *Nemarluk: King of the Wilds*,[19] published in 1941, drew a highly romanticised portrait of Aboriginal tribal life under a Northern Territory chief. The character of Idriess' book can be gauged from his own comparison of the chief with American author Edgar Rice Burroughs' fanciful creation, Tarzan of the Apes. Idriess called his chief 'a living Tarzan of the Wilds'. And in one of his later works, *The Red Chief*,[20] Idriess offered a heroic picture of the life and death of a warrior chief. The book is prefaced by the 'real' story of the desecration of the chief's grave site by a white scientist, who is collecting skeletal remains for research. Although Idriess appropriates the dead man's life story to a European romantic tradition, the book is entirely sympathetic to a displaced Aboriginal past.

There were others, too. Bert Vickers (1903-85) was born in England, and moved to Australia in 1925 where, like so many other of these popular writers of the period, he went through a series of outback jobs before moving into journalism. Two of his works, *The Mirage*[21] (1955) and *No Man is Himself*[22] (1970), deal with the problems of race relations in Australia. *The Mirage* looks at the difficulties faced by people of part-Aboriginal descent, while *No*

Man is Himself offers an indictment of the white treatment of Aborigines. Vickers was a keen supporter of land rights, sympathetic to the Aboriginal cause; but his work conveys a sense of the failure of the Aborigine in white society.

In *Yandy*[23] (1959) Donald Stuart (1913-83) tackled the story of the 1946 Stockmen's Strike at the Pindan Co-operative, an attempt to challenge the system of Aboriginal segregation and low pay. Two other books, *Yaralie*[24] (1962) and *Ilbarana*[25] (1971) deal with Aboriginal subjects, and Stuart wrote a sequel to the second book, *Malloonkai*, in 1976. Like Idriess, Stuart's work has a tendency to romanticise its Aboriginal subjects, and this provoked at least one response – an attempt by Gavin Casey (1907-64), a journalist and short story writer, to balance the romanticism with harsh social reality. Like the earlier writers Prichard, Litchfield and Vance Palmer, Casey's novel *Snowball*[26] (1958) also examines issues of white-black interaction and intermarriage.

This infiltration of an Aboriginal presence into the popular imagination had of course been going on since the earliest days of settlement, but the distinctive difference in these works is the attempt, however imperfect, to understand Aborigines as individuals with their own cultural perspective and world view, which could be approached as something alternative to rather than inferior to European culture.

This change of attitude is most strikingly represented in a popular account of the history of Australian literature, written for children and published in 1962. *How Australian Literature Grew*,[27] by Enid Moodie Heddle & Iris Millington, contains an extensive analysis of pre-European storytelling. Chapter Two, 'Makers of Myths & Legends', states baldly that the white settlers:

> ...*knew little about aboriginal life before coming to Australia and they were wrong in thinking the country had no art and no human history recorded in words before the white men came, for the lives of the aborigines had always been filled with songs and stories of their tribal history, their laws and their customs...*

There had been many previous collections of Aboriginal 'myths and legends' by white writers. Titles such as Mary Anne Fitzgerald's *King Bungaree's Pyalla and Stories Illustrative of Manners and Customs that Prevailed Among Australian Aborigines*[28] (1891) offered 'retold' stories for a popular audience. Enid Moodie Heddle herself had produced *The Boomerang Book of Australian Legendary Tales*[29] in 1957, drawing on previous collections by well-known figures like Catherine Langloh Parker, whose own *Australian Legendary Tales* had appeared in 1896. *How Australian Literature Grew*, however, does not merely appropriate the tales for a white audience seeking new sensations. Instead, the book gives an extensive and detailed account of creation stories, their cultural significance and how they are transmitted. And in concluding this section of the book, Heddle and Millington are clear about the relativity of cultural values:

> When Roland Robinson sat down in the sand with Albert Namatjira and was shown his totem stone and told by him some of the legends of his tribe, he knew that he was listening to a man who had a knowledge of very ancient things, more important to aboriginal life than the form of art in the pictures by which most Australians know Namatjira.

The important point here is not the acceptance of Namatjira as an Aborigine of good standing in mainstream Australian culture, but the recognition and acceptance of the different scale of values in Namatjira's own culture. With its use of terms like 'totem' and 'legend' this remains the outsider's point of view, locating Aboriginal artefacts and traditions in the world of 'primitive' cultures. But the book seeks deliberately to avoid a judgement that the white valuation is superior.

Albert Namatjira's paintings, which have become highly collectable in the Australian art market, used European techniques to represent the land. For the white community of the time his work offered an acceptable and easily understood way to 'connect' with the land through Aboriginal eyes. Namatjira's painting was safe for a popular audience because it did not seem to require an effort of comprehension (though more recently it has been revalued in terms of its specifically Aboriginal understanding of the land it represents).

Namatjira himself was a victim of the double standards of effective apartheid imposed within White Australia. With the assistance of artist Rex Battarbee, Namatjira exhibited a number of times during the 1930s to the 1950s and was fêted in the southern states. But in the Northern Territory he was unable to obtain a grazing lease or build a house in Alice Springs. He was granted citizenship in 1957 (Aborigines at that time were not normally considered full Australian citizens and were regarded as ceasing to be Aboriginal if citizenship was granted), but he then fell foul of the law and was jailed for supplying alcohol to an Aborigine. He died shortly after his release. Under these circumstances, the extraordinary thing about this account of the meeting between Namatjira and Robinson is the assertion that the 'totem stone' and 'legends' might in any context be of greater value than the paintings so highly valued by the white community.

How Australian Literature Grew accepts that what is valued by indigenous culture is important for that reason alone. It accepts that the same land may be occupied by two cultures, with different value systems and different ways of communicating. It also implies that these differences do not have to be in direct competition; that they may, in fact, peacefully and rewardingly co-exist. The laws of this period still actively discriminated against Aborigines, but in some of the writing at least there were clear signs of change in social attitudes towards race relations.

All of us are bound by the cultural conditions of our childhood. We grow up believing the world is as it is; that our view of things is a state of nature. The picture of cross-cultural understanding presented by *How Australian Literature Grew* might not have been universal in 1962, or even widely held. But when a popular literary history written for children could adopt such a position, the beginnings of reconciliation seemed to be in sight.

9

Cultural Reconciliation

Early in 1942, Japan seemed poised to capture the Australian protectorate of New Guinea. White Australia's worst nightmares of invasion by the 'yellow peril' were about to come true. Then came the defeat of the previously unstoppable Japanese forces, first in the Battle of the Coral Sea, then on the Kokoda trail. These events helped focus popular perceptions of Australian identity in the modern world through two powerful emotions – terror of invasion, and pride in military victory. The pride helped reinforce a sense of Australia's capacity to defend itself without what had proved to be the illusory protection of British naval power. But any lingering complacency about the long-term security of White Australia was shattered by the narrowness of the escape from Japanese invasion. The post-war government turned to the United States for military support, and to Europe for the mass of white immigrants who could quickly populate the empty and vulnerable continent.

Australia opened its arms to the Balts, fair-skinned northerners, and other 'Aryan' types (if government ministers were aware of the ironic similarities of this immigration program to Hitler's recent racial policies, they were not about to publicise the fact). Under the assisted migration scheme, the British working classes of the old country were sold the dream of an Australian future. And, when these were still not enough, Australia took the southern Europeans, darker-skinned Mediterraneans from Italy and from Greece. Anything, rather than admit the peoples from the North, or other 'coloured races'.

Although every effort was made to preserve the monoculture, to absorb and re-educate the newcomers, and turn them into new White Australians, this influx of other cultures began to have its inevitable effect. Anglo-Australians who had grown up knowing no other culture began, like many of the demobbed service people who had served overseas, to understand that difference was not in itself a threat. Official policy might still have sought to preserve the monocultural ideal, but on the street and on the beach, in backyards and in milk bars, Australian society began to change.

The Vietnam War was the catalyst for widespread public expression of that change. When Australian forces took the fight into Asia itself, public opinion was polarised. Many people, some with memories of turn-of-the-century invasion fears, some with more immediate experience of Japanese expansion, embraced US President Nixon's 'domino theory': the belief that the fall of one south-east Asian state to communism would lead to the weakening and collapse of the next, and so on, until Australia itself was next. Others saw Australia riding on the coat-tails of America, as it had once ridden on those of Britain. They rejected involvement in yet another foreign war. And despite strict censorship, Australia did not prove immune to the sea change in attitudes among young people that swept the Western world in the 1960s: the Vietnam War became a focus for radical discontent with the values and policies of the Menzies era.

The war had other unexpected effects. Eventually the United States bowed to domestic opposition to the human and material costs of an unwinnable war, and abandoned the South Vietnamese government to its fate. The North Vietnamese victory sent a flood of refugees into neighbouring countries, and onto the sea, in search of a new life. In a world that had been changed by the war against Nazism, and the foundation of the United Nations, Australia found itself grudgingly accepting another kind of Asian invasion, based on principles of international responsibility and humanitarianism.

In 1973 the Whitlam Labor Government was voted into power, and immediately set about an ambitious program of reforms to shape the new Australia. The dismissal in 1975, when Whitlam was sacked by the Governor-General, Sir John Kerr, brought a halt to radical reform, but it also proved the final impetus for change in Australian perceptions of the relationship with Britain. Menzies' old imperial vision of a world-wide British community of nations was gradually replaced by a more narrowly defined Australian nationalism.

The changes brought about a gradual shift in public perceptions of Australia's relationship with Asia. The White Australia policy of exclusion and the successful halt to Chinese immigration at the time of Federation had turned the 'Chinese problem' of the last century into a foreign affairs issue. Now an Asian presence was once more a domestic reality.

Attitudes to Aboriginal culture had also been changing over time. In 1898 American writer Mark Twain drily summarized the ambivalent 'official' record of nineteenth-century white relations with Aborigines:

> Why, a literature might be made out of the aboriginal all by himself...In his history, as preserved by the white man's official records, he is everything – everything that a human creature can be. He covers the entire ground. He is a coward – there are a thousand facts to prove it. He is brave – there a thousand facts to prove it. He is treacherous – oh! beyond imagination! He is faithful, loyal, true – the white man's records supply you with a harvest of instances of it that are noble, worshipful, and pathetically beautiful.[1]

But even as Twain was writing, the overwhelming success of inland European settlement had turned Aborigines from an active threat into a dying curiosity. As the threat receded, the minority European position, of sympathy for persecuted fellow human beings, gradually became a majority view, particularly among urban communities. Here too, public opinion moved ahead of political change. When the 1967 referendum on constitutional change was held, it merely confirmed the widespread acceptance of Aborigines as fellow citizens. The referendum did not radically alter the petty persecution to which Aborigines had been subject for so long, but it removed much of its official status. It became possible to imagine that low pay, appalling housing, inferior medical attention, and all the other problems of marginalised groups, might be the result of intentional or unintentional disruption, neglect and discrimination, rather than evidence of 'natural' decline.

Although the direct connection between politicians and fiction had largely ended by the First World War, literature continued to play a significant role in the process of change. The *Bulletin*'s drive for a particular kind of national culture succeeded in establishing a popular sense of what was meant by 'Australian Literature', and this nationalist but Anglocentric model was given real definition in 1929 by, of all things, an American critic. C. Hartley Grattan's booklet, *Australian Literature*[2] (1929) had a foreword by Nettie Palmer, and it drew on her essay, *Modern Australian Literature*, extending her thesis into a broader canonical history, and giving Australia its first substantial national literary overview. This was later followed in 1942 by his more general book, *Introducing Australia*, a history which helped to formalise the absence of Aboriginal culture from the early canon, and the more general exclusion of popular writing about race relations.

But the success of Federation, with its sense of a national identity achieved, provided a security which would allow others to challenge the new certainties. A post-Federation generation of intellectuals, descended from the very squattocracy that had led the push for Aboriginal dispossession, and who were children when Grattan published his work, formed the backbone of an Australian literary culture that became increasingly reformist.

Patrick White (1912-90) and Judith Wright (1915-2000) were both born into established New South Wales pastoralist families, educated at private schools and sent to England to extend their education. Both became committed supporters of Aboriginal issues. White, generally reclusive, spoke out publicly on the

Vietnam War, Aboriginal affairs, and the Whitlam dismissal. He donated to Aboriginal education, as well as various arts, and used his public stature in a gesture of protest at government policies when he resigned his Order of Australia in 1976. Although White's work was generally concerned with 'universal' human issues, his treatment of Aborigines played an important role in several books. In *Voss*[3] (1957), which is based on the story of explorer Ludwig Leichhardt, and *A Fringe of Leaves*[4] (1976), which revisits the Eliza Fraser story, Aboriginal characters are peripheral to the growth through suffering of the central European character. But unlike the caricatured savages of, for example, Simpson Newland's *Paving the Way* (which also deals with shipwreck and massacre), White's Aborigines are as 'real' as his other fictional characters. *Riders in the Chariot*[5] (1961) goes further, drawing together its disparate tales through the vision of the aboriginal artist Alf Dubbo.

Poet Judith Wright was also a major supporter of indigenous land rights, and secretary of the Aboriginal Treaty Committee. Born at Thalgaroch station near Armidale, New South Wales, into a pastoralist family whose Australian connections date back to the 1820s, Judith Wright's lyrical work is preoccupied with the natural world and with the interrelationships of all living things. She has given voice to her views on Aboriginal issues in various works: *The Cry for the Dead* (1985); *We Call for a Treaty* (1985); *Born of the Conquerors* (1991). In an essay for the 1981 Tasmanian Wilderness Society Calendar, she described her involvement in the Aboriginal cause, saying that 'Those two strands – the love of the land we have invaded and the guilt of the invasion – have become part of me. It is haunted. We owe it repentance and such amends as we can make...'[6]

Both White and Wright have taken advantage of their artistic status to enter political debate: voices from the centre have spoken for those on the margins of society. Though it might be argued that White's work is concerned for indigenous culture only insofar as it has influenced white culture and attitudes, there is no doubting his genuine commitment to the need for improvement in actual living conditions. He and Wright have helped raise public awareness of the need for change.

This need, and our collective ability to address it, is also echoed in the fiction of writers such as Thea Astley (1925-2004), whose work speaks of an underlying scepticism about the human capacity for good. Astley is particularly concerned with the social condition of Australian women, portraying a bleak view of their vulnerablity as outsiders in a male-dominated national identity. Criticism of our national myths is present in her representations of conflict between the smug malice of those inside the accepted social system and the helplessness of those outside it. She once described her novels as 'a plea for charity'. Astley's outsiders include Aboriginal people, particularly in *It's Raining In Mango*[7] (1988), where descriptions of Aboriginal dispossession and slaughter are blended with other tragic stories of social ills such as economic depression, war, prostitution and incest.

Astley's story, 'Heart is Where the Home is',[8] is about the 'stolen children', describing with compassion the anguish of a young mother whose child is taken away from her by shallow 'insiders', the men, despite the well-meaning obstruction of her white employers, the Laffeys. The Aboriginal people are: 'powerless before this new white law they'd never heard of'. The story shows the police as totally insensitive to the Aboriginal perspective. They are brutal, impatient, determined to enforce 'the law', and complaining that: 'The [Aboriginal] passivity finally stuck in their guts'. George and Mag Laffey protect the mother, Nelly, then offer to take her in – but they, too, have their insensitivities: George cannot understand why Nelly cries at leaving her family who live by a creek a mile away. Nelly's response shows the misery of her situation:

> *The old men old women uncles aunts cousins brothers sisters*
> *tin humpies bottles dogs dirty blankets tobacco handouts*
> *fights river trees all the tribe's remnants and wretchedness,*
> *destruction and misery.*
>
> *Her second skin now.*

> 'Not same,' she whispered. And she cried them centuries of
> tribal dream in those two words. 'Not same.'

This process of raising public awareness was carried into the universities when, in the 1960s, 'Australian Literature' finally became an academically acceptable course. Although the canon that was taught remained for a long time fairly narrow and culturally Anglocentric, the inclusion of reformist writers led inevitably to change.

In the publishing world, companies like Angus & Robertson maintained a consistent presence in the local market, offering some resistance to the monolithic industry agreements that had divided the English-speaking world between British and American zones of interest, and locked up Australian distribution for the British companies. The establishment of an Australian arm of Penguin gave a major boost to the local product, helping supply texts for the new tertiary courses.

There had also been a gradual shift in attitude towards censorship. The breakthrough for imported works came with the famous Lady Chatterley trial when D. H. Lawrence's book, *Lady Chatterley's Lover*, for so long banned as obscene, was finally ruled acceptable on the grounds that it was serious art. Australia's various defamation laws remain among the most draconian in the western world, which severely limits direct criticism of politicians, but at least it is now possible to read what is read in other western countries, and enter a wider debate.

The Whitlam government's foundation in 1973 of the Australian Council of the Arts (which became the Australia Council in 1975), with its programs of official support grants, helped create a vigorous literary scene that matched the rebirth of the local film industry. A younger generation of writers was given the financial support to develop their ideas and a new generation of now established writers such as Thomas Keneally and Randolph Stow enlivened Australian writing.

A new phenomenon also came about: the birth of an Aboriginal literature in English. As *How Australian Literature Grew* pointed out in 1962, Aboriginal cultures have their own rich, diverse and important oral traditions. Despite being first belittled and then collected by a nineteenth-century European culture which had sought to distance itself from its own oral traditions, many of these oral cultures have survived. More than a century and a half of mass slaughter, persecution, neglect and enforced assimilation has not succeeded in eliminating the older tradition, which has been supplemented by the development of new cultural amalgams created by extensive dispossession and displacement. Inevitably, perhaps, this new literature in English began as a response to white Australian literary representations of the Aborigine. The poem by Oodgeroo of the tribe Noonuccal (formerly known as Kath Walker), 'We Are Going'[9] (1964), is couched as a reply to Henry Kendall's romanticised vision of Aboriginal decline, 'The Last of his Tribe' (1864) (see Chapter 2). Its voice looks for a way to de-romanticise the realities of dispossession and decline, articulating the thoughts of a tribal remnant returning to its old haunts: 'We are as strangers here now, but the white tribe are the strangers...' The poem ends with a blunt statement of the situation:

> The bora ring is gone.
> The corroboree is gone.
> And we are going.

Oodgeroo Noonuccal's view that Aboriginal Australians should take their rightful place in this country without having to surrender their own culture is indicative of the views expressed by the first groups of Aboriginal writers, including poet, playwright and editor Jack Davis and politically provocative playwright Kevin Gilbert. Further Aboriginal writers, such as Bobbi Sykes, Robert Merritt, Sally Morgan, Gerald Bostock, Lionel Fogarty, Faith Bandler, Archie Weller, Ruby Langford Ginibi, and Bill Neidjie, to name a few, have since joined earlier Aboriginal writers in creating a vibrant new literature of Australia, a literature which covers a wide range of individual Aboriginal experience, including the problems of urban displacement and the plight of 'stolen children', together with the broader issues of relationships with the land itself and the role of Aboriginal cultures in modern Australia.

As early as the 1880s poet George Gordon McCrae had put forward his belief that wider understanding in the white community of Aboriginal myth and legend would provide the most effective basis for bridging the cultural divide between the two groups. It is a view that is being vindicated in more recent works, particularly in the retelling of Aboriginal stories in works for children. A case in point is the work of Dick Roughsey (whose tribal name Goobalathaldin meaning 'Water standing on end', or Rough Sea, has been anglicised to Roughsey). Roughsey combines traditional Aboriginal painting techniques with work in western oils, and has produced such extraordinary children's picture books as *The Giant Devil Dingo* (1973), *The Rainbow Serpent* (1975) and, with (white) writer Percy Trezise, *The Quinkins* (1978), *Banana Bird and the Snake Men* (1980), *Turramulli the Giant Quinkin* (1982), *The Magic Firesticks* (1983), *Gidga* (1984) and *The Flying Fox* (1985). Books such as these are re-working Aboriginal myth and legend, deliberately merging oral, pictorial, and written literature into a new form.

This is a process that is also occurring in fiction, in the work of writers such as Western Australian Kim Scott, whose first novel, *True Country*[10] (1993), tackled the difficulties faced by those who are part descended from Aborigines and looking for cultural identity.

True Country is a publication by the Fremantle Arts Centre Press (now Fremantle Press), which reflects one aspect of Federal government support since the mid-1970s for Australian writing, giving publishing access through small presses to a number of promising new indigenous writers. Their success has been matched by a wider acceptance amongst mainstream publishers like the University of Queensland Press, which has been instrumental in encouraging writing by and about Aborigines.

The development of an Aboriginal literature is paralleled by the emergence of 'multicultural writing', a product of the enormous cultural diversity introduced to Australia by post-war migration. Many of today's 'multicultural' writers were born in Australia, but are part of a generation that was been encouraged by multicultural policies of the 1980s and 90s to move beyond their parents' more limited choice between assimilation or isolation. It has become possible to celebrate difference and to chart the difficulties of co-existence in the urban communities which are the centres of muticulturalism.

The change in the direction of Australian literature now underway at universities can be represented by the presence of writers such as George Papeallinas (who has lectured in creative writing at the University of Technology, Deakin University and The University of Melbourne) as writers-in-residence. In his collection, *Ikons*[11] (1986), Papaellinas, who was born in Sydney of Greek Cypriot parents, writes of the experiences of cultural uprooting. The other side of the migrant experience, the difficulties faced by native-born Anglo-Australians in coming to terms with their new neighbours, has also been tackled, by writers like well-known Western Australian novelist Tim Winton, whose short story, 'Neighbours',[12] offers an entirely positive picture of what can be gained in the encounter between cultures. As is so often the case, the voices of popular literature are in the vanguard of social change.

This emergence of vigorous new Aboriginal and multicultural voices has begun the process of countering some of the dominant literary prejudices of the past. While all of this appears encouraging, however, it would be wrong to assume a social Darwinist view, that 'improvement' is a natural process. This dangerously comfortable misconception has been encouraged in Australia by the self-censorship that has accompanied the construction of a national literary identity: the construction and rewriting of the literary canon in the twentieth century has brought Australia into line with Britain and America by focusing attention on 'serious' and 'literary' writing. This tends, in retrospect, to distort the balance of a literature which, unlike the English or American models, came into existence in a period of mass readership. Popular writing, which formed the bulk and often the most influential portion of Australian writing, has been sidelined. With it has gone much of the overt racism which, even today, tends to be treated as an unfortunate and marginal aspect of the literature of the past. It is too easy to look back and say that our culture has outgrown the lapses of its colonial past. We need to face squarely the racist and xenophobic reality of the once dominant white world view – the view that played a central role in the creation of modern Australia.

Simpson Newland, writing at the end of the nineteenth century, recognised the scale and the thoroughness of what took place then: in the face of an aggressively self-assured white society, indigenous culture stood no chance of effective resistance. Then, as now, land rights were recognised as the most important element in cultural survival:

> ...the European he [the Aborigine] placed in the category of the animals he thought it his duty to destroy in any and every way. In his eyes the white man was the personification of ruthless, all-absorbing power; never satisfied without the whole of the country; before whom his people absolutely withered away, even when not actively ill-treated, as was too frequently the case.
>
> Under the most favourable circumstances for the aborigine, the stranger took complete possession of his country and destroyed his game, thus compelling him to depend largely on the intruder for subsistence, or driving him back upon hostile tribes. This engendered the bitterest hate though it might be masked under the most abject subserviency. The process began with the coastal tribes and has continued throughout the whole of inhabited Australia. From the first colonization to the present time, no adequate reserves have ever been set aside for the unfortunate people whom we have dispossessed and all but annihilated. This is a black indictment to make, but the sting is in its truth. Those who have seen the process must unhesitantly though reluctantly admit that the darkest stain on Australia's fair name is her treatment of the aboriginal race. We found them a happy,

> *healthy people and wherever we have come in contact with them, in less than fifty years we have civilized them off the face of the land, or such a miserable remnant is left that it were a mercy if it had gone too.*[13]

The fact that this process of 'civilisation' was so successful goes some way to explaining the current level of misinformation about Australia's past. It has proved too easy for some politicians to claim that the mistreatment lies in the past, somewhere out of sight and out of our area of responsibility. Quite apart from ignoring the evidence of very real present-day social and economic problems amongst the remnant indigenous cultures, however, such a denial of the past can also lead to a dangerous level of misunderstanding in policy debates.

Even commentators sympathetic to the plight of Aborigines can find themselves unintentionally downplaying the significance of past racism. In an article for the Melbourne *Age*, 'Weighing up the facts on genocide claims',[14] visiting philosopher Raymond Gaita problematises the use of the term 'genocide' by the Human Rights Commission report, *Bringing Them Home*, in its description of the post-war forced assimilation policy. In his article, Gaita makes it clear that, for all its cruelty, the policy of forced assimilation never involved genocide by mass killing, and that such a solution was never officially contemplated. He differentiates Australian culture from those cultures in which such genocide has occurred, or might be contemplated: 'A genocidal intention formed in a culture where mass murder is unthinkable', he says, 'is radically different from a genocidal intention formed in a culture where it is seriously an option.'

This is a comforting position for Australian society, setting it apart – according to Gaita – from Nazi Germany, Cambodia, Rwanda and Bosnia. But the mass killing of Aborigines by settlers has been well documented; and a number of the texts we have examined in this book show that genocide – to be realised by officially sanctioned mass killing – was indeed a significant feature of thinking in some parts of Australian political life from at least the 1880s to the 1920s (the period when the Nazis came to power in Germany). Exclusion (to deal with the Chinese) and assimilation (to deal with Aborigines) became the favoured options in a federated White Australia, but the possibility of 'race war' was seriously canvassed by major political figures.

A common belief in the essential humanity of Australian culture is important for the successful resolution of such major issues as those raised by the stolen children report. It is equally important that Australians understand how little has, at times, separated our culture from those cultures where genocide by mass killing has actually occurred. We have been fortunate that circumstances have so far never combined to allow such policies to be sanctioned here. Indeed, the extraordinary thing about Australia is that is has managed to produce such a humane and essentially tolerant society out of such racist beginnings as the White Australia policy and enforced assimilation. But we would be dangerously complacent if we chose to regard even the most extreme forms of genocide as inconceivable in our culture.

Conclusion

The proposed Voice to Parliament is about the future of Australia. The time has come for the nation to recognise the biases of the past, and attempt to make space for different ways of thinking – ways which will create a new, inclusive history that will serve us better than the colonial half-truths currently hampering our national identity. The extracts you have been reading in *Aliens & Savages* chart the changes in public perception thought that have brought us to this point.

When William Dampier published *A New Voyage Around the World* in 1697, he described his encounter with 'the miserablest people in the world'. Exactly three hundred years later, in 1997, the Australian Reconciliation Convention took place. That Convention revealed both the need and the desire for policy changes in relations between mainstream Australia and its indigenous communities. But in the same year, the nervous responses by many politicians and pastoralists to the Mabo and Wik High Court decisions revealed a lingering suspicion that 'progress', 'development', and 'economic stability' (neat phrases, but vague concepts) were threatened by any resurgence of indigenous cultures.

Although nothing in either the Mabo or the Wik judgements implied any displacement of pastoralists by an Aboriginal reoccupation of land, the idea of 'co-existence' raised the old spectres of dispossession. After all, as the Australian invasion fictions show, peoples who occupy land they or their forebears have taken from its original inhabitants are likely to be keenly aware of the possibility of displacement in their turn.

There is – as Senator Pat Dodson demonstrates in his 2023 essay, 'A firelight stick on the hill'[1] – an eerie sameness about the political rhetoric surrounding previous attempts to redress historical injustices. Successive conservative governments espoused an official policy of 'Assimilation', by which they meant denying any separate cultural identity for First Nations people. Listen to the language. In 1963, Paul Hasluck, minister for territories in the conservative Menzies government, insisted that 'Aborigines should not be made the subject of special laws... Let them come within the laws made for all Australians'.[2] And this was John Howard, staunch opponent of Reconciliation in any form, speaking against the Hawke Labor Government's legislation to create the Aboriginal and Torres Strait Islander Commission in 1990:

> *The ATSIC legislation strikes at the heart of the unity of the Australian people. In the name of righting the wrongs done against Aboriginal people, the legislation adopts the misguided notion of believing that if one creates a parliament within the Australian community for Aboriginal people, one will solve and meet all of those problems.*[3]

Howard stuck to this position throughout the ensuing years: one of his first acts when he defeated Labor Prime Minister Paul Keating in the 1996 election was to scuttle Keating's Mabo social justice package, framed with the help of the Native Title Social Justice Committee; in 2000 Howard pointedly ignored draft legislation presented for Aboriginal Reconciliation by a committee chaired by Dr Evelyn Scott; in 2004 Howard legislated ATSIC out of existence altogether. Howard's successors have continued his rhetoric: in 2017 then Prime Minister Malcolm Turnbull abandoned the idea of a Voice, on the grounds that it would be perceived as a third house of parliament; more recently former Prime Minister Tony Abbot claimed that the voice will mean two classes of Australian 'with the few given a special right to influence legislation over and above that accorded to the many';[4] and the current Leader of the Opposition, Peter Dutton, insists that the Voice will 're-racialise the nation', while his deputy, Sussan Ley, has repeatedly made nonsensical claims that a voice would threaten events such as Anzac Day and Australia Day.

The upcoming referendum on an Aboriginal and Torres Strait Islander Voice to Parliament has provoked some extreme – at times downright uncivil – discourse. It has been represented by opponents as racially divisive, as though the constitutional *status quo* occupies a benign and neutral position. It does not. Australian Federation in 1901 was grounded in a long and dishonourable history of racism – the colonies came together in a mutual desire to entrench a White Australia policy in the face of Imperial opposition. Now, with the eyes of the world upon us, the rhetoric of home-grown racists is similarly defiant.

It is unfortunate that the current discourse surrounding the Voice to Parliament is taking place in a climate of economic uncertainty, of rising interest rates and growing inflation. Back in the late 1990s, the more hostile responses to the Mabo and Wik judgements were reinforced by prevailing global economic conditions. And apart from damaging the wider social fabric of the nation, the doctrine of economic rationalism had, by then, also helped to reinstate a popular perception of Aboriginal groups as direct competitors for limited economic resources. Such 'rationalism' is a modified version of social Darwinism, one in which the survival and prosperity of the economically 'fittest' is assumed to benefit society as a whole by improving the quality of its human and economic stock. It does not.

Survival of a biologically 'inferior' race was once seen as a threat to the natural advancement of the human species. In the 1990s, Aboriginal claims for security of Native title were represented by their opponents as a threat by an 'inferior' economic system to the general advancement of the nation's wealth through mining and farming – claims that, like so many others, have proved illusory.

This racist rhetoric was taken up enthusiastically by Pauline Hanson and her supporters, who tapped into the nervousness of ordinary Australians who were (as they are now) counting the cost of rising inflation and increasing interest rates. In 1997, when journalist Paul Kelly wrote about 'The Challenge of Pauline Hanson', in *The Weekend Australian*,[5] he noted that 'Hanson...symbolises an alienation within part of the community caused by a conjunction of forces – globalisation, economic restructuring and social changes – where people need scapegoats to explain their frustration.'

The economic situation (then, as now) owes a great deal to the 1980s policies of British Prime Minister Margaret Thatcher, a firm believer in the economic principles of capitalism spelt out by Adam Smith in *The Wealth of Nations* – those same principles which so profoundly affected the first settlement of Australia. Industrialists of the Victorian period took to heart Smith's ideas on capital and the free market, while Karl Marx identified them as the root of social inequity. The twentieth century was dominated by the struggle between modified forms of these two opposed ideologies. When Mrs Thatcher appealed directly for a return to 'nineteenth-century values', she was looking for a way to end this impasse. She, and other Western leaders who followed her (including United States President Ronald Reagan, and Australia's John Howard) succeeded. State communism collapsed in Europe, and the 'triumph of the West' was announced (prematurely, as we now see).

But the cost for ordinary citizens has been high. David Leser summed up the situation in 1996 when he wrote of 'Pauline Hanson's bitter harvest':

> *To be Australian today is, for many people, to be deeply insecure about the future. You can't see this trauma in the economic indicators so much as you can in the faces of those in dole queues, in companies being downsized, in workplaces of increasing stress and competition, in traffic snarls, in isolated country towns, behind the walls of disintegrating family homes... The Australian psyche has*

> taken a pummelling. People are bewildered and
> apprehensive. They let fly at easy targets – welfare
> recipients, Aborigines, migrants. It's called the politics of
> downward envy. The politics of resentment.[6]

Does this sound familiar? When ordinary individuals feel disempowered by any social system, it is far easier to blame a visible 'competitor' than it is to tackle difficult and complex long-term issues of change and reform. 'Downward envy' refers to the popular belief that somebody got something they weren't entitled to have – or something you didn't get but feel *you* are entitled to have. It is a blame game that creates an atmosphere which allows easy scope for disingenuous conflation of the issues, producing a political environment in which demagogues flourish.

In addition to the obvious attractions of scapegoating, the other important factor in this reactionary political equation is the power of the comforting myth of a golden past. As journalist Paul Kelly pointed out back in 1997:

> *Hanson's ideology is essentially an old-fashioned racial*
> *isolationism which strikes a chord within elements of the*
> *national psyche. It is potent precisely because it is a mirror*
> *of what Australia once was. Hanson is an echo of the past*
> *and she trades on this nostalgia.*[7]

This, too, is still with us. While the frustrating sense of disempowerment felt by many at the end of the twentieth century mirrored the working-class frustration expressed a century earlier by Henry Lawson in 'Faces in the Street', the retreat to nostalgia was (and is) something different. Part of it is a nostalgia for better economic times. The generation that lived through the Great Depression of the 1920s and 1930s placed a high value on the economic security of post-Second World War Australia; and subsequent generations that have grown up unused to any real inequity have taken for granted that this quality of life will continue. It follows that the ordinary Australian faced today with massive social change is likely to resent it, to look for someone to blame, and to hanker after an ordered way of life somewhere in a half-remembered past.

We can see this currently playing out in the deliberately ageist attacks on 'Boomers' (a derogatory epithet for the post-war generation), as if their modest success in paying for the homes they have worked for somehow denies similar home ownership to later generations. Nobody would deny that the current generation is struggling – or that the elderly retirees of the post-war generation are a soft target. This, too, is the politics of downward envy, cynically reframed for the circumstances of the current decade, politically manipulated to split the inter-generational vote and divert attention from the real underlying causes of our ongoing socio-political-economic predicament. It is, alas, becoming increasingly obvious that a great deal of rhetoric issuing from opponents of the Voice is designed, likewise, to frame hostile responses as genuine economic issues. Immigrant groups, in particular, have been targeted with assertions that giving one racial group 'special status' will financially disadvantage others. There have already been unsubstantiated claims that the Voice will make ordinary Australians pay more tax: Laura Tingle's recent analysis piece for ABC News[8] points to an anonymously letter-boxed leaflet claiming that the Voice will expose Australians to reparations and financial settlements – including rates, land taxes and royalties. This leaflet shamelessly appropriates the artwork of indigenous artist Danny Eastwood (who emphatically repudiates its misuse). The tone of the leaflet is hysterical, but the intention is clear. Tingle points out that it leverages the same politics of downward envy and resentment that John Howard's government used to demonise single mothers as lazy welfare cheats; the same technique that Scott Morrison's government used to justify hounding welfare recipients through the infamous Robodebt scheme. And, sadly, it is the same technique that has frequently painted indigenous communities as a drain on the national economy. It points to a disturbing strain of cruelty in populist politics: a level of deliberate institutionalised cruelty that some voters are all too willing to accept.

Neither side of politics in Australia has had a monopoly of racism, as the fictions of William Lane and Kenneth MacKay so clearly demonstrate, and the populist battle for hearts and minds is fought out, now as then, in the media of the day. The forms might have changed, but the principle is the same.

When the One Nation Party was launched, it was heralded by the publication of *Pauline Hanson: The Truth*. The launch was a major media event, carefully stage-managed to generate maximum publicity, but with copies of the book limited to such small numbers that any informed response was severely limited. Like so many politicians engaging in Australian race debates, Hanson was skilful in her manipulation of the popular press to achieve maximum publicity. Myths of Aboriginal cannibalism described in Hector Holthouse's *River of Gold*, and selectively quoted in *Pauline Hanson: The Truth*, were given a new lease of life by 60 Minutes.[9] In a special report on 'Unknown Australia', the program gave a perfect illustration of rumour in action: extracts from Holthouse were read as background to travelogue visuals, and given 'factual' status by the addition of nineteenth-century illustrations. No reference was made to Hanson; no attempt was made to question the truth of the stories. To a casual observer, the program appeared to offer independent corroboration of the claims made by *The Truth*.

This technique of elision and obfuscation has been recently reprised by the Murdoch media in support of the 'No' vote. In a concerted campaign of misdirection, multiple arms of the Murdoch press empire – television, print, radio and digital – have quoted or paraphrased comments made several years earlier by 'Yes' campaigner Thomas Mayo. At the time he linked the restorative action aims of the 'Pay the Rent' movement[10] with a possible indigenous advisory body. Mayo has since specifically rejected this connection – a detail which has been overlooked, minimised, or manipulated to make him appear deliberately disingenuous in various articles and interviews. Journalists have even resorted to quoting other Murdoch outlets as 'evidence' (Chantelle Francis, for example, writing for nine.com, cites a Ben Fordham interview on 2GB radio).[11] As with the 'corroboration' of Hanson a quarter-century ago, this kind of disingenuous cross-referencing produces an illusion of truth clearly intended to direct – or misdirect – its audience to an apparently widely-supported conclusion.

There is no simple antidote to such half-truths, misdirection and misinformation. Only one thing is certain – all of us must consider and learn from the past if we are to make informed, intelligent decisions on such important questions as our political future.

In his 1997 address to the Reconciliation Convention in Melbourne, 'Chances Lost – Chances Taken', ABC Radio National presenter, Bill Bunbury, reminded his audience of the dangers of forgetfulness:

In parts of white Australia right now there is a sad sense of denial, a refusal to acknowledge our past. People are accused of being 'black armbanders' if they want to talk about this part of our history... When truth is a casualty, evil follows.

I'll go further and paraphrase Edmund Burke, who observed that to ignore evil is to allow it to happen. We saw that in Germany earlier this century. Evil exists in any society and can only be countered by honesty.[12]

These words still resonate today. Australia is a nation whose very institutions have been built on racism; whose politicians, whether conservative or radical, have been governed by it. And, as Edmund Burke and George Santayana have both reminded us, a true understanding of our past will always be essential if we are to make change for the better a permanent part of our future. We are in danger of forgetting what the tropes of racist rhetoric really look like: a recent anti-Voice cartoon in *The Australian Financial Review*[13] caused a furore, but many of those leading the response somehow saw the implications of the representation of the 'little princess' (Teal MP Kate Chaney) sitting on Daddy's knee (Michael Chaney, Chairman of Wesfarmers) while an indigenous man ('Yes' spokesman Thomas Mayo) dances for money – but they missed the social Darwinist reference to the organ grinder and his dancing monkey. Less sophisticated observers didn't: some indigenous social media websites reported being bombarded with pictures of monkeys and apes.

The Australian Electoral Commission is investigating the author of the anonymous 'No' pamphlet described by Laura Tingle – on the technicality of failing to include a statement of authorisation, as required by law for political advertising. The Commission has also, however, made clear that there is no requirement for truth in such advertising – as has been made abundantly clear with the release of the official 'Yes' and 'No' statements.

Patrick Dodson concluded, in his essay 'A firelight stick on the hill': 'While maintaining the colonial stories, truth-telling must reveal and adjust the stories of war, destabilisation and assimilation. There can be no place for triumphalism'.[14] *Aliens & Savages* is our contribution to national truth-telling. The extracts in this book show how the marginalisation of First Nations people has been done; how it has always been done; how it is still being done. We began this new edition by asking what has changed in the 25 years since this book was first published. Now, we invite you to judge for yourself.

Endnotes

Introduction

1. Albanese, Anthony, 'Lowitja O'Donoghue Oration', Adelaide, 29th May 2023.
2. Editorial, *The Sydney Morning Herald*, 10th June, 2023.
3. Anderson, Pat, cited in Flanagan, Richard, 'Our inauthentic heart: What the Voice to Parliament means for the stories we tell', *The Monthly*, May 2023, p.33.
4. Flanagan, Richard, 'Our inauthentic heart: What the Voice to Parliament means for the stories we tell', *The Monthly*, May 2023, pp.28-38.
5. George Santayana, *The Life of Reason or the Phases of Human Progress*, Scribner's, New York, 1905-6.
6. Charles Dickens, *Hard Times for These Times* (1854), Penguin, 1969, p.90.
7. Tench, Watkin 1789 and 1793, *1788: Comprising A Narrative of the Expedition to Botany Bay (1798) and A Complete Account of the Settlement at Port Jackson (1793)*, ed. Flannery, Tim 1996, The Text Publishing Company, Melbourne.
8. See White, Richard 1981, *Inventing Australia: Images and Identity 1688–1980*, George Allen & Unwin, Sydney, Ch. 5, 'The National Type', pp. 63–84; and Ch. 8, 'Diggers and Heroes', pp. 125–139.
9. A Lady Long Resident in New South Wales 1841, *A Mother's Offering to her Children*, The Gazette Office, Sydney. (See Healy, J. J. 1978 and

1989, *Literature and the Aborigine in Australia*, University of Queensland Press, Brisbane, pp. 31–2.)

10. Burke, Janine 1991, 'The Use of Stories: A Tale for my God-daughter at Midnight', *Millennium*, ed. Daniel, Helen 1991, Penguin, Melbourne. pp. 323–4.

Chapter One

1. de Quiros, Fernandez 1605, cited in Day, David 1996, *Claiming a Continent: A History of Australia*, Angus & Robertson, Sydney, p. 16.
2. Carstenz, Jan 1623, cited in Day, p. 18.
3. See Day, p. 20.
4. Dampier, William 1697, *A New Voyage Round the World*, reprinted in *William Dampier: Buccaneer Explorer*, ed. Norris, Gerald 1994, Folio Society, London.
5. Cook, James 1773, *Journal of the 'Endeavour', 1768–1771*, Facsimile edition 1968, South Australian Libraries Edition, Adelaide; cited in Reynolds, Henry 1989, *Dispossession: Black Australians and White Invaders*, Allen & Unwin, Sydney, p. 98.
6. Tench, Watkin 1789, *A Narrative of the Expedition to Botany Bay*, reprinted as *1788: Comprising A Narrative of the Expedition to Botany Bay (1789) and A Complete Account of the Settlement at Port Jackson (1793)*, ed. Flannery, Tim 1996, The Text Publishing Company, Melbourne.
7. Tench, Watkin 1793, *A Complete Account of the Settlement at Port Jackson*, as above.
8. Wentworth, William Charles 1823, 'Australasia: A Poem Written for the Chancellor's Medal, at the Cambridge Commencement, July 1823', Whittaker & Co., London.
9. Tompson, Charles 1826, 'A Song, Written for the XXVth January Last, being the XXXVIth Anniversary of the Establishment of this Colony', from his collection *Wild Notes, from the Lyre of a Native Minstrel*, Government Press, Sydney; reprinted 1973, Sydney University Press, Sydney with introduction by G. A. Wilkes & G. A. Turnbull.

10. Lang, John Dunmore, Speech to the Moreton Bay Friends of the Aborigines, reported in *Moreton Bay Courier* 19 January 1856; cited in Reynolds, Henry 1989, *Dispossession*, Allen & Unwin, Sydney, p. 5.

11. Tompson, Charles 1826, 'Blacktown', *Monitor*, 2 June 1826.

12. Anon. 1826, 'The Native's Lament', *Colonial Times*, 5 May 1826.

13. Ayliffe, Ettie A. (pseud. Mrs J. A. Bode) 1886, 'Lubra', from collection, *Original Poems*; reprinted in *The Poet's Discovery: Nineteenth-century Australia in Verse*, 1990, eds. Jordan, Richard D. & Pierce, Peter, Melbourne University Press, Melbourne, pp. 398-99.

14. Dunlop, Eliza Hamilton 1838, 'The Aboriginal Mother (from Myall's Creek)', *Australasian*, 13 December 1838.

15. Roderick, Colin 1952, *Ralph Rashleigh, from the original manuscript written by James Tucker in 1844-45*, Angus & Robertson, Sydney; reprinted 1992. Also published 1929 as *The Adventures of Ralph Rashleigh*, Jonathan Cape, London.

16. Newland, Simpson 1893, *Paving the Way: A Romance of the Australian Bush*; reprinted 1954, Rigby, Adelaide.

Chapter Two

1. Auster (pseud.) 1847, 'The Tasmanian Aborigine's Lament and Remonstrance When in Sight of His Native Land from Flinders Island', *Courier*, 9 October 1848.

2. Chambers, Robert 1844, *Vestiges Of Creation*, 'The Origin of the Animated Tribes', 3rd edn. 1845, Chambers; excerpted in *The Portable Victorian Reader* 1976, ed. Haight, Gordon S., Penguin, Melbourne, p. 510.

3. Darwin, Charles 1859, *The Origin of Species by Natural Selection: or, The preservation of favoured races in the struggle for life*, J. Murray, London; reprinted 1968, ed. Burrow, J. W., Penguin, Harmondsworth.

4. Spencer, Herbert 1852, 'The Development Hypothesis', *Leader*, 20 March 1852, pp. 280-1.

5. Aeneas (pseud.) 1844, articles in *The Colonial Literary Journal*, 29 August and 5 September 1844; cited in *Dispossession* 1989, Reynolds Henry, Allen & Unwin, Sydney, pp. 108-9.

6. Wentworth, William Charles, speech cited in *Frontier* 1987, Reynolds, Henry, Allen & Unwin, Sydney, p. 111.

7. Lang, John Dunmore, ibid.

8. Clarke, Marcus 1872, article in *The New Era*, supplement to the *Australasian*, 29 April 1872, p. 2.

9. Anon. 1873, *An Account of a Race of Human Beings with Tails*, A. T. Mason, Melbourne.

10. Granville, Austyn 1892, *The Fallen Race*, F. T. Neally, Chicago and New York.

11. Favenc, Ernest 1894, 'A Haunt of the Jinkarras', *Tales of the Austral Tropics*, Orgood McIlwain & Co., London.

12. Kingsley, Henry 1859, *The Recollections of Geoffrey Hamlyn*, Macmillan, London.

13. *The Holy Bible* (Authorised King James Version), 'The Revelation of St John the Divine', ch. 21, verses 1–3.

14. Wells, H. G. 1898, *The War of the Worlds*, William Heinemann, London.

15. Kendall, Henry c. 1862, 'Aboriginal Death Song', *Poems & Songs*, Mr Clarke, Sydney; reprinted in *Leaves From Australian Forests: Poetical Works of Henry Kendall*, 1991, Weldon Publishing, Sydney, pp. 349–50.

16. Kendall, Henry n.d., 'John Dunmore Lang'; reprinted in *Leaves From Australian Forests: Poetical Works of Henry Kendall*, 1991, Weldon Publishing, Sydney, pp. 341–2.

17. Kendall, Henry 1864, 'The Last of His Tribe', collected in *Leaves from Australian Forests*, 1869, George Robertson & Co., Sydney; reprinted in *Leaves From Australian Forests: Poetical Works of Henry Kendall*, 1991, Weldon Publishing, Sydney, p. 92.

18. Stephens, James Brunton 1873, 'To a Black Gin', *The Black Gin and Other Poems*, George Robertson & Co., Sydney.

19. Henry 1877, 'Ode to a Black Gin', *Town and Country Journal*, 17 March 1877.

20. Kendall Henry 1879, 'Jack the Blackfellow', *Sydney Mail*, 23 August 1879.

21. Kendall, Henry 1879, 'Black Jemmy', *Freeman's Journal*, 9 August 1879.

22. McCrae, George Gordon 1867, 'Mamba ("The Bright-Eyed"): An Aboriginal Reminiscence', H. T. Dwight, Melbourne.

23. Gilmore, Mary 1932, 'The Waradgery Tribe', *Under the Wilgas*, Robertson & Mullens, Melbourne; reprinted in Selected Poems, 1998, ETT Imprint, Sydney.

24. Oodgeroo of the tribe Noonuccal (formerly known as Kath Walker) 1964, 'We Are Going', *My People*, 3rd edn. 1990, Jacaranda Press, Milton, Queensland.

25. Clarke, Marcus 1877, *The Future Australian Race*, pamphlet, A. Messina & Co., Melbourne.

Chapter Three

1. Hughes, Robert 1997, *American Visions*, Harvill, London.

2. Warburton, Peter 1875, *Journey Across the Western Interior of Australia*, Sampson, Marston, Low & Searle, London; reprinted 1968 with introduction and additions by Charles H. Eden, ed. Bates, H. W., Libraries Board of South Australia.

3. Lumholtz, Carl 1889, *Among Cannibals*, J. Murray, London; reprinted 1980, Australian National University Press, Canberra.

4. Newland, Simpson 1893, *Paving the Way: A Romance of the Australian Bush*; reprinted 1954, Rigby, Adelaide.

5. Pemberton, R. J., 'Bully Beef and Biscuits', unpublished reminiscences in possession of authors, Newcastle, New South Wales.

6. Hanson, Pauline et al 1997, *Pauline Hanson: The Truth*, self-published, Ipswich, Queensland.

7. Holthouse, Hector 1967, *River of Gold: The Story of the Palmer River Goldrush*, Angus & Robertson, Sydney and Melbourne.

8. Favenc, Ernest 1896, *Marooned on Australia: Being the Narration by Diedrich Buys of his Discovery and Exploits in Terra Australis Incognita about the year 1630*, Blackie, London.

9. Dampier, William 1697, *A New Voyage Round the World*, James Knapton, London; extracted in *William Dampier: Buccaneer Explorer*, 1884, ed. Norris, Gerald, Folio Society, London.

10. Anon. 1888, *The Battle of Mordialloc or How We Lost Australia*, Samuel Mullen, Melbourne.

11. Article 1883, *Bulletin*, 9 June 1883; excerpted in *The Oxford Companion to Australian Literature*, 1994, eds. Wilde, William H., Hooten, Joy & Andrews, Barry, Oxford University Press, Melbourne, 2nd edition, p. 5.

12. Murphy, G. Read 1894, *Beyond the Ice: Being a Story of the Newly Discovered Region Round the North Pole*, Sampson, Low, Marston & Co., London; excerpted in *Australian Science Fiction*, 1982, Ikin, Van, University of Queensland Press, Brisbane and Academy Chicago, Chicago, p. 66.

13. Favenc, Ernest 1876, 'In the Desert', *Australasian Sketcher*, 30 September 1876.

14. Collins, Tom (pseud. Joseph Furphy) 1903, *Such is Life*, *Bulletin*, Sydney; reprinted 1969, Angus & Robertson, Sydney.

15. 'Recruiting' (sea shanty) 1889, *The Native Companion Songster*; reprinted in 1956 and 1990, Edwards, Ron, The Overlander Songbook, University of Queensland Press, Brisbane, pp. 209-10.

16. Becke, Louis, 'A Dead Loss', collected in *South Sea Supercargo* 1967, ed. Grove Day, A., University of Hawaii Press, Honolulu.

17. Gunn, Mrs Aeneas 1908, *We of the Never Never*, Hutchinson of Australia, London and Melbourne.

18. Favenc, Ernest 1894, 'Spirit Led', *Tales of the Austral Tropics*, Orgood, McIlwain & Co., London, p. 74.

19. Lawrence, D. H. 1923, *Kangaroo*, Martin Secker, London.

20. Kirmess, C. H. 1909, *The Australian Crisis*, George Robertson & Co., Melbourne.

21. Cox Erle 1925, *Out of the Silence*, E. A. Ridler, Melbourne; republished, unabridged 1947, Robertson & Mullens, Melbourne; reprinted 1981, Angus & Robertson, Sydney.

Chapter Four

1. Wakefield, Edward Gibbon 1829, 'A Letter from Sydney', *A Letter from Sydney and Other Writings*, Dent, London.

2. See *The Oxford Companion to Australian Literature*, 1994, eds. Wilde, William H., Hooten, Joy & Andrews, Barry, Oxford University Press, Melbourne, 2nd edition, p. 162.

3. Chandler, J. 1893, *Forty Years in the Wilderness*, E. Wyatt, Printer, Melbourne.

4. Thatcher, Charles 1857, 'Chinese Immigration', *Thatcher's Colonial Songster, containing all the choice local songs, parodies etc of the celebrated Charles R. Thatcher*, Charlwood & Son, Melbourne.

5. Meng, L. Kong, Cheok Hing Cheong & Louis Ah Mouy 1878–79, *The Chinese Question in Australia*, pamphlet, F. F. Bailliere (publisher to the Victorian Government), Melbourne.

6. *Melbourne Punch*, 16 January 1879.

7. Cited in *The Oxford Companion to Australian Literature*, 1994, eds. Wilde, William, H., Hooten, Joy & Andrews, Barry, Oxford University Press, Melbourne, 2nd edition, p. 162.

8. Anon. 'Dick the Digger: A Tale of the Buckland', in *Colonial Songster: contains several new Irish Colonial songs and a choice selection of popular songs of the day*, 1884, Small, J., A. T. Hodgson, Castlemaine, Victoria; excerpted in *The Oxford Companion to Australian Literature*, 1994, eds. Wilde, William, H., Hooten, Joy & Andrews, Barry, Oxford University Press, Melbourne, 2nd edition, p. 162.

9. A.S.O.W.A. (pseud.) 1886, 'John Chinaman My Jo', *Inquirer*, 3 November 1886.

10. Anon. 1870, 'Only Thirteen', *Melbourne Punch*, 14 July 1870.

11. Editorial, *Melbourne Punch*, 2 January 1873.

12. Walch, Garnet 1867, 'Stroke Oar's Story', *The 'Fireflash', four oars and a coxswain: where they went – how they went – and why they went: and the stories they told last Christmas Eve*, Gordon & Gotch, Sydney.

13. Traditional.

14. Lawson, Henry 1912, 'Ah Soon', *Lone Hand*, 1 August 1912, Sydney; reprinted in *Henry Lawson: Stories for Senior Students*, 1962, ed. Roderick, Colin, Angus & Robertson, Sydney, p. 181.

15. Anon. 1885, *The Fall of Melbourne*, novella published in *Sydney Quarterly Magazine*, Vol. 2, No. 6, June 1885.

16. Anon. 1888, *The Battle of Mordialloc or How We Lost Australia*, Samuel Mullen, Melbourne.

17. Palmer, Vance 1954, *The Legend of the Nineties*, Melbourne University Press, Melbourne, p. 158.

18. The Sketcher (pseud. William Lane) 1888, *White or Yellow?: A Story of the Race War of AD 1908*, serial in *The Boomerang*, 18 February–5 May 1888, Brisbane.

19. Hanson, Pauline 1996, maiden speech, 10 September 1996, *Hansard*.

20. Editorial, *Brisbane Courier*, 7 May 1888.

21. Mackay, Kenneth 1895, *The Yellow Wave: A Romance of the Asiatic Invasion of Australia*, Richard Bentley & Son, London.

22. Mackay, Kenneth 1896, *NSW Parliamentary Debates*, Legislative Assembly, 13 October 1896.

23. Parkes, Sir Henry 1891, speech on 13 March reported in *Official Report of the National Australasian Convention Debates 2 March to 9 April*, Sydney.

Chapter Five

1. Clerk, Nellie S. 1887, 'Federation', *Songs from the Gippsland Forest*, Mirboo North.

2. Rata (pseud. Thomas Roydhouse) 1904, *The Coloured Conquest*, NSW Bookstall Co., Sydney; excerpted in *Australian Science Fiction*, 1982, Ikin, Van, University of Queensland Press, Brisbane and Academy Chicago, Chicago.

3. Kirmess, C. H. 1909, *The Australian Crisis*, George Robertson & Co., Melbourne.

4. See Meaney, Neville 1996, '"The Yellow Peril", Invasion Scare Novels and Australian Political Culture', *The 1890s: Australian Literature and*

Literary Culture, University of Queensland Press, Brisbane, fn. pp. 347–8.

5. Deakin, Alfred 1901, speech cited in *A Short History of Australia*, 1963, Clarke, Manning, Mentor, New York; reprinted 1969, p. 185.

6. Fox, Frank 1907, 'Secret No. 1 – The Incident of the Microphone', from series of short stories, 'The Secrets of a Prime Minister', *Lone Hand*, June–August 1907.

7. Fox, Frank 1908, *From the Old Dog: Being the Letters of the Hon. –, ex-Prime Minister to his Nephew . . .*, Thomas C. Lothian, Melbourne.

8. Fox, Frank 1923, *Beneath an Ardent Sun*, Hodder & Stoughton, Toronto, London, New York.

Chapter Six

1. Pullar, A. J. 1933, *Celestalia: A Fantasy A. D. 1975*, Canberra Press, Sydney.

2. Cox, Erle 1939, *Fool's Harvest*, Robertson & Mullens, Melbourne.

3. Curtin, John 1942, New Year's Speech to Australia, 1 January 1942.

4. Hay, John (pseud. John Warwick Dalrymple-Hay) 1968, *The Invasion*, Hodder & Stoughton, Sydney.

5. Hanson, Pauline et al 1997, *Pauline Hanson: The Truth*, self-published, Ipswich, Queensland.

6. Henderson, Ronald E. 1992, *The Last White Rose? The White Race, Survival or Oblivion?*, self-published, Berry, New South Wales.

Chapter Seven

1. Hugo (pseud.) 1832, 'The Gin', *Sydney Gazette*, 14 July 1832.

2. H. L. (pseud.) 1844, 'The Aborigine's Complaint', *Port Phillip Gazette*, 10 August 1844.

3. Commentary, *Melbourne Review*, April 1877, Vol. 2, No. 6, p. 218.

4. Watson, J. B. 1885, 'Concerning Colonial Federation', *Queensland Review*, August 1885, Vol. 1, No. 1, p. 85.

5. Commentary, *Publisher*, 1 October 1886, Vol. 1., No. 1, p. 2.

6. Dilke, Sir Charles 1907 (1868), *Greater Britain: A Record of Travel in English-Speaking Countries*, Macmillan, London.

7. Besant, Sir Walter 1897, *The Rise of the Empire*, Horace Marshall, London.

8. Paterson, A. B. 1892, 'The Ballad of G. R. Dibbs'; reprinted in *The Sting in the Wattle: Australian Satirical Verse*, 1993, University of Queensland Press, pp. 33-4.

9. The Sketcher (pseud. William Lane) 1888, *White or Yellow? A Story of the Race War of AD1908*, serial in *The Boomerang*, 18 February–5 May 1888, Brisbane.

10. Lawson, Henry 1888, 'Faces in the Street', *Bulletin*, 28 July 1888.

11. Rosa, Samuel 1894, *The Coming Terror: A Romance of the Twentieth Century*, self-published, Sydney.

12. Palmer, Nettie 1924, *Modern Australian Literature (1900–1923)*, Lothian, Melbourne and Sydney.

13. Sinnett, Frederick 1856, 'The Fiction Fields of Australia', *Journal of Australasia*, Vol. 1, June-December.

14. Rosa, Samuel 1920, *The Invasion of Australia*, Judd Publishing Co., Sydney.

Chapter Eight

1. Hancock, W. K. 1930, *Australia*, Ernest Benn, London.

2. Ingamells, Rex 1938, *Conditional Culture*, F. W. Preece, Adelaide.

3. Ingamells, Rex 1952, *Aranda Boy: An Aboriginal Story*, Longmans & Green, London.

4. Stephensen, P. R. 1936, *The Foundations of Culture in Australia: An Essay Towards National Self-Respect*, Miles, Gordon NSW.

5. Watson E. L. G. 1913, 'Out There', *English Review*, no details.

6. Litchfield, Jessie 1930, *Far North Memories*, Angus & Robertson, Sydney.

7. Palmer, Vance 1928, *The Man Hamilton*, Lock, London and Melbourne.

8. Palmer, Vance 1930, *Men Are Human*, S. Paul, London.

9. Prichard, Katherine Susannah 1928, *Coonardoo (the well in the shadow)*, Cape, London; reprinted 1956, 1979, Angus & Robertson, Sydney and Melbourne.

10. Letter from the Bulletin editor, S. H. Prior, to Vance Palmer, cited in *Sense and Censorship*, 1990, Pollak, Michael, Reed Books, Sydney.

11. Eldershaw, M. Barnard (pseud. Marjorie Faith Barnard and Flora Sydney Patricia Eldershaw) 1947, *Tomorrow and Tomorrow* (censored), Georgian House, Melbourne; 1983, *Tomorrow and Tomorrow and Tomorrow*, second edition (restored text), Virago, London.

12. Herbert, Xavier 1937, *Capricornia*, Publicist Publishing Co., Sydney; reprinted 1938, 1974, Angus & Robertson, Sydney.

13. Bruce, Mary Grant 1942, *Billabong Riders*, Ward Lock, London and Melbourne.

14. Bruce, Mary Grant 1924, *Billabong Adventurers*, Ward Lock, London and Melbourne.

15. Upfield, Arthur 1929, *The Barrakee Mystery*; reprinted 1965, Heinemann, London.

16. Martin, A. E. 1950, 'The Power of the Leaf'; reprinted 1989, *Dead Witness*, Knight, Stephen, Penguin, Melbourne.

17. Marshall, James Vance 1959, *Walkabout* (first published as The Children, Michael Joseph, London); revised 1971, Michael Joseph, London.

18. Idriess, Ion 1931, *Lasseter's Last Ride*, Angus & Robertson, Sydney.

19. Idriess, Ion 1941, *Nemurlak: King of the Wilds*, Angus & Robertson, Sydney.

20. Idriess, Ion 1953, *The Red Chief*, Angus & Robertson, Sydney and London; reprinted 1965, Pacific Books, Melbourne.

21. Vickers, Bert 1955, *The Mirage*, Australasian Book Society, Melbourne.

22. Vickers, Bert 1969-70, *No Man is Himself*, Australasian Book Society, Sydney.

23. Stuart, Donald 1959, *Yandy*, Australasian Book Society, Melbourne.

24. Stuart, Donald 1962, *Yaralie*, Michael Joseph, London.
25. Stuart, Donald 1971, *Ilbarana*, Georgian House, Melbourne.
26. Casey, Gavin 1958, Snowball, Angus & Robertson, Sydney.
27. Heddle, Enid Moodie & Millington, Iris 1962, *How Australian Literature Grew*, F. W. Cheshire, Melbourne.
28. Fitzgerald, Mary Anne 1891, *King Bungaree's Pyalla and Stories Illustrative of Manners and Customs that Prevailed Among Australian Aborigines*, W. Brooks, Sydney.
29. Heddle, Enid Moodie 1957, *The Boomerang Book of Legendary Tales*, Longman, Melbourne.

Chapter Nine

1. Twain, Mark 1898, *Following the Equator*, Harper, New York.
2. Grattan, C. Hartley 1929, *Australian Literature*, University of Washington Book Store, Seattle.
3. White, Patrick 1957, *Voss*, Eyre & Spottiswoode, London.
4. White, Patrick 1976, *A Fringe of Leaves*, Cape, London.
5. White, Patrick 1961, *Riders in the Chariot*, Eyre & Spottiswoode, London.
6. See *The Oxford Companion to Australian Literature*, 1994, eds. Wilde, William H., Hooten, Joy & Andrews, Barry, Oxford University Press, Melbourne, 2nd edition, p. 829.
7. Astley, Thea 1988, *It's Raining in Mango*, Penguin, Melbourne.
8. Astley, Thea 1988, 'Heart Is Where the Home Is', *It's Raining in Mango*, Penguin, Melbourne.
9. Oodgeroo of the tribe Noonuccal (formerly known as Kath Walker) 1981, 'We Are Going', *My People*, 3rd edition 1990, Jacaranda Press, Milton, Queensland.
10. Scott, Kim 1993, *True Country*, Fremantle Arts Centre Press, South Fremantle, Western Australia.
11. Papaellinas, George 1986, *Ikons*, Penguin, Melbourne.
12. Winton, Tim 1985, 'Neighbours', *Scission*, Penguin, Melbourne.

13. Newland, Simpson 1893, *Paving the Way: A Romance of the Australian Bush*, Gay & Bird, London; reprinted 1984, Rigby, Adelaide.
14. Gaita, Raimond 1997, 'Weighing up the facts on genocide', *The Age*, 19 July 1997, Melbourne.

Conclusion

1. Dodson, Patrick, 'A firelight stick on the hill', *The Monthly*, July 2023, Melbourne.
2. Hasluck, Paul, April 1963 speech to Parliament, quoted in Dodson, Patrick, as above.
3. Howard, John, quoted in Dodson, Patrick, as above.
4. Abbott, Anthony, quoted in Flanagan, Richard, 'Our inauthentic heart: What the voice to parliament means for the stories we tell', *The Monthly*, July 2023, Melbourne.
5. Kelly, Paul 1997, 'The challenge of Pauline Hanson', Weekend Australian, 26–27 April 1997, Sydney and Melbourne.
6. Leser, David 1996, 'Pauline Hanson's bitter harvest', Age Good Weekend, 30 November 1996, Melbourne.
7. Kelly, Paul 1997, 'The challenge of Pauline Hanson', Weekend Australian, 26–27 April 1997, Sydney and Melbourne.
8. Tingle, Laura, 'With Robodebt and anonymous No Voice campaign, politics has descended into a dark place, feeding off downward envy', *abc.net.au*, posted 15 July 2023.
9. 'Unknown Australia', 60 Minutes, 15 June 1997, Channel 9, Willoughby NSW.
10. Pay the Rent is now formalised as a grassroots indigenous organisation in Victoria which solicits donations from businesses and organisations as a form of 'rent' for the land they occupy, the money to be used for furthering the betterment of indigenous peoples outside the structures of government.
11. Chantelle Francis, 'Prominent Voice campaigner's vision for Aussies to 'Pay The Rent' resurfaces', nine.com.au, posted 21 June 2023.

12. Bunbury, Bill 1997, 'Chances Lost – Chances Taken', address to Australian Reconciliation Convention, 26–28 May 1997, Melbourne.
13. Cartoon [Advertisement], Advance Australia Ltd, authorised Sheahan, Matthew, *The Australian Financial Review*, 6 July 2023, Sydney.
14. Dodson, Patrick, 'A firelight stick on the hill', *The Monthly*, July 2023, Melbourne.

Bibliography

A.S.O.W.S.A. (pseud.) 1886, 'John Chinaman My Jo', *Inquirer*, 3 November 1886.

Aeneas (pseud.) 1844, articles in *The Colonial Literary Journal*, 29 August and 5 September 1844; cited in Reynolds, Henry 1989, *Dispossession: Black Australians and White Invaders*, Allen & Unwin, Sydney.

Alexander, Michael 1971, *Mrs Fraser on the Fatal Shore*, Simon & Schuster, New York.

Anon. 1826, 'The Native's Lament', *Colonial Times*, 5 May 1826.

Anon. 1837, *Narrative of the Capture, Sufferings and Miraculous Escape of Mrs Eliza Fraser*, publisher unknown, New York.

Anon. 1837, *Authentic particulars of the dreadful wreck of the Stirling Castle, and horrible treatment of the crew by savages: with the interesting life, wonderful adventures and horrid sufferings of Mrs Fraser as related by herself before the Lord Mayor of London*, pamphlet, printed and distributed by J. Wilson, Bideford.

Anon. 1870, 'Only Thirteen', *Melbourne Punch*, 14 July 1870.

Anon. (pseud. Chesney, Sir George Tomkyns) 1871, *The Battle of Dorking: Reminiscences of a Volunteer*, *Blackwood's Magazine*, May 1871, London. Anon. 1873, *An Account of a Race of Human Beings with Tails*, A. T. Mason, Melbourne.

Anon. 1884, 'Dick the Digger: A Tale of the Buckland', in *Colonial Songster, contains several new Irish Colonial songs and a choice selection of popular songs of the day*, ed. Small, J., Hodgson, A. T., Castlemaine, Victoria; excerpted in *The Oxford Companion to Australian Literature* 1994, eds. Wilde, William H., Hooten, Joy & Andrews, Barry, Oxford University Press, Melbourne.

Anon. 1885, *The Fall of Melbourne*, *Sydney Quarterly Magazine*, Vol. 2, No. 6, June 1885.

Anon. 1888, *The Battle of Mordialloc or How We Lost Australia*, Samuel Mullen, Melbourne.

Anon. 1889, 'Recruiting' (sea shanty), *The Native Companion Songster*; reprinted in *The Overlander Songbook*, 1956 and 1990, ed. Edwards, Ron, University of Queensland Press, Brisbane pp. 209–10.

Astley, Thea 1988, 'Heart Is Where the Home Is', *It's Raining In Mango*, Penguin, Melbourne.

Astley, Thea 1988, *It's Raining in Mango*, Penguin, Melbourne.

Auster (pseud.) 1847, 'The Tasmanian Aborigine's Lament and Remonstrance When in Sight of His Native Land from Flinders Island', *Courier*, 9 October 1848.

Ayliffe, Ettie A. (pseud. Mrs J. A. Bode) 1886, 'Lubra', from collection *Original Poems*; reprinted in *The Poet's Discovery: Nineteenth-century Australia in Verse*, 1990, eds. Jordan, Richard D. & Pierce, Peter, Melbourne University Press, Melbourne.

Barrett, Charles 1948, *White Blackfellows: the strange adventures of Europeans who lived among savages*, Hallcraft, Melbourne.

Becke, Louis n. d., 'A Dead Loss'; collected in *South Sea Supercargo* 1967, ed. Grove Day, A., University of Hawaii Press, Honolulu.

Becke, Louis 1894, *By Reef and Palm*, Angus & Robertson, Sydney.

Becke, Louis, 1895, *His Native Wife*, Alexander Lindsay, Sydney

Becke, Louis 1896, *The Ebbing of the Tide*, T. F. Unwin, London.

Besant, Sir Walter 1897, *The Rise of the Empire*, Horace Marshall, London.

Boldrewood, Rolf (pseud. Browne, Thomas Alexander) 1881, *Robbery Under Arms: a story of life and adventures in the bush and in the goldfields of Australia*, serial in *Sydney Mail*; first book edition 1888–89, Dymock's Book Arcade, Sydney; second edition, Macmillan, London; reprinted 1980, Currey O'Neill, Blackburn, Victoria.

Boswell, Ron 1997, speech to Parliament, 18 June 1997.

Bruce, Mary Grant 1924, *Billabong Adventurers*, Ward Lock, London and Melbourne.

Bruce, Mary Grant 1942, *Billabong Riders*, Ward Lock, London and Melbourne.

Bunbury, Bill 1997, 'Chances Lost – Chances Taken', address to Australian Reconciliation Convention, 26–28 May 1997, Melbourne. Burke, Janine 1991, 'The Use of Stories: A Tale for my God-daughter at Midnight', *Millennium*, ed. Helen Daniel 1991, Penguin, Melbourne.

Casey, Gavin 1958, *Snowball*, Angus & Robertson, Sydney.

Chambers, Robert 1844, 'The Origin of the Animated Tribes', *Vestiges of Creation*; excerpted in *The Portable Victorian Reader* 1976, ed. Gordon S. Haight, Penguin, Melbourne.

Chandler, J. 1893, *Forty Years in the Wilderness*, E. Wyatt, Printer, Melbourne.

Clarke, Marcus 1872, article in *The New Era*, supplement to the *Australasian*, 29 April 1872.

Clarke, Marcus 1877, *The Future Australian Race*, pamphlet, A. Messina & Co., Melbourne.

Clerk, Nellie S. 1887, 'Federation', *Songs from the Gippsland Forest*, Mirboo North.

Coleridge, Samuel Taylor 1797, 'Kubla Khan, or, A Vision in a Dream, Christabel and Other Poems; reprinted 1951, *Coleridge, Selected Poetry and Prose*, ed. Schneider, Elizabeth, Holt, Rinehart & Winston Inc., New York.

Coleridge, Samuel Taylor 1798, 'The Rime of the Ancient Mariner', *Lyrical Ballads with a Few Other Poems* (William Wordsworth and S. T. Coleridge), Cottle, Bristol; reprinted 1951 in *Coleridge, Selected Poetry and Prose*, ed. Schneider, Elizabeth, Holt, Rinehart & Winston Inc., New York.

Collins, Tom (pseud. Joseph Furphy) 1903, *Such is Life*, Bulletin, Sydney; reprinted 1969, Angus & Robertson, Sydney.

Cook, James 1773, *Journal of the 'Endeavour', 1768–1771*, Facsimile edition, 1968, South Australian Libraries Edition, Adelaide.

Cox, Erle 1925, *Out of the Silence*, E. A. Ridler, Melbourne; republished, unabridged 1947, Robertson & Mullens, Melbourne; reprinted 1981, Angus & Robertson, Sydney.

Cox, Erle 1939, *Fool's Harvest*, Robertson & Mullens, Melbourne.

Curtis, John 1838, *Shipwreck of the Stirling Castle: containing a faithful narrative of the dreadful sufferings of the crew and the cruel murder of Captain Fraser by the savages: also the horrible barbarity of the cannibals inflicted upon the Captain's widow, whose unparalleled sufferings are stated by herself and corroborated by the other survivors*, G. Virtue, London.

Dampier, William 1697, *A New Voyage Around the World*; reprinted in *William Dampier: Buccaneer Explorer*, 1994 ed. Norris, Gerald, Folio Society, London.

Darwin, Charles 1859, *The Origin of the Species by Natural Selection: or, The preservation of favoured races in the struggle for life*, J. Murray, London; reprinted 1968, ed. Burrow, J. W., Penguin, Harmondsworth.

Day, David 1996, *Claiming a Continent: A History of Australia*, Angus & Robertson, Sydney.

Deakin, Alfred 1901, speech cited in Clarke, Manning 1963, *A Short History of Australia*, Mentor, New York; reprinted 1969.

Defoe, Daniel 1719, *Robinson Crusoe*; reprinted 1956, Harper & Rowe, New York.

Defoe, Daniel 1722, *Moll Flanders*; reprinted 1965, Harper & Rowe, New York.

Devaney, James 1929, *The Vanished Tribes*, with illustrations by Ray Wenban, Cornstalk, Sydney.

Dickens, Charles 1854, *Hard Times*, serial in *Household Words*, April–August 1854, London; reprinted 1969, Penguin, London.

Dilke, Sir Charles 1907 (1868), *Greater Britain: A Record of Travel in English-Speaking Countries*, Macmillan, London.

Dunlop, Eliza Hamilton 1838, 'The Aboriginal Mother (from Myall's Creek)', *Australasian*, 13 December 1838.

Eldershaw, M. Barnard 1947, *Tomorrow and Tomorrow* (censored), Georgian House, Melbourne; 1983, *Tomorrow and Tomorrow and Tomorrow* (restored text), Virago, London.

Favenc, Ernest 1876, 'In the Desert', *Australasian Sketcher*, 30 September 1876.

Favenc, Ernest 1894, 'A Haunt of the Jinkarras', *Tales of the Austral Tropics*, Orgood McIlwain & Co, London.

Favenc, Ernest 1894, 'Spirit Led', *Tales of the Austral Tropics*, Orgood McIlwain & Co, London.

Favenc, Ernest 1896, *Marooned on Australia: Being the Narration by Diedrich Buys of his Discovery and Exploits in Terra Australis Incognita about the year 1630*, Blackie, London.

Fitzgerald, Mary Anne 1891, *King Bungaree's Pyalla and Stories Illustrative of Manners and Customs that Prevailed Among Australian Aborigines*, W. Brooks, Sydney.

Flanagan, Richard, 'Our inauthentic heart: What the Voice to Parliament means for the stories we tell', *The Monthly*, May 2023.

Fox, Frank 1907, 'Secret No. 1 – The Incident of the Microphone', *The Secret of the Prime Minister*, Lone Hand, June–August 1907.

Fox, Frank 1908, *From the Old Dog: 'Being the Letters of the Hon. – –, ex-Prime Minister to his Nephew . . .'*, Thomas C. Lothian, Melbourne.

Fox, Frank 1923, *Beneath an Ardent Sun*, Hodder & Stoughton, Toronto, London, New York.

Gaita, Raimond 1997, 'Weighing up the facts on genocide', *The Age*, 19 July 1997, Melbourne.

Gibbings, Robert 1937, *John Graham, Convict 1824: an historical narrative*, Faber & Faber, London.

Gilmore, Mary 1932, 'The Waradgery Tribe', *Under the Wilgas*, Robertson & Mullens, Melbourne; reprinted in *Selected Poems*, 1998, ETT Imprint, Sydney.

Goodwin, Ken & Lawson, Alan (eds.) 1990 and 1994, *The Macmillan Anthology of Australian Literature*, Macmillan, Melbourne.

Granville, Austyn 1892, *The Fallen Race*, F. T. Neally, Chicago and New York. Grattan, C. Hartley 1929, *Australian Literature*, University of Washington Book Store, Seattle.

Green, H. M. 1984, *H. M. Green's History of Australian Literature*, two vols. , revised by Green, Dorothy, Angus & Robertson, Sydney.

Gunn, Mrs Aeneas 1908, *We of the Never Never*, Hutchinson of Australia, London and Melbourne.

H. L. (pseud.) 1844, 'The Aborigine's Complaint', *Port Phillip Gazette*, 10 August 1844.

Hancock, W. K. 1930, *Australia*, Ernest Benn, London.

Hanson, Pauline 1996, maiden speech to Parliament, 19 September 1996.
Hanson, Pauline et al 1997, *Pauline Hanson: The Truth*, self-published, Ipswich, Queensland.

Hay, John (pseud. John Warwick Dalrymple-Hay) 1968, *The Invasion*, Hodder & Stoughton, Sydney.

Healy, J. J. 1978 and 1979, *Literature and the Aborigine in Australia*, University of Queensland Press, Brisbane.

Heddle, Enid Moodie 1957, The Boomerang Book of *Legendary Tales*, Longman, Melbourne.

Heddle, Enid Moodie & Millington, Iris 1962, *How Australian Literature Grew*, F. W. Cheshire, Melbourne.

Henderson, Ronald E. 1992, *The Last White Rose? The White Race, Survival or Oblivion?*, self-published, Berry, New South Wales.

Herbert, Xavier 1937, *Capricornia*, Publicist Publishing Co., Sydney; reprinted 1938, Angus & Robertson, Sydney.

Herbert, Xavier 1975, *Poor Fellow My Country*, William Collins, Sydney.
Hergenhan, Laurie (ed.) 1988, *The Penguin New Literary History of Australia*, Penguin, Melbourne.

Holthouse, Hector 1867, *River of Gold: The Story of the Palmer River Goldrush*, Angus & Robertson, Sydney and Melbourne.

Holy Bible (Authorised King James Version), 'The Revelation of St John the Divine', ch. 21, verses 1–3.

Hughes, Robert 1997, *American Visions*, Harvill, London.

Hugo (pseud.) 1832, 'The Gin', *Sydney Gazette*, 14 July 1832.

Hume, Fergus 1886, *The Mystery of a Hansom Cab*, self-published, Melbourne; reprinted 1985, with an Introduction by Stephen Knight, The Hogarth Press, London.

Idriess, Ion 1931, *Lasseter's Last Ride*, Angus & Robertson, Sydney.

Idriess, Ion 1941, *Nemurlak: King of the Wilds*, Angus & Robertson, Sydney. Idriess, Ion 1953, *The Red Chief*, Angus & Robertson, Sydney and London; reprinted 1965, Pacific Books, Melbourne.

Ingamells, Rex 1935, *Gumtops*, F. W. Preece, Adelaide.

Ingamells, Rex 1938, *Conditional Culture*, F. W. Preece, Adelaide. Ingamells, Rex 1952, *Aranda Boy: An Aboriginal Story*, Longmans & Green, London.

Kelly, Paul 1997, 'The challenge of Pauline Hanson', *Weekend Australian*, 26–27 April 1997, Sydney and Melbourne.

Kendall, Henry n. d. 'John Dunmore Lang'; reprinted in *Leaves from Australian Forests: Poetical Works of Henry Kendall* 1991, Weldon Publishing, Sydney.

Kendall, Henry c. 1862, 'Aboriginal Death Song', *Poems & Songs*, Mr Clarke, Sydney; reprinted in *Leaves from Australian Forests: Poetical Works of Henry Kendall* 1991, Weldon Publishing, Sydney.

Kendall, Henry 1864, 'The Last of his Tribe', collected in *Leaves from Australian Forests* 1869, George Robertson & Co., Sydney; reprinted in *Leaves from Australian Forests: Poetical Works of Henry Kendall* 1991, Weldon Publishing, Sydney.

Kendall, Henry 1877, 'Ode to a Black Gin', *Town and Country Journal*, 17 March 1877.

Kendall, Henry 1879, 'Black Jemmy', *Freeman's Journal*, 9 August 1879.
Kendall, Henry 1879, 'Jack the Blackfellow', *Sydney Mail*, 23 August 1879.
Kingsley, Henry 1859, *The Recollections of Geoffrey Hamlyn*, Macmillan, London; reprinted 1935, Home Entertainment Library, Sydney. Kirmess, C. H. 1909, *The Australian Crisis*, George Robertson & Co., Melbourne.

Lady Long Resident in New South Wales, A 1841, *A Mother's Offering to her Children*, The Gazette Office, Sydney.

Lamarck, Jean Baptiste Pierre Antoine de Monet 1809, *Philosophie Zoologique*, Dentu, Paris.

Lane, William 1888, 'Leader of the Week: Australian Nationality', *Boomerang*, 28 April 1888.

Lang, John Dunmore 1856, Speech to the Moreton Bay Friends of the Aborigines, reported in *Moreton Bay Courier*, 19 January 1856; cited in Reynolds, Henry 1989, *Dispossession: Black Australians and White Invaders*, Allen & Unwin, Sydney.

Lawrence, D. H. 1923, *Kangaroo*, Martin Secker, London.

Lawson, Henry 1888, 'Faces in the Street', *Bulletin*, 28 July 1888.

Lawson, Henry 1912, 'Ah Soon', *Lone Hand*, 1 August 1912, Sydney; reprinted 1962 in *Henry Lawson: Stories for Senior Students*, ed. Colin Roderick, Angus & Robertson, Sydney.

Leser, David 1996, 'Pauline Hanson's bitter harvest', *Age/Sydney Morning Herald Good Weekend*, 30 November 1996, Melbourne and Sydney. Litchfield, Jessie 1930, *Far North Memories*, Angus & Robertson, Sydney.

Longfellow, Henry Wadsworth 1864, 'Excelsior', *The poetical works of Henry Wadsworth Longfellow*, William P. Nimmo, Edinburgh; reprinted 1934, *The Poetical Works of Henry Wadsworth Longfellow*, Oxford University Press, London.

Longfellow, Henry Wadsworth 1855, *The Song of Hiawatha*, Dent, London; reprinted 1960 and 1972, Dutton, New York.

Lyell, Sir Charles c.1830–33, (1853, 9th edition) *Principles of Geology: or The modern changes of the earth and its inhabitants considered as illustrative of geology*, J. Murray, London.

Lumholtz, Carl 1889, *Among Cannibals*, J. Murray, London; reprinted 1980, Australian National University Press, Canberra.

McCrae, Gordon George 1867, 'Mamba ("The Bright-Eyed"): An Aboriginal Reminiscence', H. T. Dwight, Melbourne.

McCrae, Gordon George 1867, *The Story of Balladeado*, H. T. Dwight, Melbourne.

Mackay, Kenneth 1895, *The Yellow Wave: A Romance of the Asiatic Invasion of Australia*, Richard Bentley & Son, London.

Marshall, James Vance 1959, *Walkabout* (first published as *The Children*, Michael Joseph, London); revised 1971, Michael Joseph, London.

Martin, A. E. 1950, 'The Power of the Leaf'; reprinted 1989 in *Dead Witness*, Stephen Knight, Penguin, Melbourne.

Meaney, Neville 1996, '"The Yellow Peril", Invasion Scare Novels and Australian Political Culture', *The 1890s: Australian Literature and Literary Culture*, University of Queensland Press, Brisbane, fn. pp. 347–48.

Meng, L. Kong, Cheok Hing Cheong & Louis Ah Mouy 1878–79, *The Chinese Question in Australia*, pamphlet, F. F. Bailliere (publisher to the Victorian government), Melbourne.

Murphy, G. Read 1894, *Beyond the Ice: Being the Story of the Newly Discovered Region Round the North Pole*, Sampson, Low, Marston & Co, London; excerpted in *Australian Science Fiction* 1982, Van Ikin, University of Queensland Press, Brisbane and Academy Chicago, Chicago.

Newland, Simpson 1893, *Paving the Way: A Romance of the Australian Bush*; reprinted 1954, Rigby, Adelaide.

Odets, Clifford 1929, *Till the Day I Die*, collected 1939, *Six Plays of Clifford Odets*, Modern Library, New York.

Oodgeroo of the tribe Noonuccal (formerly known as Kath Walker) 1964, 'We Are Going', *My People*, 3rd edn. 1990, Jacaranda Press, Milton, Queensland.

Palmer, Nettie 1924, *Modern Australian Literature (1900–1923)*, Lothian, Melbourne and Sydney.

Palmer, Vance 1928, *The Man Hamilton*, Ward Lock, London and Melbourne.

Palmer, Vance 1930, *Men Are Human*, S. Paul, London.

Palmer, Vance 1954, *The Legend of the Nineties*, Melbourne University Press, Melbourne.

Papaellinas, George 1986, *Ikons*, Penguin, Melbourne.

Parker, Catherine Langloh 1896, *Australian Legendary Tales: Folk-lore of the Noongahburrahs as told to the piccaninnies*, D. Nutt, London; Melville, Mullen & Slade, Melbourne.

Parkes, Sir Henry 1891, Speech on 13 March reported in *Official Report of the National Australasian Convention Debates 2 March to 9 April*, Sydney.

Paterson, A. B. (Banjo) 1892, 'The Ballad of G. R. Dibbs'; reprinted 1993, *The Sting in the Wattle: Australian Satirical Verse*, University of Queensland Press, Brisbane.

Pemberton, R. J. 'Bully Beef and Biscuits', unpublished reminiscences in possession of authors.

Prichard, Katharine Susannah 1915, *The Pioneers*, Hodder & Stoughton, London.

Prichard, Katharine Susannah 1921, *(The) Black Opal*, Heinemann, London.

Prichard, Katharine Susannah 1926, *Working Bullocks*, Jonathan Cape, London.

Prichard, Katherine Susannah 1928, *Coonardoo (the well in the shadow)*, Cape, London; reprinted 1956 and 1979, Angus & Robertson, Sydney and Melbourne.

Pullar, A. J. 1933, *Celestalia: A Fantasy AD 1975*, Canberra Press, Sydney. Rata (pseud. Thomas Roydhouse) 1904, *The Coloured Conquest*, NSW Bookstall Co, Sydney; excerpted in *Australian Science Fiction*, 1982, ed. Van Ikin, University of Queensland Press, Brisbane and Academy Chicago, Chicago.

Reynolds, Henry 1987, *Frontier: Reports from the Edge of White Settlement*, Allen & Unwin, Sydney.

Reynolds, Henry 1989, *Dispossession: Black Australians and White Invaders*, Allen & Unwin, Sydney.

Roderick, Colin 1952, *Ralph Rashleigh*, from the original manuscript by James Tucker in 1844-45, Angus & Robertson, Sydney; reprinted 1992.

Rosa, Samuel 1894, *The Coming Terror: A Romance of the Twentieth Century*, self-published, Sydney.

Rosa, Samuel 1920, *The Invasion of Australia*, Judd Publishing Co., Sydney. Roughsey, Dick 1973, *The Giant Devil Dingo*, Collins, Sydney.

Roughsey, Dick 1975, *The Rainbow Serpent*, Collins, Sydney.

George Santayana, *The Life of Reason or the Phases of Human Progress*, Scribner's, New York, 1905-6.

Scott, Kim 1993, *True Country*, Fremantle Arts Press, South Fremantle, Western Australia.

Sinnett, Frederick 1856, 'The Fiction Fields of Australia', *Journal of Australasia*, Vol. 1, June–December.

The Sketcher (pseud. William Lane) 1888, *White or Yellow?: A Story of the Race War of AD 1908*, *Boomerang*, 18 February–5 May 1888, Brisbane.

Smith, Adam 1776, *An Inquiry into the nature and causes of the Wealth of Nations*; reprinted 1811, John Maynard, London.

Spencer, Herbert 1852, 'The Development Hypothesis', *Leader*, 20 March 1852.

Stephens, James Brunton 1873, 'To A Black Gin', *The Black Gin and Other Poems*, George Robertson & Co., Sydney.

Stephensen, P. R. 1936, *The Foundations of Culture in Australia: An Essay Towards National Self-Respect*, Miles, Gordon, NSW.

Stuart, Donald 1959, *Yandy*, Australasian Book Society, Melbourne.

Stuart, Donald 1962, *Yaralie*, Michael Joseph, London.

Stuart, Donald 1971, *Ilbarana*, Georgian House, Melbourne.

Stuart, Donald 1976, *Malloonkai*, Georgian House, Melbourne.

Swift, Jonathon 1726, *Gulliver's Travels*; reprinted 1958 in *Gulliver's Travels and other writings*, ed. Quintana, R., Random House, New York.

Tench Watkin, 1788: *Comprising A Narrative of the Expedition to Botany Bay (1789) and A Complete Account of the Settlement at Port Jackson(1793)*, ed. Tim Flannery 1996, The Text Publishing Company, Melbourne.

Thatcher, Charles 1857, 'Chinese Immigration', *Thatcher's Colonial Songster, containing all the choice local songs, parodies etc of the celebrated Charles R. Thatcher*, Charlwood & Son, Melbourne.

Thatcher, Charles 1859, *Thatcher's Colonial Minstrel: a new collection of songs by the inimitable Thatcher*, Charlwood & Son, Melbourne.

Tompson, Charles 1826, 'A Song, Written for the XXVth January Last, being the XXXVIth Anniversary of the Establishment of this Colony', from collection, *Wild Notes, from the Lyre of a Native Minstrel*, Government Press, Sydney; reprinted 1973, Sydney University Press, Sydney, with introduction by G. A. Wilkes & G. A. Turnbull.

Tompson, Charles 1826, 'Blacktown', *Monitor*, 2 June 1826.

Trezise, Percy & Roughsey, Dick 1980, *Banana Bird and the Snake Men*, Collins, Sydney.

Trezise, Percy, & Roughsey, Dick 1982, *Turramulli the Giant Quinkin*, Nelson, Melbourne.

Trezise, Percy & Roughsey, Dick 1983, *The Magic Firesticks*, Collins, Sydney.

Trezise, Percy & Roughsey, Dick 1984, *Gidga*, Collins, Sydney.

Trezise, Percy & Roughsey, Dick 1985, *The Flying Fox Warriors*, Collins, Sydney.

Tucker, James 1929, *The Adventures of Ralph Rashleigh: a penile exile in Australia, 1825–1844*, Jonathon Cape, London; reprinted 1970 Lloyd O'Neil, Melbourne. Revised edition: *Ralph Rashleigh* 1952, ed. Colin Roderick, Angus & Robertson, Sydney; reprinted 1992.

Twain, Mark 1898, *Following the Equator*, Harper, New York.

Upfield, Arthur 1929, *The Barrakee Mystery*; reprinted 1965, Heinemann, London.

Vickers, Bert 1955, *The Mirage*, Australasian Book Society, Melbourne.

Vickers, Bert 1969–70, *No Man is Himself*, Australasian Book Society, Sydney.

Wakefield, Edward Gibbon 1829, 'A Letter from Sydney', *A Letter from Sydney and Other Writings*, Dent, London.

Walch, Garnet 1867, 'Stroke Oar's Story', *The Fireflash, four oars and a coxswain: where they went – how they went – and why they went: and the stories they told last Christmas Eve*, Gordon & Gotch, Sydney.

Walker, Jamie 1997, 'Hanson haters', *Weekend Australian*, 12–13 July 1997, Sydney and Melbourne.

Warburton, Peter 1875, *Journey Across the Western Interior of Australia*, Sampson, Marston, Low & Searle; reprinted 1968 with introduction and additions by Eden, Charles H., ed. Bates, H. W., Libraries Board of South Australia.

Watson, E. L. G. 1913, 'Out There', *English Review*, no details.

Watson, J. B. 1885, 'Concerning Colonial Federation', *Queensland Review*, August 1885, Vol. 1, No. 1.

Wells, H. G. 1898, *The War of the Worlds*, William Heinemann, London.

Wentworth, William Charles 1823, 'Australasia: A Poem Written for the Chancellor's Medal, at the Cambridge Commencement, July 1823', Whittaker & Co., London.

White, Patrick 1957, *Voss*, Eyre & Spottiswoode, London.

White, Patrick 1961, *Riders in the Chariot*, Eyre & Spottiswoode, London.

White, Patrick 1976, *A Fringe of Leaves*, Cape, London.

White, Richard 1981, *Inventing Australia: Images and Identity 1688–1980*, George Allen & Unwin, Sydney.

Wilde, William H., Hooten, Joy & Andrews Barry 1985, *The Oxford Companion to Australian Literature*, 2nd edition, 1994, Oxford University Press, Melbourne.

Winton, Tim 1985, 'Neighbours', *Scission*, Penguin, Melbourne.

Wright, Judith 1985, *The Cry for the Dead*, Oxford University Press, Melbourne.

Wright, Judith 1985, *We Call for a Treaty*, Collins/Fontana, Sydney.

Wright, Judith 1991, *Born of the Conquerors: Selected Essays by Judith Wright*, Aboriginal Studies Press, Canberra.

Acknowledgements

The authors wish to acknowledge the Woiworung and Boonwurrung people who are traditional Custodians of the lands on which *Aliens & Savages* was researched, written and revised.

They also wish to thank the following people for their support, aid and inspiration with this new edition: Louise Berry, Jack Dann, Mike Enstice, Rob Gerrand, David Grigg, Susanne Shaw.

Extracts from *Billabong Riders* and *Billabong Adventurers* by Mary Grant Bruce; *Coonardoo* by Katherine Susannah Prichard; *Capricornia* by Xavier Herbert; and *Tomorrow and Tomorrow* by M. Barnard Eldershaw are reproduced with the permission of Curtis Brown, Sydney.

Extracts from 'We Are Going' by Oodgeroo of the tribe Noonuccal (formerly known as Kath Walker) in *My People*, 3rd edition, 1990, Jacaranda Press are reproduced with the permission of Jacaranda Press.

Extracts from *Ralph Rashleigh* by Colin Roderick, from the original manuscript written by James Tucker in 1844–45, are reproduced with the permission of Colin Roderick.

Extract from 'The Waradgery Tribe' by Mary Gilmore is reproduced with the permission of ETT Imprint.

Extracts from *It's Raining in Mango* by Thea Astley are reproduced with the permission of Penguin Australia.

Extract from 'The Use of Stories: A Tale for my God-daughter at Midnight' by Janine Burke is reproduced with the permission of the author.

Extracts from *We of the Never Never* by Mrs Aeneas Gunn are reproduced with the permission of A. P. Watt Ltd on behalf of Peta Paine Nominees Pty Ltd.

www.ingramcontent.com/pod-product-compliance
Lightning Source LLC
Chambersburg PA
CBHW010706020526
44107CB00081B/2665